Dream
SIGHT

About the Author

Dr. Michael Lennox is one of America's most recognized and respected dream experts, having spent the last twenty years interpreting thousands of dreams in workshops, in the media, and for corporate and private clientele. With a doctorate in psychology, Dr. Lennox has been deeply influenced by Carl Jung's theories on dreams. He is also a noted astrologer, intuitive, and authority on all matters of spiritual psychology. A highly sought after media expert, Dr. Lennox has been seen internationally by millions of viewers, beginning with the Sci Fi Network's *The Dream Team with Annabelle and Michael*, which premiered in January 2003. Since then, he has also been featured on the Emmy Award winning reality show *Starting Over*, Soap Network's *Soap Talk*, MTV's *Myths and Urban Legends*, *National Lampoon's Editorial Desk*, *The Wayne Brady Show*, *The Gregory Mantell Show*, as well as local news broadcasts in Los Angeles and Denver. His frequent radio appearances showcase his work on a monthly basis on Sirius Satellite Radio's Playboy Channel, The Rolonda Watts Internet Radio Show, and with Canada's premiere talk jock Andrew Krystal in Toronto. He lives and practices in Los Angeles.

Dream SIGHT

A Dictionary and **Guide** for Interpreting Any Dream

DR. MICHAEL LENNOX

Llewellyn Publications
Woodbury, Minnesota

Book design by Donna Burch
Cover art © Art Explosion Image Library, © Dover
Cover design by Ellen Lawson
Editing by Sharon Leah
Interior art © Art Explosion Image Library

ISBN 978-0-7387-2602-1

Llewellyn Publications
A Division of Llewellyn Worldwide Ltd.
2143 Wooddale Drive
Woodbury, MN 55125-2989

Printed in the United States of America

Contents

Acknowledgments . . . 1
Introduction . . . 3

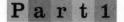

ALL ABOUT DREAMING

Chapter 1
WELCOME TO DREAM SIGHT . . . 9
The Three Steps of Dream Sight . . . 12
   The Universal Landscape . . . 12
   The Dreaming Lens . . . 14
   The Personal Focus . . . 15
Identifying the Universal Landscape . . . 18

Chapter 2
DREAMS: THE BASICS . . . 23
The Battle of the Century: Freud versus Jung! . . . 23
Dreams Defined . . . 27
Character Aspects . . . 29
The Shadow . . . 32
Archetypes . . . 35
The Collective Unconscious . . . 38

Chapter 3
TYPES OF DREAMS . . . 43
Overview . . . 43
Compensatory Dreams . . . 44

Recurring Dreams . . . 47
   Stress-related Recurring Dreams . . . 47
   Process-based Recurring Dreams . . . 50
Precognitive Dreams . . . 53

Chapter 4
THE DREAM WORK . . . 57
Overview . . . 57
Writing Your Dreams Down . . . 60
Rumination . . . 62
Identifying the Theme . . . 65
Free Association . . . 67
Automatic Handwriting . . . 72
Dream Sight Revisited . . . 77
Continuums of Meaning . . . 78
Dream Sight Structure . . . 79
The Sections Explained . . . 79
   Universal Landscape . . . 79
   Dreaming Lens . . . 80
   Personal Focus . . . 80

Part 2
THE DREAM DICTIONARY . . . 81

Glossary of Terms . . . 371
Index . . . 377

ACKNOWLEDGMENTS

There are many people to whom I am incredibly grateful; foremost are all those who said to me along the way, "When is your book going to be done? I definitely want a copy!" The anticipation and desire expressed by this legion of friends, colleagues, and acquaintances was integral to my constant battle with writer's block, procrastination, and my ever-present desire to lie on the couch and watch movies. If I had known how long it takes to write a book like this, and how difficult the process is, I might never have undertaken the challenge.

Many thanks must be given to Lynn Pentz for getting the ball going; she was first to tell me I needed to examine how I interpreted dreams and formulate a structure that could be presented to others. My deepest gratitude goes to Lawrence Monoson: life is much more interesting now as a result of his staggering capacity for truth and courageous mirroring. He provided the challenge and the inspiration that helped me to finish this project with enthusiasm and focus.

I celebrate the hundreds of dreamers I have had the privilege of working with over the years, and I wish to thank them all. Several must be mentioned by name by virtue of their direct contribution to this book: my thanks to Scott S., Todd S., Jan E., Robbie P., Michelle D., Dave

S., Andy S., Virginia S., Jason G., and Tracy P. To my gentle readers: Jan, Olenka, and Virginia, I am indebted.

My first editor, author Robin Palmer, and I met in an unlikely setting for a professional partnership to form, and I am grateful for the ridiculously casual conversation that led us to a wonderful collaboration. Additional thanks to Andy Schreiber for his keen eye, flawless grammatical acumen, and a willingness to lend his generous support.

I am certain I neglected to mention by name some people who contributed directly to the examples in these pages. Suffice to say that what I do is meaningless without those who shared their souls with me by revealing themselves as they shared their dreams.

INTRODUCTION

A dream which is not interpreted
is like a letter which is not read.
—THE TALMUD

Are dreams deep, meaningful experiences that can reveal unconscious desires or simply random brain activity? I have been asked this question over and over again. At the end of the day, the truth is that we really don't know what dreams are or why we have them. The scientist believes that truth is only what can be measured in a laboratory. The mystic believes that dreams are unmistakably the living realm of the soul. Since I consider myself half scientist and half mystic, I appreciate everything that dreams have to offer us, and I thrill with every new piece of information provided by the latest advances in neuroscience. I know dreams offer remarkable insight, and we can unlock secrets and reveal amazing elements of the human mystery when we examine them.

My experience tells me there is absolutely no wrong way to do dream work. The more objectivity we can bring to the process the deeper we are likely to go. This book stresses the importance of universality. By understanding the universal language of dreams, we can begin to know what our unconscious minds are trying to tell us.

The unconscious mind expresses itself in symbols, and these symbols form a language of their own. When I listen to someone describe a dream, I hear it as a story told in this symbolic language. Because it is not my dream, there is no emotional charge to me from these symbols. This leaves me free to apply a universal meaning when I interpret dream images, and I can do so more intensively than if I felt a personal attachment to the dream itself. After enough experiences of this detachment with other people's dreams, I found that I could approach my own dream work with this same objectivity.

It made sense that if I could learn to be objective about my dreams, other people could do this for themselves as well. All that is needed is a fundamental understanding of the universal meaning of a dream image and a way to identify what that meaning is. This is deceptively simple, but not always easy to accomplish.

A number of years ago, a young woman in her mid-twenties came to me because she had been having recurring nightmares about killing her own babies immediately after giving birth to them. The images absolutely horrified her and she was convinced that they must be confirmation of darkly sinister associations with motherhood that were worming their way into her consciousness. She was terrified about what this might mean for her potential future as a mother. After having different versions of this disturbing dream for several weeks, she finally followed her friend's suggestion and set up an appointment with me.

She described the dreams, and they were indeed horrific, bloody, and, for her, very frightening. After taking the few requisite moments to validate that these dreams were indeed disturbing, I introduced her to the universal symbolic meanings of the two images that were most prominent.

I explained that babies connect to anything new, like ideas, projects, intentions, or experiences. This is an easy interpretation to understand. I went on to describe murder as a deliberate death. While this may look, at first, like a scary image with negative connotations, death is, in fact, a very positive symbol; it represents the ultimate transformation, as death is the end of one thing and the beginning of something new. Death is always going to be followed by rebirth.

After she took this in, I asked her if anything in her life looked like the new prospects that a baby might represent. She said she had, indeed, been struggling with a writing project. I encouraged her to say more about that. She explained that she had been working on a creative project and had thrown out a number of rough drafts and started over again. When I asked if the nightmares coincided with moments when she had thrown out a draft and started again, her eyes widened with that look that says—"aha!"

In this woman's case, the babies represented the precious first drafts she was birthing through her creativity. The gruesome murders were her psyche's way of expressing the regret she felt over having to reject her unsatisfactory creations. The images were grotesque and horrifying, but had nothing to do with her becoming a murderous mom. However, she was unable to separate herself from the feelings that these images brought up. Her emotional attachment to her dream made it impossible for her to see what was so clear to me.

This case is typical of what dreamers experience. Dreams are intensely personal; they happen inside of us, and it is natural that the images that appear in them would be intrinsically bound up with the feelings they inspire. Time and again, dreamers get lost when searching for meaning in their dreams, distracted by these emotions. Feelings are reactive by nature. They respond to stimulation and help us move through our lives effectively. But this reactivity can just as easily distract us when we get stuck in highly charged moments. This happens everywhere in life: in our thoughts, in our relationships with others, in our daily lives, while driving the car and, of course, in our dreams. The best course of action in all of these situations is a measure of detachment. There is a very specific way to approach interpreting dreams, which is to stay one step removed from any personal reaction. By staying detached from the emotional aspect of dreams, we are allowed to create the deepest and most rewarding experience of them.

This should not be confused with the feeling sensations of the dream itself, or the visceral emotional aftermath of the dream content, which I discuss further in Chapter 4. What I am referring to here is the intellectual, chaotic inner dialogue some dreamers will engage in about the judgments they have about the disturbing images of some of their more upsetting dreams after the fact.

This book teaches how to recognize the universal meaning associated with the symbols in dreams. A three-step process called "Dream Sight" is used to approach any image that appears in a dream and find a universal meaning for it. After this universal meaning is found and melded with the context of the dream itself, and after any personal associations to the dream are applied, an interpretation that is both profound and valuable is possible.

The unconscious mind is waiting. Enjoy!

Part 1

ALL ABOUT DREAMING

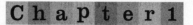

Chapter 1
WELCOME TO DREAM SIGHT

*You see things; and you say, 'Why?' But I dream things that
never were; and I say, 'Why not?'*
—GEORGE BERNARD SHAW

My fascination with dreams began pretty early. There are very few
things I can remember about the first five years of my life, but one
memory is of talking to my mother about my dreams. The most potent one was of being in this vast space where I was aware of things
above me being extremely huge and things below me being inconceiv-
ably small. Later, I recognized the dream as symbolically representing the concept of infinity. Another dream I remember well was of
what I have described as "forks and knives moving." Talking about my
dreams was one sure way of capturing my mother's attention. It was

an experience that I would later find replicated over and over again in my life, because people are endlessly fascinated with dreams.

All throughout my childhood, my imagination was my best friend. Dreams became as big a part of my inner life as anything that occurred on the outside. When I was a teenager, my mother was pursuing graduate studies in social work, and the books on her shelf captivated me. One day, I spotted Freud's *Interpretation of Dreams*. I poured through it ravenously. As precocious as I was at fifteen years old, I don't imagine that I understood any of it, but I definitely got one very important piece of information from those pages, which is that a dream is something that comes from the inside of a person's mind and that by interpreting it, something of value can be gained.

What happened next is, without a doubt, the most important part of my tale. Unfortunately, I have no idea when, where, or how it happened, but I know it connects to that ubiquitous social phenomenon wherein people are always saying to each other, "Wow, I had such a weird dream last night!"

I have to jump back to my early childhood again. My mother was fond of her LP records (long-playing 33⅓ records), and there was always music playing in my home during the weekends. She exposed me to classical music, folksingers, and a smattering of Broadway show scores, one of which was *Fiddler on the Roof*. In *Fiddler*, there is a wonderful sequence where Tevye tells his wife about a dream he had. On the record, Tevye's wife says, "Tell me what you dreamed, and I'll tell you what it meant." I can't overstate how strongly that imprinted on my brain. That simple comment about Tevye's dream and, more importantly, Golde's interpretation of it was to be one of the most salient experiences of my life.

So, a decade later, as my teenaged friends began to mention their dreams when we were out and about, I found myself unable to stifle the impulse to quote Golde. I can't quite imagine what presumptuousness prompted me to make such an outlandish offer. Not being one to typically hold back my impulses, that's just what I did. As a result, an amazing thing began to happen. I would listen to the dream, and my imagination would be ablaze. I would then offer some thoughts about what the dream might mean from this imaginative place. I had absolutely no idea what I was doing, but from the very first, people began to respond with curiosity and more surprisingly, satisfaction. I clearly had a gift and, thus, I began interpreting dreams. By the time I was in my mid-to-late twenties, I had interpreted hundreds of dreams for people. It was not unusual for my phone to ring and me to hear, "My friend so-and-so tells me that you can tell me what my dream means!" I was hooked.

Cut to the new millennium. Much has changed in my life, and I have now officially dedicated my life to dreams and dream interpretation. I earned my master's and doctorate degrees in psychology. I was even tapped by the media to showcase my work in the first-ever television show centered on the topic, the very short-lived "The Dream Team with Annabelle and Michael" on the Sci Fi Channel. My then-manager, a very savvy woman by the name of Lynn Pentz said to me, "Michael, you are going to have to figure out exactly how it is that you do what you do when you interpret a dream so that you can describe it to others and eventually teach them how to do it for themselves."

My first response to Lynn's suggestion was that I started to cry. The idea seemed overwhelming. I had absolutely no idea how I did what I did, I only knew it was something I could do. My understanding of dreams comes fast—very fast—and when I share my interpretations with a dreamer, there is the inevitable "aha" that lets me know I am on the right track. Sure, there are certain foundational precepts that I learned and applied over the years, but the act of interpreting was just too ingrained in my thinking for me to ever imagine being able to understand how it actually happened.

I did, however, take the proposition very seriously. And for the weeks that followed, I did my best to watch myself with my mind's eye and ear and see if anything occurred to me. And much to my surprise, something did.

When I heard a dream, it was like I heard a *story*. The dreamer would give a narrative description of the dream, but I found that wasn't what I listened to. It seemed that the language of dreams was symbolic and it was the symbols that I actually paid attention to. They lined up inside my head in such a way that I heard the story as told to me in this language. The process was lightening fast, but I could see that this was something I could innately understand, much like I imagine it would be to be bilingual. The act of me speaking an interpretation was me translating the symbols back into a story. What I was translating was *a story about the story* of the dream itself.

This is the process of looking at the meaning of dreams that I decided to call "Dream Sight." It is a theoretical structure of how to discover the meaning of any symbol that appears in a dream and is directly based on my personal process of interpretation. It reveals the meaning of specific dream imagery by examining a symbol in three separate steps. By looking at something first from a universal perspective, then considering the contextual elements from the dream itself, and lastly adding personal thoughts and feelings, the resulting interpretation will reveal what the unconscious mind is trying to reveal in the purest way possible. At first, this may feel laborious and overly cerebral. However, with practice, Dream Sight becomes more and more organic, and it allows us to connect with a more informative and valuable meaning of our dreams.

The Three Steps of Dream Sight

The Universal Landscape

The first step of Dream Sight is called the "Universal Landscape." Something is considered to be *universal* when it would be recognized or understood by most people. The greater the number of people who connect to something, the more universal that thing is. Love is a universal concept because all human beings understand what love feels like. Fear is another one of these familiarly experienced emotions. All of us can relate to love and fear as universal elements of being alive and human.

The unconscious mind expresses in symbols. These symbols emanate out of the imagination, or what is known as the collective unconscious, which will be covered in more detail in Chapter Two. When dreaming is looked at from this perspective, it becomes easier to accept that for every image our mind can conjure, there exists in the imagination of *all human beings* some association with that particular image. Most people will agree with the association, even if their own personal thoughts and feelings *about the image itself* differ. This is what is meant by "universal." Universality indicates that the meaning of a symbol is likely to resonate with all people no matter what their cultural background, personal feelings, or personal understanding are with regard to the context of the dream.

I used the image of a landscape to evoke the sense that if a whole bunch of people were standing in one place looking at something off in the distance, they would all, because of their similar proximity, see essentially the same thing—a landscape. Everyone would have the same general view. Ten people looking down on a valley from the same hilltop would all agree that the tall, spindly thing on the left is definitely a tree. But one person might decide it's an apple tree, while another is certain it's a weeping willow, and still another might decide it looks like a dormant tree that is waiting for spring to come so it can bloom again. No matter what individual distinctions are being made, however, everyone can agree: it's a tree.

Let's use an example of an image that might appear in a dream and actually identify the meaning from this perspective of the Universal Landscape free of any personal associations. To make this fairly clear, we'll use a nice, juicy term that just might evoke a powerful response in some individuals. It's one of the most frequent images I hear about in dreams: the police. The police are guardians of law and order in our society. They, therefore, represent obeying the rules and the potential consequences of dangerous choices; and if police appear in a dream, everyone understands the Universal Landscape that is associated with police.

There are people who have very negative connotations with police officers and still others who have a very positive identification with them. On a personal level, this might change how we would interpret a dream with a police officer in it (however, that comes later in the process). To truly achieve a deep, satisfying interpretation, we must detach ourselves from any personal associations and understand what is universal about a dream symbol. *Guardians of law and authority* would be the Universal Landscape of Police in a dream. What the Police do in a dream and how each of us feels about the police on a personal level are the second and third elements of Dream Sight—the "Dreaming Lens" and "Personal Focus."

The Dreaming Lens

The second step of Dream Sight is to incorporate the context of the dream itself, which will deepen the interpretation. Keeping with the visual analogy, I call this second step the "Dreaming Lens." Remember the hilltop with the tree in the valley below? That was the Universal Landscape. Now imagine looking at the tree through a camera. The tree is visible, but the lens of the camera blocks out the rest of the valley. Each one of us standing on the hilltop will have a slightly different view because of our unique position, the kind of camera we use, and so forth. Our unique Dreaming Lens is akin to a camera lens in that an image is presented through the dream.

So let's go back to our dream police. If a police officer pulls me over and issues a citation for speeding in a dream, I can add to the interpretation that the *guardian of law and order* has stopped me on my path to inform me that I have broken the law. This invites me to consider what I may be trying to get away with—something that is not in my best interest—or where I may be moving too fast in my inner life.

The Personal Focus

Only after completing these two steps is it time to add personal meaning to the interpretation. The "Personal Focus" is obtained by fine-tuning the Dreaming Lens through which the Universal Landscape is viewed. We can do this by combining whatever personal associations we might have with the symbol in question. This includes ideas that come from our individual values and beliefs as well as life experiences and our various cultural backgrounds.

To round out our example, and sticking with the image we've been working with, let's decide that our fictitious dreamer has great reverence and respect for officers of the law. In fact, some of the people whom he admires in his family chose this profession. Now the officer in his dream can be interpreted as a part of his personality (we will discuss in Chapter 2 how all people in dreams are parts of the dreamer) that he instinctively trusts and respects. Viewed through the Personal Lens, we can see that this dream can be interpreted as meaning he is moving too fast in some area of his life, and an unconscious part of his personality that knows right from wrong is warning him that if he is not more careful, there may be challenging consequences. By investigating dream symbols in this particular order—first for universal meaning and then for personal meaning, a deeper and more powerful interpretation is free to emerge.

Additionally, the Personal Lens is where we can consider all the different possible meanings that could be associated with an image without regard to universality. These can include mundane facts, historical information, and how things work and function, as well as awareness of different perspectives that might be within specific issues. Just about any information connected to a symbol can inform the interpretation of it, provided it is introduced after it has been identified in the Universal Landscape.

To illustrate this principle more clearly, let us use another example in which two people have essentially the same dream. The primary image is that of a snake. Dreamer number one is terrified of snakes, while Dreamer number two finds them interesting and even a bit erotic.

While hiking down a path alone somewhere in nature, the dreamer comes upon a large snake in the middle of the path. Encountering the snake stops their hike and the dreamer regards the snake from a safe distance before waking up.

The fact that snakes shed their skins, which is symbolic for discarding the old to make room for the new in one fell swoop, makes change and transformation the Universal Landscape for snake. In addition, many varieties of snakes are capable of killing, and death is always symbolically linked with rebirth, which is the ultimate of transformations. Even the fact that their long, straight shape can be formed into a circle is symbolically suggestive of the cycles of change that are so much a part of life.

The Dreaming Lens in this dream is the same for both dreamers—the presence of the snake in the middle of their path has halted their progress. Now the meaning of the dream can be expanded—this is a dream about some path in life that each dreamer is on. Since the dreamers are alone, we can assume the dream reflects their own private journey as opposed to public life. Some element of change or transformation is occurring in their lives as represented by the snake appearing on their respective paths. This apparent obstacle has caused them to stop and consider what direction to take and what to do next.

Now we come to the Personal Focus, which is going to be very different for our two dreamers and, therefore, result in a different final interpretation for each. Dreamer number one is afraid of snakes, so whatever change in life this dream is expressing is accompanied by some level of fear. Dreamer number two is also facing a shift in life, but one that is intriguing and inviting by virtue of having a Personal Focus of snakes as an object of fascination. Without using the process of Dream Sight, both dreamers would be stuck and confused by thoughts that the dream means something about snakes and how they feel about them instead of seeing the dream as representing of change or transformation, which their unconscious minds are asking them to explore.

Here is an example from another client whose dream included the tried-and-true image of a baby that we have already identified as representing a new construct in the dreamer's life. Notice how the meaning shifts completely after using Dream Sight to explore the dream more effectively.

A man in his early thirties finds a baby in his office. He spends the rest of the day trying to hide it from his boss and coworkers.

When I asked what he thought this dream was about, he expressed fears of one day becoming a father, because he does not know how to relate to babies and prefers the company of children who are old enough to speak articulately and communicate easily with adults. He and his wife have no immediate plans to start a family. He naturally associated the dream with his fears around fatherhood but didn't understand why it produced such acute anxiety.

The assumption that he had this dream because of his fatherhood anxiety was too literal. By confining its interpretation to the personal realm, the dream's value is severely limited. Because a baby is at the beginning of its life, filled with all that is to come, the Universal Landscape for the symbol of a baby in a dream is all about new beginnings and possibilities. All human beings would innately understand this perspective, no matter what their personal association with having a baby might be, as long as they *disconnected their understanding* from any strong, personal associations they might have.

When I asked if there was anything in his life that was new or just beginning to appear on the horizon, the man expressed that he was faced with a new project at work that demanded a lot of his attention.

After I asked him if he felt any anxiety coming up with regard to the project, he confessed that was, indeed, the case. When introduced to the notion that the baby in his dream might represent the new project at work, he had an immediate epiphany. In his new understanding of the dream, the baby represented the delicacy of the new project. His need to hide the baby from his coworkers in the dream related to the fact that he felt he had been hiding his anxiety from them. By masking his fear, he thought he was being a more effective project leader. However, the dream also indicated that this wasn't working out quite as well as he thought. In this way, a generalized, overly-personal interpretation of the dream was converted to a more accurate and helpful one. He felt he would be able to return to work with more confidence and authenticity, because he was no longer trying to hide his real feelings; he also felt that he could relate to his coworkers from a more real and grounded place.

Identifying the Universal Landscape

By now it should be clear how important it is to discover what the Universal Landscape for a symbol that you are attempting to interpret might be. There are hundreds of terms outlined in the second part of this book where this is already done for you. However, this is nothing compared to the infinite number of images that are likely to appear in your dreams; many of them will not be found within these pages. Therefore, learning how to think in terms of universal meaning will be a crucial part of your ongoing dream work.

The concept of universality refers to themes and images that are common to all people. That which is purely universal knows no boundaries of geography, culture, history, or belief and affects all human beings in the same way. Fundamental experiences such as love, grief, joy, fear, and aggression are felt by everyone worldwide.

All images have some universal meaning and the job of the dream interpreter is to find a kernel of universal meaning that can be associated with the symbol being considered. The secret is to momentarily forget about your personal view and consider what meaning would find the greatest resonance with the most people. Rather than solely applying to specific groups of like-minded individuals, the notion of "the most people" needs to apply to entire populations. The larger the population that would identify with a particular meaning or perspective of a symbol, the more universal that symbol would be considered.

One of the most effective ways of discovering what the Universal Landscape might be for a symbol is by examining its use or its essence. While the use of something applies to its function, its essence connects to its purpose. Although these may seem barely distinguishable from each other, they are, in fact, quite different. Use takes into account what something does, therefore, helping define how we relate to it and how it relates to us. On the other hand, the essence of something connects to its purpose, thereby informing us of why we relate to it the way we do.

Here is an example of a specific image, and how considering its "use" and its "essence" can help us interpret the dream in which it appears: a refrigerator keeps a certain amount of confined space at a specific, desired temperature that is colder than the room in which it stands. This is what it *does*, which, therefore, defines its "use." Its *purpose*, which is to lengthen the life of our perishable foods, connects to the "essence" of a refrigerator.

One of my all-time favorite examples comes from a woman who described a dream in which she found a disembodied head in a refrigerator. Using principles of universality and some common sense thinking, she told me that the head represented thoughts or ideas that she had not incorporated into her day-to-day thinking. I was thrilled and thought she was right on track. But the refrigerator had her stuck. In order to discover the Universal Landscape for refrigerator and further inform her understanding of this dream, I encouraged her to turn to the use and essence of the symbol "refrigerator." She thought for a moment and then began to muse out loud. The *use* of the refrigerator told her that the head was going to be kept cold, which didn't resonate with her. Next, she considered that the *essence*, or purpose, of a refrigerator is to preserve and extend the life of something to keep it fresh. Now came the "aha" moment, and she suddenly got excited. This was now a dream about ideas whose time had not yet come, however, the ideas had to be kept fresh—preserved—for later use. This tied directly into a decision she was facing and was not quite ready to commit to.

To further illustrate this concept, I will use the example of a bomb appearing in a dream. Its *use* relates to the creation of sudden, intense combustion. It isn't until the *essence* of deliberate destructiveness with an implied target is added to the definition that we have something with which to work, though. If I have a dream in which I am carrying a bomb from one place to another, I could now consider both the danger of sudden combustion as well as deliberate destructiveness that the bomb represents. These minute distinctions will pay off powerful dividends when the symbols with which we work are of a more esoteric nature and, therefore, more challenging.

Let's look at a few more examples to make this concept as clear as possible. The *use* of a hat is to cover and protect the head. The *essence* of a hat is to adorn and express. Because a hat is worn on the head, the symbolic meaning must connect with the concept of thoughts or thinking. Therefore, the Universal Landscape—the universal symbolism, of a hat in a dream will connect to protecting or hiding private thoughts, but with the added texture of expressing public thoughts in a creative way.

The *use* of a jar is often to hold or contain liquid or fluid substances, whereas its *essence* relates to the preservation of what is inside it. In a dream, the universal meaning of a jar embodies the need to preserve something, or a sense that something from the past is currently available, because it has been preserved in the unconscious through the symbol of the jar.

The *use* of a pool is to hold a large amount of water. Its *essence* aligns with relaxation and fun. Because water is always symbolically associated with emotions, an interpretive meaning that connects water to a pool's *use* would be a gathering of emotions, whereas a meaning that grounds itself in a pool's *essence* might connect to a need for more freedom or levity. Both are credible interpretations.

The definitions contained in Part 2: The Dream Dictionary will become accessible in such a way that even when working with symbols that are not found within these pages, the Dream Sight process will be a guide for interpreting dreams.

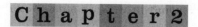
Chapter 2
DREAMS:
THE BASICS

The interpretation of dreams is the royal road to knowledge
of the unconscious activities of the mind.

—SIGMUND FREUD

The Battle of the Century: Freud versus Jung!

Dreams have been a central part of humanity since the time when people first began to gather around fires and live in community with each other. One of the most intriguing notions I have ever heard about some of these early cultures is that what happened in dreams was considered the "real" world and waking life was the illusion. I think this beautifully illustrates our innate desire to connect to the spiritual side of life. My love of dreams comes right out of this idea that the inner world is the one really worth exploring; everything else is just a series of to-do lists.

I could spend a lot of time on what we know today about early human's relationship with dreams and the spiritual practices led by Shamans in cultures around the globe from the time before recorded history. However, that would really be best left to minds far more informed about such things than I. Therefore, I will start with modern psychology and the fascinating work done in the late nineteenth and early twentieth century by two men who truly changed the course of our understanding of the human mind: Sigmund Freud and Carl G. Jung.

Freud is often credited for discovering the unconscious mind. He did not. The unconscious was well known by the time he was a young man. He is even credited for creating what was the first case of psychoanalysis. He didn't do that either. Freud's teacher and colleague, a guy named Breuer, did that. Freud helped Breuer with some research that involved the diagnosis and treatment of a young Viennese woman. What is even less known is that the young woman got much worse, not better. The diagnosis was egregiously wrong and the whole affair ended with a startling level of controversy that included the two colleagues lying about the case in the published version of their results. However, the work itself led Freud to identify the structure of the unconscious mind in a model that is still used today. Now, *that* is a pretty powerful accomplishment.

What Freud did for the emergence of modern dream work is also extraordinary. Furthering the work started by Breuer, Freud developed the free association talk therapy that eventually became psychoanalysis. During this exploration, he found that by examining and interpreting the dreams of his patients, enormous insights and connections to their waking life revealed themselves. He published a book about this, which hit the world with a dull thud (it didn't sell more than six hundred copies). Of course, *The Interpretation of Dreams* has since become perhaps the most famous work on the subject ever.

The story of Freud and Jung is a fascinating tale of bitterness and rivalry. Both men were brilliant theorists, and their work had enormous impact on the human condition. Very excited about the work Freud was doing, Jung, himself a near-famous up-and-coming young doctor, traveled from Switzerland to Vienna to study with him. Jung was captivated by the idea of dreams being what Freud so aptly called "the royal road to the unconscious." Freud, the older of the two, thought he had found in Jung his perfect apostle. In fact, both men felt they were at the beginning of a life-long association. It was not. In fact, it ended badly—very badly. Freud demanded rigid loyalty from his followers that left absolutely no room for disagreeing with him. Jung was authoritative and opinionated, and often brutal in his expression of those opinions. The character traits of the two men didn't mix well.

The role of dreams was central to their discussions. Freud's utter obsession with sex permeated all his theories to an extent that is considered almost ridiculous today. This is where he and Jung departed. Here's a bit of what Freudian dream interpretation might look like. You dream of climbing stairs: that represents sex. You dream of a mountain; that's a penis. You dream of a cave in the mountain: that's a vagina. A train is a penis. It goes through a tunnel: that's intercourse. And at the end, you both smoke a cigarette and, well, everyone knows what that means.

By all accounts, Jung liked sex just as much as the next person. He knew, however, that there was much more to the story of dreams than that. Freud felt that the sex drive was the only mechanism that inspired human beings. Jung's instincts told him that there were many drives and the human mind was far more sophisticated and interesting. He left Freud, headed back to Switzerland and devoted the rest of his life to figuring it all out.

Over the years, Jung began to treat the local, wealthy neurotics in his own analytic style. Dream interpretation became a foundational pillar of that work. One thing he noticed was that all of his patients seemed to have the same dreams; falling, flying, losing their teeth, and being chased all recurred with alarming regularity, even in his own dreams. When he later traveled to Africa and spent some time with tribal communities, he was astonished to learn that these aboriginal people were having the very same dreams as his white, upper-class Swiss patriots. Everybody was falling, flying, loosing their teeth, and being chased. Of course, the Africans were being chased by lions and the Swiss were being chased by bankers or assailants with guns, but the essential content was the same. Jung surmised that there must be some plane of thought that all people share, regardless of where they live, what culture they come from, or how they have been raised. Thus was born his notion of the Collective Unconscious, which will be discussed at length later in this chapter.

Both Jung and Freud traveled extensively to lecture about their work. One time, they even came to the United States together in an attempt to reconcile, but the effort resulted in another very bad ending. However, the outcome of their travels was that psychoanalysis became very fashionable in Europe and later the United States. In urban settings, people began to hear of Freud and read his books. While Jung was less well-known, the following that grew up around him was a thriving community of analysts and laypersons alike. His work has permeated into theories of personality that are used today everywhere from Fortune 500 companies to online dating services that match people up based on compatibility.

The influence of both men is nothing short of staggering. The use of dreams as a tool for self-investigation was foundational in both of their work. The media has done the rest, with themes of psychology and dream interpretation finding their way into novels, plays, and films throughout the twentieth century. The explosion of popular psychology in the 1970s solidified the notion that the unconscious mind is rich with meaning and revelation, and that by investigating dreams, each of us can tap into a deeper level of understanding ourselves in a profoundly satisfying way.

Dreams Defined

The question I am asked every time I appear on a television or radio show is, of course, "What are dreams?" I am the expert, so certainly I should have some brilliant answer that is definitive, satisfying, and absolute. If only that were true. The bottom line is, we have absolutely no idea what dreams are or why we have them. Neuroscience is making enormous strides in understanding more and more about the function of dreams with regard to memory formation, learning and cognition, and mood stabilization. But these answers focus on the technical aspects of the brain during the dreaming process and do nothing to elaborate on the psychic, emotional, and spiritual reasons why we dream.

My personal challenge with this is that most of the scientists who make these discoveries pepper their published research with various snipes at the more mystical function of dreams, as if to say, we now know dreams have a regulatory neurological function, therefore, the notion that dreams have any deeper meaning has been proven wrong. While this annoys me quite a bit, I take solace in the fact that the mystics of the world have always been way ahead of the scientists in knowing the truth.

For the purpose of dream work and dream interpretation, let's just decide that dreams are messages from the unconscious mind. They reveal us to ourselves by providing glimpses of information ordinarily hidden beyond the boundaries of the conscious mind. Presented through the language of symbols, dreams are like raw materials mined from the depths of the human psyche. When satisfyingly interpreted, they are transformed into precious gems that adorn the path of self-discovery and self-investigation.

In both the Introduction and Chapter 1, I referred to the experience I have as a dream interpreter that just delights me to no end. It's when I see a sense of recognition wash over the dreamer's face, and their eyes widen with delight and amazement in that "aha" moment. Sometimes, the person will even cry. Now does any of this make the interpretation true, right, or real? I have no idea. What I do know is this: someone presents a dream and in prompting them to explore the associations they have with the symbols, together we arrive at a possible interpretation. There is a moment of identification with the interpretation that is palpable, visceral, and very rewarding to the dreamer. This may not make it true, but it certainly makes it valuable.

So, if dreams are to be considered messages from the unconscious, we must accept that the unconscious *really is* unconscious. That is to say, we really do not know most of what is rumbling around outside of our conscious awareness. Besides, whatever is happening in the brain during the dreaming process that can (and certainly ought to) be described in scientific, technological terms, there is also something mystical occurring. Somehow, a doorway opens between these two otherwise separate realms of the mind. By taking a look at dreams through interpretation, we are actually engaging in a conversation between the unconscious and conscious mind.

It's kind of like a knock-knock joke. You have a dream in which the brain is saying, "Knock, knock." Remembering the dream, and after spending some time thinking about it, you say back to your unconscious, "Who's there?" The next night in another dream the unconscious mind says, "Boo!" The next day, after thinking about the second dream, you say back to your unconscious mind, "Boo who?" And in yet another dream on another night, the joke is completed with the punch line.

From day to day, night to night, dream to dream, we participate in a sophisticated, on-going series of knock-knock jokes through which the unconscious and the conscious mind have a dialogue. The more we dialogue in this fashion, the better we will know ourselves. The better we know ourselves, the more effective we will be as people facing life on its own terms; living fully, with consciousness, awareness, wisdom, and sensitivity.

All of us are having this experience every time we sleep. Even people who can not remember their dreams are still dreaming—if we didn't dream, our heads would explode. Well, not really, but we would eventually have psychotic breakdowns. And whether we remember them or not, it is in our dreams that we actually learn and grow in wisdom. We take in information each day, download that information during the process of dreaming, and wake up the next day smarter, more conscious, and ready to face the challenges of our daily lives once again.

I believe there is an intense drive behind the unconscious mind's desire to express itself to us. There is also a built-in and powerful receptivity to engaging the unconscious in any way that expands our self awareness. The efforts we make to increase the dynamic between conscious and unconscious communication will result in an expansion of your dreaming experience—in intensity, in frequency, and in the value that we can get from interpreting them.

Character Aspects

Dreams are filled with people. Some we know, others are strangers. Sometimes, we know exactly who a dream character is despite the fact that he or she may look nothing like the person they seem to represent. And while dreams feature a myriad of settings, objects, themes, creatures—the list is endless—the bulk of our dreams contain people more than any other type of image.

There is an adage in dream work which expresses the belief that everyone in a dream is a part of the dreamer. While this is not the only way to approach the people who appear in our dreams, it is the only way that I work because, for me, it is the perspective that offers the most value. This is not to say that dreams which involve people who are close to us in our lives are not reflecting the relationships we have with them. They are. However, the dream work that I am drawn to is entirely about self-investigation. Therefore, considering every person who appears in a dream as representing a part of our own personalities is the best route to go. I call these individual representations "Character Aspects," and each one represents an aspect of the personality.

I have noticed how often we use language to describe how we feel that goes something like this: "Part of me feels one way and part of me feels another." This is a great example of how we organize our inner experiences in a compartmentalized way. Dreams operate on the same principle, but exclusively through the language of symbols. It is in this way that the people in our dreams are symbolic representations of different aspects of ourselves.

The term Character Aspect appears frequently in Part 2: The Dream Dictionary. I use it whenever the interpretation process requires incorporating the meaning of a person who has appeared in a dream. There is a very simple technique designed to aid discovery of what a specific Character Aspect means on a personal level. I call this the "Three Adjective Rule."

Give it a try right now. Choose a person and identify three adjectives that best describe him or her. Try not to think too hard about what adjectives to choose. Being as spontaneous as possible helps our unconscious minds work with us to find the right words. While it isn't always necessary to use three, it is helpful in order to see if a theme emerges.

I'll share a few examples from my own life. A professor of mine from graduate school was very analytical and, at times, harshly critical—that's the polite version to describe him. If he showed up in a dream, I knew that he was a Character Aspect of the critical part of me.

On the other side of the spectrum, I have a close friend who is one of the warmest, most affectionate individuals I have ever known. If she were to appear in a dream, she would be a Character Aspect of my own capacity for warmth and affection.

Let's use an example from a real dream of an actual client. A woman had a dream in which her high school English teacher was standing at the back of the conference room where she was soon to give a presentation to coworkers. When asked for three adjectives to describe the English teacher, the dreamer replied "negative," "harsh," and "demanding." It was easy for her to understand and even express to me how nervous she was about the upcoming presentation. But it was through examining her high school English teacher as a Character Aspect of herself that she was able to relieve some of her anxiety and realize that she was her own worst critic.

It is hard to envision people we know as parts of our own personalities. In these cases, it's best to attempt to stay very detached and consider how *someone else* might describe the people who show up in our dreams. In that way, it is possible to reach a more objective sense of these people as Character Aspects of ourselves.

Of course, the dream world is also populated with people we have never met. When this is the case, we have to use whatever information there is from the dream and any details we can remember about them. The less stuff offered by the dream, the more work it will take to discover what Character Aspects might be represented by these strangers.

Sometimes this is not at all easy to do, especially if a Character Aspect represents personality elements that we don't readily relate to. I ran into this with a client who so resisted this idea that it took every ounce of my patience to guide her through the process. She was a woman in her late twenties, and her dream was about an older, female boss who she worked for many years prior to when she had the dream. When picking the three adjectives, she came up with "aggressive," "powerfu,l" and "unethical." It was clear to me that the merciless boss-lady from the dream was a Character Aspect of the part of the dreamer who was capable of being ruthless and unconcerned with the moral constructs of right and wrong.

My client didn't like this process one bit. In her waking life, this young woman certainly did her best to do the right thing in every situation and would hardly be considered ruthless. Ironically, while she railed against the idea I asked her to consider, she became quite ruthless in her defensiveness. She finally relented and understood what I was trying to convey when I explained to her that all things live inside of us; the good as well as the seemingly bad.

To be truly effective with dream work, there must be a willingness to explore all sides of ourselves. Remember that the unconscious mind knows the totality of who we are—even the parts that are ugly, unpleasant, and hidden away from conscious awareness. This hidden part of ourselves is called the Shadow, which brings us to one of the most powerful and important concepts of effective dream work.

The Shadow

The Shadow is my absolute favorite part of dream work. In fact, the notion of the Shadow impacts all areas of self-investigation. Jung actually considered the Shadow to be an Archetype, which I discuss in the next section of this chapter. I am more inclined to describe the Shadow as an area of the unconscious. And as its name implies, it is home to all the elements of the human condition that are dark and shadowy.

The Shadow is that portion of the unconscious where we hide parts of ourselves that we think are distasteful, hated, rejected, disowned, and unacceptable. By burying these rejected parts deep within the hidden recesses of our minds, we are able to remain blind to them in our conscious awareness. The basic idea behind this is that *all the potential expressions* of the human condition are contained within every individual. For example, murderous rage lives in everyone. For the most part, few of us will ever act on those impulses; but by virtue of being human, every quality that can be expressed—including those that are dangerous, shameful, and otherwise objectionable—is housed in the Shadow area of the mind, safely out of view.

For the average person, an endless variety of dark, socially unacceptable emotions remain safely tucked away and never see the light of day outside of our dreams. By allowing them to reside in the Shadow, we can be fully human and still function properly within society. The undesirable aspects of the Shadow are capable of being more fully expressed in our dreams precisely because they are not subject to the same editing process that our thoughts and behaviors are in waking life.

Many of the Character Aspects that appear in our dreams are Shadow characters. Some may be people we dislike intensely in waking life. However, any Character Aspect—whether known or unknown—that exhibits rage, dangerousness, deception, or other challenging behavior in a dream might be emanating from the Shadow.

Not everything in the Shadow is horrifying. We all have innocuous or mundane characteristics in our personalities that we push below the surface if we find them unacceptable in some way. In the world of psychology, we call this process "disowning." Timidity, feelings of ineptness, confusion, and vulnerability are just a few inoffensive traits that some people might disown. No one in their right mind would ever consider me to be a shy person; but shyness lives in my Shadow. The great irony of Shadow material is that what we disown and remain unaware of is exactly the stuff that has the most influence over how we operate in the world. Dreams are amazing at revealing our Shadow to us.

It's a good idea to become acquainted with the concept of the Shadow, and to get a sense of what is Shadow material in our own waking lives in order to become effective at this part of dream work. The easiest ways to identify what is in the Shadow is to look around and notice what makes us crazy about others in our day-to-day lives. If something that someone else does or says drives us insane, chances are we have discovered something from our own Shadow.

A person who feels uncomfortable around strongly opinionated people most likely has some strong opinions hidden in their own Shadow. The quiet person who finds overbearing people repugnant to their sensibilities has a loud, overbearing Character Aspect stuffed just below the surface of their quiet, reserved exterior. Someone who is sensitive to criticism may have pushed awareness of their own critical nature into their Shadow self. A rough-edged, abrasive person who equates sensitivity with weakness might very well carry their soft, gentle side in their Shadow; in other words, a jerk may always be a jerk and have no access to the kind person buried deep inside their Shadow. A take-charge person who must always feel in control might have buried their sense of helplessness out of sight. The key point here is that something is only Shadow material if it is disowned and, therefore, rejected by the conscious self.

There are tremendous gifts associated with getting to know the disowned self. It facilitates discovering more about who we *really* are, rather than who we imagine ourselves to be or wish that we were. The more authentic we can be, the further down the path toward emotional balance we will find ourselves. Since dreams are largely based in Shadow material, doing dream work can be one of the most effective tools available to assist us on this journey.

In dreams, certain themes are clear indications that we are dealing with the Shadow. Nightmares are an obvious sign of this. However, any imagery that is overtly dark in nature, such as dreams that take place at night, settings that are inherently gloomy, or the presence of danger should also be thought of as Shadow elements.

Another clue that the Shadow is appearing in a dream is when a character appears that is unmistakably contrary to our physical appearance. If a dark-haired character appears in the dream of a light-haired person or vice versa, it could be a Shadow Character Aspect.

The same goes for differences in skin color or other distinctive physical attributes that are significantly different from our own.

When interpreting a dream, identifying the Shadow is more of a concept to consider than a specific tool to utilize. It is a framework through which to view the information being revealed by the unconscious mind. While examining these areas can be confronting and uncomfortable, it is essentially unavoidable. Our dreams offer us glimpses into often uncharted territory, much of which can be dark and scary. Effective dream work requires being thorough and courageous and when all is said and done, the Shadow is really our best friend.

Archetypes

In his writings, Jung described the notion that there are certain energies present in our universe that were here long before we humans came along. As the human race developed, we naturally formed ideas around these pre-existing energies that became part of the stories that eventually became the hallmark of emerging culture. These stories developed into the myths that formed the early pagan religions of Greece and later Rome.

Plato described Archetypes as ideal forms of certain specific qualities. The gods of his culture were characters that represented these ideal forms. Aphrodite was the Goddess of Love. Aries was the God of War. The qualities here are love and aggression; the characters that embody these qualities are the Archetypes themselves: In this case and using the Roman monikers, we're talking about Venus and Mars.

In a way, Archetypal Characters are similar to and should be interpreted just like Character Aspects. However, it should be remembered that they operate on a grander scale and they possess a level of universality that reaches across the entire human race. What seems important in understanding how they impact us is the fact that all people seem to relate to them in a similar fashion. Because of the consistency of this experience, archetypal energy has created characters that appear over and over again in the stories and mythology of all cultures from the beginning of recorded time. They are as present for us today as they were thousands of years ago.

Let's go back to the notion of love as an archetypal principle as an example, because it is one that is pretty easy to relate to. Every culture throughout history includes characters that embody this basic human experience. We have already connected the dots between Aphrodite for the Greeks and Venus for the Romans. There is not a single bit of difference between these two ancient Archetypes of mythological love and say, Marilyn Monroe, with the minor exception that underneath the persona of Ms. Monroe was the tortured woman named Norma Jeane Mortenson.

Our modern-day athletes, whom we revere as heroes, are today's Archetypes of virility and strength in the way Hercules was to the Romans who worshiped him. We have, of course, connected the archetypal persona to a living, breathing human being, who has flaws, foibles, and the potential for failure, to create the inflated, perfect media *image* we admire.

It is fair to say that anyone who rises into public visibility is vibrating with an archetypal energy. Jungian psychology paved the way for contemporary psychologists to codify the Archetype, creating various sets of identifiable characters that people recognize across the boundaries of language and culture. Several key Archetypal Characters are listed as terms in the Dream Dictionary. Additionally, while choosing the terms to present in this first edition, I opted for those symbols that had more archetypal foundations than those that had less. For instance, I included "Skyscraper" because the image of this purely American symbol represents the massive upward expansion that emerged out of the enormous explosion of abundance of the last century; this is an archetypal idea that lives in the collective consciousness of the modern era. A term I considered but opted out was "Flesh-eating Bacteria." While it has certain titillation and I have heard a handful of dreamers report the image from dreams, there is much less archetypal content to this symbol. In having to make choices to cut, such a term went by the wayside. Archetypal symbols are undoubtedly going to be more valuable to more people because of their inherent universality.

While knowing the specific identity of all of these Archetypes and archetypal imagery is not necessary in order for you to be effective in your dream work, it is necessary to understand the concept. Many of the figures who appear to us in our dreams are, in fact, Archetypes and need to be interpreted as such.

You can recognize an Archetype in a dream by a number of clues. Firstly, the Archetypal Character will not be anyone you know personally. Secondly, an Archetypal Character will more often than not have a singular, specific persona as opposed to the way in which many dream characters are volatile, changeable, and unpredictable. Some examples of frequently appearing Archetypes initially identified by Jung are the King, Queen, Wise Old Man or Old Crone or Witch, the Lover, the Magician, the Trickster, the Divine Child, and the Warrior, to name just a few.

There is a style of dream that can be an indication you have had a clearly archetypal dream. Most dreams are very chaotic and frenetic, jumping from scene to scene with very little cohesiveness. An archetypal dream is more likely to exhibit one scene, one character, and very little movement. One of Jung's favorite archetypal dreams was of a wise character standing in a field of wheat. Nothing else occurred besides this one very still image and Jung spent a lot of time contemplating on what this powerful dream meant for him. Often in such dreams as this one that Jung wrote about, the character will not speak or be otherwise interactive. If a dream contains a strong, silent presence of a clearly definable character, it is an archetypal dream.

When this occurs, approach the interpretation process the same way as with any Character Aspect; however, the presence of an Archetypal character in a dream has a deeper significance. While most dreams are reflecting the experiences, challenges, and processes of everyday life, the presence of an Archetype indicates a moment in life where a major integration is occurring deep within the psyche on the soul's journey toward a higher level of evolution as a human being.

The Collective Unconscious

Earlier in this chapter, I introduced the notion of Jung's most significant discovery as it relates to dream work; the Collective Unconscious. The Archetypes and archetypal images we have just described actually exist in the Collective Unconscious and call it home.

To understand the Collective Unconscious, we must begin with the Personal Unconscious. Through the popularity of psychoanalysis that began in the 1930s, most people in the West now have a basic understanding of the unconscious. This is the part of our human mind that is on the invisible side of life; it remains hidden from our conscious awareness and the contents of it are essentially unknown to us. This is the part of the mind I like to refer to as the Personal Unconscious, but do not get too caught up in yet another technical construct that you have to understand. What I am calling the Personal Unconscious is really just another name for what we commonly understand as the unconscious mind. I use the term Personal at this point in our discussion to distinguish it from the Collective Unconscious. The notion that we have an unconscious mind is generally accepted in our day-to-day experience in popular culture. The Collective Unconscious is less familiar and less well-known. Simply put; the Personal Unconscious is what we experience as individuals and the Collective Unconscious is what we experience globally.

Truthfully, we really have no way of knowing if the unconscious actually exists, but I'm certainly convinced. Its presence is revealed to us through behaviors we cannot justify, choices we make that we don't understand, reactions to events that do not energetically match the event itself, or my personal favorite: slips of the tongue that embarrass us because they reveal hidden desires we hadn't planned to expose. It is considered by many to be a mysterious and frightening place, yet our easy access to it in dreams can be one of the most exciting aspects of being human.

It is only fitting to take a brief moment and clarify the notion of the subconscious and the unconscious. These two terms have been used interchangeably over the past one hundred thirty years and I have no desire to have the different opinions about their meaning and usage confuse the reader while using this book. There are those who would stake their reputations that these two terms have very different meanings. Just as many would blow gaskets insisting the opposite. The academic truth of the matter is this: There is absolutely no fundamental difference to each term. They have been used interchangeably by different psychological theorists over the past century, based solely on the whim of the theorists. The realm of the human mind that is unknown to use and that houses instincts, hidden tendencies, Shadow material, and all else we have been describing (like dreams, creativity, imagination, etc.) is the subconscious mind. The unconscious mind refers to the *exact same stuff!*

I have my own very specific perspective of the best use of each of these two terms. They are different words and, therefore, should have different meanings. I use the word unconscious frequently and the word subconscious almost never. This is a very definite choice and is based on the linguistic distinctions of each. I refer to the subconscious as the part of the mind that is hidden and mysterious and that will *always stay that way* (and perhaps for good reason). The flip side of this is that the unconscious mind is the part of the psyche that is disowned, hidden, and unknowable, but which *has the potential* for becoming known: through self-investigation, creative expression, risky and vulnerable communication, and dream work, of course. The unconscious, therefore, is a realm of immeasurable value. It is that which is invisible today, but may be visible tomorrow. It is the land of all human potential and I believe that it is possessed by an overwhelming desire to be known, seen, and understood.

It bears repeating that in addition to the disquieting, powerful, and frightening unseen forces that lurk below the surface of our thinking, the unconscious is also home to intuition, imagination, creativity, and spontaneity. It is also where our dreams come from. More importantly, if we can accept the existence of the unconscious mind, it may be easier to make the leap to understanding what the Collective Unconscious encompasses.

The Collective Unconscious goes even deeper than the unconscious mind. It is a realm of experience that exists in all human beings. It connects each individual to every other person living on the planet, taking us back through our genetic history and all the way to the beginning of time itself. Because it is not something that can be scientifically proven, we only know of its existence through the commonality of experience that all of us share collectively. The incredibly powerful reach of the media makes this even more intense. Who doesn't turn on the news and feel an emotional tug when confronted with events around the world. We may think this response is just personal, but there is a powerful experience of things happening in the world that is deeply felt by each of us; the depth of these feelings has its origin in the Collective Unconscious.

The real beauty of how the Collective Unconscious impacts dreaming is that, through this shared level of the human experience, an individual dreamer can connect to symbolic meaning of which they have absolutely no awareness of in waking life. That is to say, even without personal knowledge of such an image, it is possible to be aware of its symbolic meaning on a deeper level. Often this requires the dreamer to do a little research to discover what the dream is trying to tell them. Additionally, a leap of faith may be required to accept, as true, the information being offered.

A man in his forties once came to me for a session at a time in his life when there was an enormous amount of intense change. He had been laid off from a job in a successful career that he had been longing to leave for years because of a high level of burnout. He had a certain level of freedom due to profitable investments and a lucrative settlement from his job. Still, he experienced a great deal of anxiety about a choice he faced, and his dream life had exploded as he faced this significant moment.

Of the many dreams we explored, there was one that grabbed my attention right away. In the dream, he stood at the beach and off in the water was a beautiful woman who sang to him. Her voice captivated him and, in the romanticism of the moment, he was tempted to swim out to her. When we explored who she might be, he made an association between his dream-singer and a woman who lived in a far-off city, with whom he had been engaged in a long-distance relationship. While he really wanted to connect with the woman on the rock, he found himself making excuse after excuse not to jump in the water.

I pushed him to identify for himself a single sense of what held him back. I wanted him to explore a more feeling-based reason for why he didn't just dive in and swim out to the beautiful singer. After a moment, he quietly said that he didn't feel it would be safe. He felt danger out there, though he could not identify what that danger might be.

I told him a tale from Greek mythology about the Sirens—beautiful creatures that live on the rocks near the shore and use their lovely voices to lure sailors to their death. He immediately became emotional and made an association with the story of the Sirens and the ambivalence he felt toward this woman. He often felt manipulated by her, and that she used his current uncertain circumstances to try to get him to leave his home and move across the country—something he was dead set against.

At first, the interpretation landed on him with great clarity and offered him a sense of decision that brought him immense relief.

However, when I explained the notion that it was the myth itself that was responsible for this particular dream and the guidance he received, he balked. He wondered how that could possibly be true when he knew nothing about Greek mythology, and more importantly, he couldn't care less about the subject matter.

It didn't take much to convince him of the vibrant presence of the Collective Unconscious. Before long, he became one of the initiated. He now fully respects the fact that no *conscious* connection is needed in order to receive a piece of information in a dream. The Collective Unconscious connects all human beings and through it there isn't anything we can't tap into if we open our minds and hearts to the possibility of what mysteries are available through the invisible side of life.

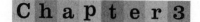

Chapter 3
TYPES OF DREAMS

Dreams are excursions into the limbo of things,
a semi-deliverance from the human prison.
—HENRI AMIEL

Overview

One of the questions I am most often asked is "Does every dream mean something?" My stock answer is always, "Only if you ask." While that response is admittedly a little flippant, what I'm really saying is that, of course, every dream has meaning. Why would something about our lives that is so rich and vibrant have meaning some of the time, but not others? Everything in life has meaning, every moment. The real question people should be asking is whether or not it is necessary to interpret every dream. And while that is an interesting notion to ponder, if I thought we had to interpret every dream we ever had, we might never get out of bed.

Different dreams do different things for us. In this way, there are a few basic categories into which most dreams fall. As a good steward of your dreaming life, it would be valuable for you to know the difference between some of these basic types of dreams. And though it is not necessary to classify a dream's type in order to interpret it, knowing these distinctions can only enhance the way you approach dream work.

Compensatory Dreams

This is the category of most of the dreams we have. Compensatory comes from the word compensate. When a thing compensates, it is making up for something that is missing or trading one thing for another. Think of compensation as synonymous for getting paid for work. This is really about balancing a situation out: I do *this* for you and you pay me *that*. Hopefully, at the end of the day both sides feel like the exchange is fair.

The human psyche is much like a happy employer-employee relationship in which I imagine the roles of who does the work and who issues the paycheck are interchangeable. At times, the dreams make the effort and we experience great transformation without having to know exactly what is happening inside our minds. At other times, we have to do the work before our unconscious selves can reap the benefits of becoming more conscious. Only then are we more self-aware and comfortable in our own skins.

Dreaming itself is designed to perform this task. Our dreams help us achieve a level of psychic equilibrium that allows us to function in our lives on a day-to-day basis. They help us learn new information, whether that information is about the algebra we are going to be tested on in math class or the mysteries of life. This occurs unconsciously, whether we remember our dreams or not.

Each time we sleep deeply enough to dream, we are enacting experiences that help us process the information that we are being bombarded with during the day. Because the language is symbolic and not literal, it is usually not clear to us, initially, what is being addressed. This is one of the reasons why dream interpretation can be so valuable. Life is a constant series of confrontations with experiences that are not only challenging in and of themselves, but many of them also tap into the memories of earlier wounds and hurts that we carry with us. By confronting and expressing our deepest fears, secret desires, and exhausting challenges in the safe confines of the dream state, we are able to wake up and return to our daily lives feeling restored to balance. In fact, sometimes, the dream world offers us a forum to process difficult emotions such as rage or grief that would be impossible to do in our daily lives without debilitating levels of confrontation or embarrassment.

The magical nature of dreams can also allow the dreamer to attain impossible desires, which can relieve certain tensions much in the same way that scratching can cause the sensation of an itch to disappear. This is sometimes referred to as "wish fulfillment." I have never liked this term. To me it implies that if you desire something that you may never achieve and then wish for it and get it in a dream, somehow that desire must be something you don't deserve. Let's just leave it with the idea that dreams can often satisfy the need to fulfill a longing or a desire so that you can awake feeling complete and not seeing your life as missing something that is not present.

Not every compensatory dream has a desirable outcome. Dreaming of having sex with a beautiful movie star may represent a wish fulfilled; but it might also be compensating for an underlying lack in the dreamer's self-esteem or perceived level of attractiveness. Also, desirable may not always be synonymous with constructive. A friend of mine exemplified this perfectly with his frequent dreams of murdering his detested neighbor. If ever there was a wish fulfillment dream, this was it. I am thoroughly convinced that if it weren't actually against the law, my friend would have murdered the guy next door. On the surface, the wish fulfilled looks like getting rid of the source of the frustration. However, the real purpose of the dream was to help my friend process his anger in such a way that he was better equipped to wake up the next morning and not have to act out his feelings, because he had actually already done so in his dreams.

I like to use examples of dreams from clients that I've worked with whenever possible. And here is one that I particularly like, because it involved the inappropriateness of using off-colored language in front of children, something that contributes much to the consternation of people who have kids of that impressionable age who will repeat every new word they learn.

The dreamer, a mother of two, had been experiencing an enormous amount of stress over family finances. The tension caused her husband and her to argue intensely, often in front of their two small children. They were sensitive enough about the impact this had on their kids and agreed to stop having such conversations in front of them, since it both upset the children and clearly wasn't helping the situation. Though the financial challenges were unchanged, the environment in the home immediately shifted, much to my client's relief. However, about two days after this agreement was made, she had this dream:

> I was in a department store and there was a man with a little baby, maybe eighteen months old. Right in front of him, I said, "Oh f**k!" He looked at me with shock and I felt terrible. I said, "I'm so sorry, I have two kids at home and I never curse … it just flew out of my mouth. I apologize for saying it in front of your child." He looked at me with a stern look that seemed to say, "Your excuses don't erase the fact that my child heard that word."

Now, we all know that expletives are expressions of violence and anger. While both my client and her husband were behaving more calm and relaxed in front of their children, since they had stopped the fighting, they no longer had a satisfying arena in which to express their enormous frustration around money. The fights didn't feel good, but they had served a purpose. This dream allowed her to release the pent-up emotional pressure, but not at the expense of her children's sensitivity. When we explored the meaning of the dream through this interpretation, she had a great epiphany. She immediately understood that her dream had compensated for the loss of the forum that the fighting had been providing. She was then able to have private conversations with her husband about the fears and frustrations she felt about money. And miraculously, though the feelings were still the same, the anger and the blame dissipated.

Recurring Dreams

Recurring dreams are not the most common dreams people have, but they are the most readily remembered and frequently talked-about dreams when I do workshops. I assume this is so because the fact that they recur keeps them in the forefront of the dreamer's mind. And this is, of course, the underlying purpose of a recurring dream. If a dream comes again and again, it is attempting to do something very specific, which is to get your attention.

I have divided recurring dreams into two very distinct categories. This is because while they both appear to fit under the same general topic heading of recurring, that is—they recur—they are very different styles of dreaming that have completely different functions. The first category of recurring dreams is stress related and the second is process related.

Stress-related Recurring Dreams

Stress is a constant companion to us in the Western world. We are born into it and for most of us, it is a way of approaching life that has become a macabre sort of paradox, which we use as an actual tool for getting through life. Presented with obligations and obstacles, we have grown to believe that in order to effectively meet those obligations and overcome those obstacles, it is the stress itself that helps us do that. This is, of course, a magnificent lie that is not only tragic in its utter fallacy, it is a misconception that is fatal. Stress kills.

There are all kinds of beneficial and scientifically proven stress combatants—exercise, meditation, and medication to yoga and breath work—the list goes on and on. However, one prominent, organic tool for reducing stress is actually built into the human mechanism; it is dreaming, which is, without a doubt, the most effective stress combatant there is.

The stress we experience throughout our lives changes. Varied circumstances, issues based on our chronology and age, and confrontations that depend on the areas of life that are causing anxiety will differ greatly. What will not always be different, however, is the way in which the unconscious mind will use dreams to regulate that stress and reduce it to non-lethal levels, allowing us to wake up each morning and do it all over again.

Because the human mind is economical, it will often turn to a recognizable image that has worked in the past to convey certain emotional states. We experience this in the form of recurring dreams, such as being chased, falling, or being naked in public, to name a few common ones that trouble us from time to time. These dreams are not usually filled with elaborate plots and characterizations, but are rather simplistic, with a familiar theme.

Dreams of being chased will likely not have much detail beyond the act of running from the enemy, who is often unknown to the dreamer. These dreams, which are remembered as frightening and usually leave us with residual anxiety, serve an important purpose when our waking lives present us with scary experiences. A person under excessive stress might experience this dream image in order to process the unconscious fears that come up as the result of chaos in their life. Surviving the danger or panic present in the dream may actually help us to navigate our daytime obstacles. It is in living out the raw blast of unbridled fear in our dreams that allows us to wake up and feel a sense of balance that, without the dream, would leave us emotionally ragged.

The dream of returning unprepared to a high school setting also falls into this category. It often recurs when someone is not feeling ready or prepared for whatever life is presenting. At a moment where the ability to perform is under scrutiny, we might have dreams of being back in high school and unprepared for a test. Any dream that points out this sort of vulnerability is helping to balance out underlying feelings of inadequacy or insecurity.

Other anxiety-based dreams include teeth falling out, being lost, or being under attack. All of these are connected to underlying feelings of fear. Since these themes commonly recur in life, they commonly recur in our dreams.

I hear over and over again from people who say they "always dream of _____ (fill in the blank)." It is not that these people have no dream imagination; it is much more about the effectiveness of the dream process as a tool for helping the mind achieve balance. As an example, say someone has a recurring dream of driving a car up a steep hill until finally the incline is so steep that their car can no longer move forward and begins to slide backward out of control. The feeling of completely losing control as the car careens backward is terrifying. Of course, as panic sets in and we plummet toward certain death, we wake up.

Some people have this dream frequently, perhaps monthly, and have done so for years. This is simply the mind's dynamic response to this particular image. It is perfectly suited to express the various stresses in our lives. It hardly matters what it is in our waking life that inspires the dream. Either an argument with a friend or worrying about paying a large credit card bill on time could illicit the very same dream. While waking-life circumstances are clearly very different in nature, the dream that helps us restore psychic balance is the same.

Process-based Recurring Dreams

The process-based recurring dream is very different from the stress-related dreams described above. These benefit the most from dream work, and they often are the reason a new client will seek out my services. It is the frightening nature of these dreams that propels people to seek out the guidance of someone like me. Although process-based recurring dreams may vary in certain ways, they are considered recurring because they show repeated themes and sometimes developing stories, when each dream builds somehow on the previous dream. In fact, a series of dreams that occurs over a period of a week or more can be alarming, with regard to the information they reveal.

When I am working in an on-going basis with a client, very often the dreams they have and record nightly during the week that may pass between sessions fall into this category. While these dreams are not necessarily frightening, they can be treated as a series that exemplify the moniker of these dreams—they are process based.

What I mean by process based as opposed to anxiety based is this: Anxiety-based dreams provide a very simple function. They take elements of our waking life that cause us anxiety and help our minds lessen that anxiety so that we can face life a bit freer of that debilitating human challenge—the anxious mind. Process-based dreams are specifically aligned with a change or transformation that someone is going through that is particular to a life circumstance or series of confronting or challenging events. The "process" that is being exemplified here is the process of growing, expanding consciousness, and changing from the inside out.

These dreams appear in varying continuity from a few times in a short period to repeatedly over many years. Usually more elaborate, they tend to involve images particular to the dreamer's life experience. These more personalized dreams usually connect to a specific emotional wound that may be being healed through the dream world. The distinction with this type of dream is that it will relate specifically to the issue being expressed. Keep in mind that, like most dreams, an interpretation will be required to uncover the meaning that lies beneath the confusing or convoluted imagery that the dream presents. This type of dream may change slightly with each recurrence and will continue till the process completes itself.

One example that should be easy to relate to connects to how dream work can help us to process loss and grief. When we lose someone through death or the end of a relationship, we often dream of that person in a way that reflects the gradual letting go that accompanies such a separation. The dreams may recur until the process of separating feels complete. Each dream may be thematically similar, but have shifting elements that embody the change taking place. Each progressive dream may show less and less proximity to the person being dreamt about. This reflects the arc of the grief process and the dreams will likely stop when that process is over.

Any dramatic life change can be expressed through a series of recurring dream images. A woman in her thirties who moved away from home after a divorce reported a recurring dream about cars after driving across the country to her new life. Each successive dream reflected her then current relationship to this life change by virtue of the condition and type of car that appeared in her dreams. The smoother her waking life seemed to go, the more effective the cars appeared to be. She could literally chart her own emotional development by the level of functioning of the cars in her dreams.

I used this story in the Introduction; however it is such a wonderful example of dream work in action, I feel comfortable using it again here. A woman in her late twenties had a recurring nightmare of being pregnant and murdering her newborn child. In each successive dream, she carried the baby to term, only to kill it after giving birth. She was horrified by this series of recurring nightmares and sought help to understand what they might mean. Once she viewed the dreams through the Universal Landscape of "babies as new directions in her life," she was able to connect the fearful dreams with the numerous first drafts of a creative project she wanted to get off the ground. The dreams expressed her trial and error approach and the frustration of having to kill off the creative impulses that didn't feel right to make space to birth something better. Once seen in this light, the dreams lost their frightening hold over her and the nightmares immediately stopped.

Though not as relevant to some, a clear example of a process-oriented recurring dream is frequently experienced by my clients who have been battling some form of addiction after achieving a level of sobriety. A recovering addict may have dreams of slipping back into their destructive behavior. Addictive behavior serves the purpose of creating an emotional buffer from life's difficulties. When a daytime experience challenges the emotional vulnerability of such a person, they may counteract overwhelming feelings by dreaming of their old form of escape. It may be the very thing that allows them to face their fears without relinquishing their success in sobriety. While such dreams are often accompanied by levels of regret as intense as if the fall off the wagon had occurred in life, these dreams usually subside as the person continues to stay sober.

Here's an example from my own life. As I was finishing this book, I felt, at times, overwhelmed with the process. At one point, I had a crisis where I was completely unable to work and had absolutely no idea why I was so blocked. Of course, I understood on an intellectual level that I was experiencing a pervading sense of dread that, although completing the book would certainly be a fairly large achievement, it would also mark the beginning of even more effort to bring my work to the world in a concrete and significant way. During this time, I had five recurring dreams of climbing Mount Kilimanjaro in three days time, with my family of origin. In the dreams, I was feeling overwhelmed at the task itself, but I was also excited by the prospect of facing the unknown dangers and felt great anticipation about what it would be like to reach the summit.

This series of dreams was clearly connected to the unconscious feelings of resistance to the hard work that my life required of me. Climbing the mountain in my dreams was the symbolic climb that my life sometimes felt like. Because my family of origin was part of these dreams, I knew that I was considering my entire life and not just this small moment in time. By working with this dream series in a very diligent manner, I found my discipline increase and my focus sharpen. And just as valuable, I was able to connect deeply and authentically to my fear, vulnerability, and utter terror at the prospect that I had to be at least willing to consider: "What if I wasn't as up to the challenge as I thought I was?" The dream work I did in the weeks following the dreams allowed me to face the fears head on. The end result was that the book was completed despite the emotional and psychic obstacles I faced.

Precognitive Dreams

Intuitive phenomena come in many different forms for many different people, but they all have one thing in common: the use or expression of what is sometimes called the "sixth sense." This is a way of synthesizing information that is not derived from the five generally accepted senses of sight, touch, smell, taste, and hearing. People with this facility are sometimes called psychic or clairvoyant. Sometimes, this innately human ability is referred to as "instincts" or "street smarts." No matter what you call it, all human beings are intuitive to some extent, although few people trust their instincts.

On the other side of this coin are the insufferable people who believe that their perceptions are so keen, they feel compelled to share their "gifts" with anyone and everyone they meet. Suffice to say that intuition is an area of the human experience that is misunderstood by most. And all too often, among those who claim to understand the phenomenon, it is misused by either overinflating the value of the information that the intuition provides or contemptuously dismissing the same information.

Intuition can be accessed without any distraction or doubtful second-guessing by people in their dreams. Some may connect so easily to their sixth sense in this way that, on occasion, they report having dreams that contain information about events that have yet to occur. This is called precognitive dreaming. There are two general types of precognitive dreaming.

The first and most common type is when a person has a dream in which the scenario and sometimes the events of a dream seem to occur in the dreamer's waking life anywhere from days to weeks or even years following the dream. Often, the dreamer doesn't recognize such a dream experience as precognitive dreaming unless a daytime event is a replay of the similar scenario in a recent dream. For example, someone may be doing their grocery shopping, and in passing another shopper, their shopping carts bump. The dreamer suddenly remembers, perhaps quite unexpectedly, that just such an interaction occurred in a recent dream—shopping cart and all. It is hard to identify if this is an actual psychic phenomenon or just a trick of a vivid imagination, but it is certainly an experience I have heard described on many occasions by people from all walks of life.

The second type of precognitive dreaming is something that might inspire a good deal of skepticism. I have never experienced it myself, so I can not validate or invalidate the accuracy of such stories from a scientific perspective. However, I can report what I have heard over the years, and I have to acknowledge that many different people at very different times have described to me such dreams in a very similar way—so much so that I am led more toward belief than disbelief that such a thing is real.

These are the dreams of people who see future events in their dreams and also experience dream-like visitations from people who have just died, without their knowledge that the person in question has indeed passed away. One example about a future event was described to me by a woman who claimed to have had precognitive dreams her entire life. She dreamed of her sister having a car accident while driving in a blue car in the rain. Indeed, several months later, her sister crashed into a railing during a rain storm in her new blue car.

This same woman said that several of her relatives came to her bedroom when she was in a semi-dream state. Then, she would learn the following day or two later that those who visited her had passed away. I have heard this same phenomenon described by many different people over the years. Again, I am not including this section because I believe in this phenomenon or that I disbelieve in it. I have simply heard the stories too many times to leave them out.

What is consistent about these types of dreams as described to me is as follows: They are not chaotic or frenetic in the way that most dreams are. They usually consist of one setting and the event that is being foretold, and they are presented with clarity, chronology, and simplicity.

When these dreams involve the passing of loved ones, they inevitably only take into account family members or people very close to the dreamer, again with a simple, one-setting clarity. The person in question may sit in silence at the edge of the dreamer's bed or say something brief and simple, such as, "Everything is going to be all right." I have found that this ability is frequently described as multi-generational within a family's ancestry. It is more often experienced by women than men, and it is not uncommon to find mothers and daughters who share the same gift.

What is important to know about precognitive dreams is that most people who have them are well aware that they will, periodically, have such a dream. I often hear from people who, having never had such a dream before in their lives, will be terrified because of a dream in which they, as an example, witness the death of a loved one. If they know of this phenomenon, they will sometimes immediately assume that this is absolutely one of those experiences and that their friend is doomed. Again, I must reiterate that unless this is something that you have a lifetime of experience with, such a dream is far more likely to be a random nightmare than a vision from the invisible world of psychic phenomena.

Chapter 4

THE DREAM WORK

A dream is a microscope through which we look
at the hidden occurrences in our soul.

—ERICH FROMM

Overview

Dreams can reveal so much. They emerge from the depths of our soul under the veil of sleep. Inside them are hidden treasures both wondrous and terrifying. Looking inward is not for the faint of heart though, for sometimes dreams expose much more than you might imagine possible.

I'm reminded of a joke I just love to tell about Sigmund Freud and his daughter Anna, when she was about eight years old. Of course, it works best when I do it with my best little girl's voice and German accent, but here's how it goes: Little Anna came down to the breakfast table one morning and, as usual, she sat on her father's lap. "Oh, Papa! I had the strangest dream last night!" she said. "Really, little Anna?" Sigmund replied. "Tell Papa your dream." "Well," she started, "It was with you and me. First, you bought me an ice cream cone. And you licked it and then I licked it and then you licked it and I licked it. Then we went for a walk in the woods and you had a very big stick, and I asked you if I could hold it and you let me hold your big stick. Then we were on a train and the train went though a long, dark tunnel . . . and then there was this BIG explosion . . . and then we both smoked a cigarette! What does that mean, Papa?" Freud thought for a moment, then grumbled uncomfortably as he hid behind his morning newspaper and grunted, "Ah . . . nothing."

This joke exemplifies the notion I mentioned in the previous chapter that if you choose to ask your dreams if they have anything to offer you, the answer is always yes. At the risk of being redundant or overstating the obvious, I love dreams. I love having them, I love hearing others tell about their dreams, I love interpreting them, I love working on my own dreams, and I love (perhaps more than anything else) that moment when a dreamer looks at me utterly flabbergasted by the insight they just received from the process of interpreting a dream. I wrote this book to share this love with anyone open to having even the slightest bit of the experience I have with the dream world. And, so, here we are at the nuts and bolts of it all.

There are several things that are important to know about doing dream work. First and foremost is that there is no single way of working with dreams; there are, in fact, many. There is no way of working with our dreams that is better than any other. Different people and different schools of thought may present themselves in such light, but I think this does a disservice to anyone interested in using their dreams to gain insight and self-awareness. Any consideration of a dream, no matter what the perspective is and what specific tools you use, is valuable and important. I am presenting the work that I do because it is just that; the work that I do. I would be hard pressed to present work that I haven't practiced myself. And I would be egregiously presumptuous if I said that my way was the only way of value.

Secondly, there is no such thing as a wrong interpretation. That's why it's called an interpretation. In fact, I detest the phrase "dream analyst" and much prefer "dream interpreter." Ironically, no matter how many times I have told people in the media to please refer to me as a dream interpreter, more often than not, I am introduced as a dream analyst. It may seem insignificant, but to me there is a huge difference.

An analysis is the separation of the whole of something into its parts. It is finite. To analyze something is to find out exactly what is in it, no more no less. To interpret is to present the meaning of something convoluted in understandable terms. There is nothing finite about that. An analysis is complete when every part is discovered and labeled, and then it is done forever. An interpretation is complete when some level of understanding is reached, and new levels of meaning can be reached over and over again by going deeper with each subsequent exploration. That is why I love the one and loathe the other.

Like most things in life, the more you put into it, the more effort you apply, the more there is to be gained from dream work. I like to think that there are five different steps or levels of working with a dream, each one slightly more beneficial than the one that precedes it:

- Remembering a dream brings it into consciousness, therefore, elevating the value it can offer in the search for personal understanding.

- Thinking about and processing the information it presents by ruminating on a dream will deepen the experience.

- Writing a dream down will reinforce the impact of the effort and lock the unconscious expression in the conscious mind.

- Discussing it with another person is going one step further, as an objective viewpoint is always going to help us see something that we would be unable to see on our own.

- Responding to a dream with a creative endeavor, such as drawing or writing a poem, takes this process to its highest level. The unconscious mind expresses itself through creative means and this kind of dream work is the most powerful there is.

It is not necessary to work with every bit of a dream. Whatever fragments that are remembered, or chosen to work with, will always lead to the perfect level of insight needed to examine a dream. Feeling frustrated or doubtful about accuracy only undermines our sense of well-being and is in opposition to the way in which unconscious material becomes conscious. Do not try and overcomplicate the process. Go slowly if necessary. Be open-minded. Be patient with dreams and, most of all, be patient with the process. And remember, how a dream is interpreted becomes part of the process itself. The scenes that are remembered, the words used to describe them, and the way that is chosen to work with a dream are both significant and revealing.

Writing Dreams Down

There's just no way around this: serious dream work means being willing to write them down. Every person's capacity for remembering their dreams is different. Some can recall all of them down to the smallest detail, whereas others never remember any of their dreams. Most people fall somewhere in between, and it is common to go through different phases where sometimes a lot of dreams are remembered, and at other times, very few.

A more powerful relationship with your dreams can be developed by writing them down. Writing by hand is more primitive and engages the unconscious more readily than using a computer or making a voice recording. I unequivocally recommend longhand on a pad or

in a journal, however, in this day and age of computers and digital recording equipment, I can certainly understand the appeal of the new
technology. And truly, the bottom line is that the ritual of attending to
this task can only bring benefits.

Whatever is used as a dream journal should be kept near the bed-
side, because the most effective time to write them down is immediately upon waking. Dream imagery tends to be gone in a flash, so
it is best to record them as soon after waking as can be comfortably
managed. Some of the most valuable dreams come in the middle of
the night, so it can be handy to have a dream journal right there to
grab and jot something down upon waking up from a dream, because
dreams are often lost if the dreamer falls back asleep.

When writing about a dream, put down anything that is remembered from the dreams, no matter how short or seemingly limited in
scope. People who do not easily remember everything may have to
coax their dreams into staying present after they are awake. The smallest detail, no matter how fragmented, is important. Even writing "I
don't remember any dreams from last night" will start the ball rolling.
After a time, dreams do become more vivid and detailed, and remembering them becomes easier to do.

Dreams occur in the three-dimensional space of our imagina-
tions. This can be a very confusing and chaotic place that rarely makes
any logical sense. Writing is linear and has the effect of taking what
is floating around in our minds and grounding it in a structure that
will allow us to begin working with it in a manageable way. Also, the
very words we use to describe a dream can become as informative
and valuable as the dream itself. After all, the way a dream is remembered and described also emanates out of the unconscious mind. How
a dream is described can be interpreted as well, offering additional
revealing information about what may be going on inside the mind of
the dreamer at the time of a dream.

If there isn't enough time to write down an entire dream, choose a few key images and record those. Reading about the dream images at a later time may trigger a deeper sense of the dream, even if the dream itself has been forgotten.

Always notice the feelings that come up when writing down a dream. Record whether or not the dream itself had an emotional component. Also notice what emotional state lingered after the dream, because any feeling associated with a dream is an important clue in the game of deciphering the hidden information it has to offer. Additionally, it is important to date entries so that correlations can be made between dreams and life events when we look back on dreams that occurred at certain times in our lives.

Rumination

To ruminate on something is to contemplate it over and over again. This is the simplest form of dream work, and we practice it any time we have afterthoughts about a dream. The thing that turns this type of dream work from daydreaming into an actual tool is the magic ingredient of intention. Thinking about something over and over again is, at best, a distraction and, at worst, an obsession. Neither adds anything of value to the person doing the thinking, but adding intention to the process changes everything.

If you look the word up in the dictionary, intention basically has something to do with purpose. In the world of self-investigation, however, it has a much more powerful meaning. In this regard, an intention is an emotionally charged idea—a magic ingredient—that may be added to any activity, and has the power to raise the stakes of the desired experience. Just as purging closets will result in more room for storage, so will adding the intention of *clearing out the psychic debris of things that haven't been paid attention to in a while* create a significant shift in the level of personal serenity.

Adding intention to ruminating about a dream allows the mind to propel this spontaneous process into a powerful level of self-investigation. The intention is to focus so gently on the dream as it is reviewed over and over in an organic way so that new ideas, fresh perspectives, and spontaneous associations can rise up out of our unconscious minds. Ultimately, the intention for all dream work is to have a deeper experience of ourselves and the level of consciousness through which we respond to all that happens in our lives.

This is most effectively done if we have written our dreams down and have set up a quiet place in which to read without being disturbed. Read and reread the dreams that were written in a journal, and then read them at least one more time. Random thoughts will probably interrupt this process. When this occurs, gently bring attention back to the dreams while also being mindful about where thoughts drift to, because some random thoughts may, in fact, connect to a dream as it is relived in the mind's eye. Sometimes, a plethora of pointless information about unrelated issues must be sifted through, but don't give up before the miracle happens. When least expected, an association, interpretive image, or related idea may become a conscious thought that can expand understanding of the meaning of a dream.

This technique doesn't work as well for people who experience a lot of chatter that is not easily quieted. However, with patience for the inevitable dead ends and alleys that are often the products of a busy head, this process can be surprisingly effective and has the added benefit of being a meditative discipline.

Rumination is also something that can be done with another person or with others in a group in the form of discussion. Having people with whom dreams can be discussed is a luxury and a delight. The intimacy and sense of connection this creates between people is one of the most joyful experiences I have ever witnessed or have had myself.

Here is a dream where rumination was the primary modality of the interpretation. Lawrence, a man in his thirties, had this dream while he was exploring a relationship with a woman he had recently met.

I dreamed I was driving my SUV at a high rate of speed, and the woman I'm dating was in the passenger seat. Suddenly, the car veered slightly out of control. After regaining control, I apologized for driving too fast. A police car appeared in front of me. I decided to follow what became a caravan of police cars, setting a slow and deliberate speed, which made me feel safe. Then we hit a patch of ice, which caused me to lose control and the truck went over a cliff. I knew we were going to die. I was comfortable with my own death, but had a wave of guilt about killing the girl and about the reaction of her family.

The truck is the first image that stuck out for me; vehicles represent how we move through our lives and this entire dream centers around how Lawrence is progressing through his life at the time of this dream. When I asked for more information, he told me that this was the actual truck he drives every day. This lets us know that we were investigating how his life was currently moving and where it was (or wasn't) going. I asked for associations about the woman in the passenger seat and he confirmed that he was, indeed, dating her in his waking life and that he felt ambivalent about continuing the relationship. After encouraging him to go deeper, he revealed that not only was he not sure he wanted to continue, he was having a lot of feelings come up around what it would be like to end the relationship and experience the fallout from other people's reaction to that choice.

In order to get a better handle on the dream, I needed to know what stuck out the most for Lawrence. When I asked, he surprised me by saying it was the moment when he apologized for driving too fast. While ruminating about this idea, he talked about his own tendency to drive aggressively and that it seemed odd that he felt the need to apologize for driving fast in the dream. It didn't take long before he was musing that perhaps he was really talking about the movement toward commitment: it was the relationship that was moving too fast.

I then asked him to talk about the patch of ice. At first, he only related to the dream context itself and the icy road being the real culprit for causing the accident. When I want to lead someone toward a more universal meaning associated with a symbol, I ask a simple question. "So, what exactly *is* ice?" "It's frozen water," he replied. Lawrence has been doing dream work for long enough to know that water always represents some element of the dreamer's emotions. He stopped dead in his tracks, looked straight at me and began to laugh. "I guess my feelings for her are starting to cool off." So not only did his icy feelings impact how he was moving down the road of his life, it had the additional impact of sending him over a cliff, clearly indicating the demise of the connection between the two of them.

We then started to discuss the ambivalence Lawrence felt about actually breaking up with her. He recognized that police are authority figures who connect symbolically to the concepts of right and wrong. He went on to express that the most prevalent reaction to the accident in the dream was his concern for how she was affected. Indeed, he was more preoccupied by how her family and friends would view his culpability in the crash than the event itself. As a result of interpreting this dream, Lawrence was able to confront his struggles around being concerned with what other people think and how their reactions have kept him from doing what's right and best for him. Shortly after doing this dream work, he ended the relationship and has experienced a significant shift in putting his own needs first in a healthy way.

Identifying the Theme

Part of interpreting a dream can involve the themes that a dream might be expressing about life at any given moment in time. The risk of introducing this idea is that people might overcomplicate this and, therefore, miss the value. Thematic consideration is a subtlety of dream work and not a mainstay. As such, it should be treated as something that can add color to a palette, but should not be confused with the paper and paint brush that is being worked with.

Using a movie such as *The Wizard of Oz* might be a good way to make this point with a little more clarity. The meaning of this movie can be identified by virtue of interpreting the plot: A young girl gets swept into a faraway land where fantastical creatures help her find her way home. We could do the same through the perspective of the characters themselves: There's a man made entirely out of straw and burlap. Another is constructed out of tin. And these are just two; there are dozens more and they are equally fascinating.

I could write an entire chapter about *The Wizard of Oz* through the symbolic meaning of the strange creatures that populate the land that is located just over the rainbow. But the theme of the film connects with the idea that is the intended message behind all of the plot lines, the characters, and how they interact with each other. Here, it has to do with going on a long expedition, only to find one's way back home and the sense of self that can only come from venturing into the depths of the unknown first. It is the classic hero's journey.

Let's turn to a dream to illustrate this process. This one comes from a young man in his late twenties, a dreamer named Efram. When he described the dream to me, he said:

I was walking my sister's dog, a big powerful animal that was really pulling on the leash, to the side and back. I'm trying to go in one direction and he's resisting and pulling behind me. He finally pulls so hard that he pulls the leash out of my hand and runs away, back behind me. I went to tell my sister what happened— that I lost her dog and that I wasn't strong enough to hold him. Her reaction was very nonchalant.

In an effort to work on this dream from a thematic approach, I used an assignment that draws parallels between dreams and films.

I asked Efram to think of a title for the dream, and what he came up with was "Dog Gone Mad." He chose the title because of the humorous play on words from the phrase "Dog gone it," with which he was familiar. While this particular phrase may not be popular today, and I'm not entirely certain it would be spelled the way I just did, suffice to say, it is generally used to express frustration.

Now that his dream had a title, it was time to identify the theme. Since in the dream, Efram was struggling to be in control of something (the dog), the theme he assigned to the dream was of being effective in the world. So we have a title and a theme and are now free to consider what the dream was trying to tell him. Going back to the title, he noticed that he chose to include the word "mad" in it. Combining the theme and the title, we are clearly in an investigation of Efram's effectiveness (or lack thereof) in the world, and just how mad he is about that.

Now the doors really opened up. He wondered why his sister didn't show any anger in the dream when he was certain, based on her personality, that she would. She was, in fact, nonchalant and accepting.

In this family, Efram was never shown how to express direct feelings of anger. Instead, he learned how to battle for control in other less obvious and passive-aggressive ways. In his own life, by acting "nonchalant" to his own anger, it showed up as conflict that seemed to come out of nowhere and where there was no winner. He would not have made these connections without the introduction of the title and the theme he chose to work with. By approaching the dream work from a thematic perspective in this way, the level of the interpretation was deeper and of more value. And this brings me to repeat once again an old adage—trust your instincts!

Free Association

The role that free association has with psychoanalysis and later, with dream work is nothing short of remarkable. In early treatment of mental illness, before Freud was even on the horizon, big strides had been made using the newly discovered technique of hypnosis. Physicians were finding it possible to learn things about their patient's fantasies and hidden thoughts that turned out to be quite profound and revelatory when a patient was under hypnosis.

One famous patient that I discussed in Chapter 2 was the first such hysteric—neurotic patient—to move the cumbersome method of hypnosis to a more conversational style of simply saying whatever came into her mind. She called this process "chimney sweeping" and found it very refreshing. So, in a way, the person who should really be credited for creating psychoanalysis is neither Freud nor his teacher Breuer, but the patient herself—the infamous Anna O.

The significant chain of events is hidden in this transition from one way of working to a second, and to yet a third way. Anna suffered from trance-like states in which she mumbled incoherently. When she was under the influence of hypnosis, her physician was able to discover that her ramblings, which were very poetic and expressive in nature, were actually morbid fantasies of death and loss. However, she grew tired of the hypnotic experience and preferred to just talk extemporaneously, allowing her thoughts to wander in a seeming aimless fashion. Of course, the wanderings were hardly aimless and by continuing to analyze the content of her expressions, more was being revealed about her unconscious thoughts, feelings, and deep conflicts. By the time Freud entered the picture and began to use the same free-form talking technique to explore Anna's dreams, the dynamism of the psychoanalytic process was born. Freud recognized, among other things, that there was no such thing as purely random expression when someone was on the couch.

The power of this approach is as vibrant today as it was two centuries ago. The unconscious mind is always engaged with us and eagerly waits for moments to express itself. It does this by words we choose to use, details of a story we might leave out, other details we might add, even if they aren't quite true. The association from one thought to another is so revealing, if people were truly aware of how much they expose in this way, most people would go about life never uttering a word. However, when used as a constructive tool, especially when images that appear in dreams are the subject matter, truly remarkable information can be culled from the depths of the psyche.

This method is probably most effectively used in modern psychotherapy when it comes to dream work. It's almost ridiculously simple. Overexplaining it runs the risk of causing us to wonder that if something is so simple, it couldn't possibly also be powerful and profound. It involves taking a symbol that appears in a dream and making an association to another image based on the original. The idea is to say what comes to you right away, without over-thinking it. I'll provide some simplistic examples: I say dog and you might say cat. I say up, you say down. I say sunshine, you say rain. Now let's say not everyone will be driven by the extrapolation of opposites. I say flower, you say love. I present sandwich, and you say Swiss cheese.

These simplistic examples might make it look like the object is to come up with worlds and ideas that are trite and simplistic, but that is not it at all. The idea is to truly consider the supplied image and associate it with an idea: a past experience, a notion, a belief, a person, or concept that has a personal connection to it. This process requires an absence of judgment or second-guessing and should be done quickly and impulsively. In other words, trust intuition and don't think too much. This is, in reality, a visceral experience and not a mental one.

When I was a kid, we did a lot of kite flying in the park. I was woefully inadequate at getting the thing off the ground and as a result, I did not enjoy this experience. Not ever. If I had a dream about flying a kite and I thought (or was directed by a therapist or dream partner) to make an association with kite-flying, I might come up with the notion of being humiliated. This comes straight out of my eight-year-old experience of humiliation that I hated so much. This association between kite-flying and humiliation won't be found in a dream dictionary. But if I were using this technique, I would have hit pay dirt with this memory resurfacing as a result of using free association to go deeper with a dream. The point is that a powerful association does not have to be rational. In fact, the more illogical the association, the more likely it becomes that we have tapped into something unconscious.

Free association provides a simple way of uncovering surprising depth and meaning to dream work and pinpointing an elusive interpretation. Simply take the symbol in question and make an association. Then, see where it leads you. This can be done with a partner who listens or as part of a discussion; it can also be done in written form as a part of journaling.

For example, a man had a dream in which a puppy is one of the dream characters. When asked to make an association for puppy, he told a story about when he was a boy and had kept a puppy under the porch for three days before his mother found out and made him give it away. Since dogs represent loyalty and enthusiastic affection in the Universal Landscape of Dog, the dream clearly involved these qualities in the dreamer's life. By adding the personal association of a sad moment when he had to give up love and affection, which the puppy provided, the man was able to dramatically access more potent material with which to work. In this way, he could apply what he discovered to the circumstances in his current life situation.

Here is another example: A woman dreamed of a large warehouse where she was held prisoner by an unseen authority. A warehouse is a storage facility. This setting tells us the dreamer is examining old material that she has been storing up for many years. When asked to free associate about this image, she ruminated that warehouses store things, like clothes. From there, she associated about what clothes meant to her. This led to a story about getting ready for her high school prom, which, in turn, led her to an association with being thin enough for her liking.

The dream dislodged a previously denied body-image issue that had troubled her on an unconscious level all her life. Now in her early thirties, this dream and the association that followed allowed her to see that her own self-judgment about her body and her eating habits were the "unknown authority" that held her prisoner. Remember that a warehouse can store almost anything; her particular *association* was an array of clothes. Her unconscious mind was working with her to bring these specific body-image issues closer to her conscious awareness so she could address them with more clarity.

When the image of the prom popped into her head, seemingly out of nowhere, it surprised her. Free association is an organic process and our minds will indeed surprise and sometimes delight us. We can not make wrong associations, so allow ideas to flow spontaneously without holding back or judging what comes up. If an association doesn't feel like it has hit something important, do an association to the image that *does come*, and the unconscious will deliver more hints to the conscious mind.

One technique for doing this is to write associations in list form, stopping when something feels important. Using the sample dream above, our dreamer might have written her list, thus: Warehouse. Storage. Clothes. Fashion. Popularity. Prom night. This last association is underlined because it was the one that sparked an epiphany in the dreamer. This is how to know when something has value and makes a powerful association. This is when I see people's eyes widen and hear them say, "Now, *that's* interesting."

Here's another example of using free association. This time the dreamer connected a dream about an unknown house to a house from his childhood that contained some very potent memories. The man dreamed of being in a lavish house. The dream consisted primarily of wandering through the house going from room to room looking for some unknown but important thing, which he never was able to find. He woke up frustrated and angry.

When he practiced free association on the house in the dream, the first thought that emerged was its similarity to the beautiful home of a childhood friend. Associating further, he thought about a particular evening when he stayed over for dinner at that house. He remembered an embarrassing incident where he ate a great deal of food at the dinner table only to get sick and then have the need to excuse himself to the bathroom periodically and throw up. This led to an association with utter humiliation and feeling terribly embarrassed. House. Wealth. Vomiting. Embarrassment. Rejection. Undeserving.

The interpretation started with the dreamer searching for his sense of self (a house represents the self in dreams), and being unable to do so was represented by the lost object. The process of free association added the element of emotional embarrassment and feeling undeserving of abundance, which was represented by the richness of the surroundings in the dream house. Ironically, this man was about to start a new, very high-paying job and this dream allowed him to process his strong undercurrent of feeling undeserving, when it came to accepting abundance in his life.

Automatic Handwriting

Automatic handwriting is a technique that Jung developed while he was in what he usually referred to as his "creative illness." A creative illness is a very fancy name for a nervous breakdown. It's kind of like this: You lose your mind and the men in the white coats take you away, or you lose your mind and spend time doing meditation and making art, and it's called a creative illness. Another lofty moniker for such an experience that is a bit darker is often referred to as "the Dark Night of the Soul." That's also code for midlife crisis. I had one of my own and as much as it sounds like I'm belittling the process and being cynical, the truth as I know it is this: If your life circumstances bring you face to face with an existential crisis of identity and purpose, and you choose to utilize that time to explore your unconscious mind, you have the opportunity to mine gold. For it is in such times that the doorway between the conscious and the unconscious is the most easily traversed. Jung understood this and unashamedly took advantage of this availability to explore areas of the psyche that generally remained hidden. In doing so, he made discoveries about the human condition that we take for granted today. In his time, however, his discoveries made him a pioneer of enormous courage.

One of the tools that he stumbled upon during this time was what he dubbed "automatic handwriting." He had already formulated the theory that the various Character Aspects he encountered in his dream world lived inside his unconscious mind. When he would awaken from powerful dreams, he would do anything he could to keep the connection to his unconscious open and available. In an attempt to do this, he decided to communicate with one of them directly through his already avid journaling.

Here's where his stroke of genius came into play. He recognized that his dominant hand, with which he did all his writing, was intrinsically bound to his conscious mind. He then wondered if his non-dominant hand offered some indirect connection to his unconscious. The experiment worked like a charm, and he indeed found that if he sat down with a particular Character Aspect in mind and wrote out a question on the page with his dominant hand and then switched his pen to the other hand, a fascinating thing occurred. Thoughts began to pour onto the page that did not appear to be emanating from his ego mind, but rather from someplace deeper. The answers always surprised him and this technique became a staple for all Jungian analysts who followed in his footsteps.

A client of mine was dealing with debilitating, chronic pain due to some fused vertebrae in her neck. For a period of several weeks prior to a scheduled surgery, her dreams contained many images of her neck in various expressions of challenge. One had a beautiful scarf that began to slowly strangle her. In another more gruesome dream, her neck actually began to separate her head from her body with a sort of hinge-like mechanism. The interpretations were so apparently literal because of the specific injury and pending surgery. So we tried automatic handwriting to see if anything interesting might emerge. Below is what came up.

Delores: OK neck of mine! You and I seem to be working at cross-purposes for a while now. You have been a real pain in the neck.

Pain in the Neck: You are the one to talk. It is because of you that I am being this pain. You gotta learn how to speak up!!

Delores: What was the purpose of your coming on as such a strong pain when I first saw Dr. Jones?

Pain in the Neck: Because you were following Dorothy down the yellow brick road, hoping that the healer you were seeking would show you where your home was. The pain was there to teach you to listen to your own knowing. And just like Dorothy, you found the old man behind the curtain. You had all the answers all the time.

Delores: So, you mean I think I didn't actually believe I was going to get better?

Pain in the Neck: You felt that your healing was not up to you. Your pain got worse because you were giving too much power to others—the doctors—the "experts." Sometimes, they're wrong!

Delores: Geez, you are very preachy. You seem like you think you know it all. I decided to go to Dr. Jones. I thought I was following my own guidance.

Pain in the Neck: Uh-huh...so what did you find?

Delores: I did strengthen my connection to myself and to the Divine, but not because of (pause). I don't understand why you are being so tenacious about being a pain in my neck.

Pain in the Neck: This is reality, baby. You have a lot of years of wear and tear, accidents and ageing have made me a little rusty and frozen from lack of use. I need some outside intervention. Dr. Jones may be just great, but you are the one who has to believe it's possible and be willing to say so out loud.

This woman didn't realize just how much her thoughts and the challenges to her spiritual belief system were impacting how much pain she was in. This automatic handwriting *completely* changed how she interacted with her surgeon and other physicians. She is well on her way to having a more pain-free existence.

Fran was in her forties and preparing to go to nursing school in order to expand her career opportunities in the health field. About to take a math test that was part of qualifying for the master's level course of study, she had this dream:

> *I was at the airport preparing to travel to Mexico and realized I had forgotten my purse. In a panic, I wanted to call my ex-husband to remind him to bring it to me, but I couldn't remember the phone number and was not able to find it in the phone book.*

We had to identify the theme of this dream before Fran could get to an interpretation that had real value. The meaning of the symbol of the purse provided an initial theme for this dream, but as Fran discovered, the obvious might have been accurate, but ultimately not as satisfying. I asked Fran to make an association with what a purse represented for her. She immediately associated Purse with having ready access to the things we need with us to be at our most effective; such as money, grooming tools, and other necessities.

The dream certainly exhibited her stress around not being ready for the changes she faced (the plane trip symbolized a major, fast transition in her life). She did, indeed, feel ill-prepared for what lay ahead of her. Phone numbers are our access to effective communication with others, especially in times of need. Forgetting the phone number may have reflected her sense of isolation and an inability to connect to her support system. Interestingly, in this case, she looked to her ex-husband to for help. He was definitely not a member of her inner circle at the time, so it was interesting to see how he played into this scenario.

Not remembering the digits necessary to reach him offered an additional ironic and subtle interpretation: In her waking-life, Fran experienced fears about her knowledge and skills. Comfort with numbers would be essential for her performance on the pending math examination she would shortly face. Additionally, she traveled to a Spanish-speaking country, something akin to taking a test where the language of math is more foreign than familiar.

All of these interpretations are accurate and insightful and they resonated with Fran on a cerebral level. However, she continued to feel dissatisfied; it was far too troubling a dream to be dismissed as just an expression of stress around a math class. In order to go deeper, I suggested doing some automatic handwriting with the other character that appeared in the dream, her ex-husband, William. Here's a snippet of what came up:

Fran: I've been trying to reach you. I need my purse.

William: What's that got to do with me?

Fran: I need you to bring it to me.

William: You can't do anything right. Do I have to do everything for you?

Fran: What's that supposed to mean?

William: This is why I always had to do everything.

Fran: Well, not any more. That's why I left you.

William: You are lost without me.

Fran: You are so wrong about that, William. You don't have any control over me any more!

The dialogue may read as fairly mild, but doing it brought up a lot of emotions for Fran. Finally, she reached a deep and full understanding of the dream. She recognized that she was anxious about going back to school and passing the math test; it was, in fact, a bit of a hurdle for her to get over. But the real juice of what the dream revealed connected to the ways in which her ex-husband always held her back. Of course, in many ways, she allowed him to hold her back. In leaving him, she took the risk of freeing herself from his controlling ways, but the dream illuminated that she was still stuck in this same pattern of not taking full control of her own life and destiny. The insights that came from examining it courageously and thoroughly showed her that she was finally ready to take responsibility for her own choices and take the risks she had always yearned for.

Dream Sight Revisited

And so ends the first part of this book and Part 2: The Dream Dictionary begins with the next chapter. It bears repeating that there are many ways to approach dream work, and no one way is better than any other. The most important thing to remember when working with dreams is to find the approach that resonates the most and provides insight and satisfaction. The techniques presented in these first chapters are the basics that make up the work I have done over the years. They are simple enough to be accessible to the beginner and go deep enough for the seasoned dreamer to bring their work to a higher level.

Time and time again, I have seen people react with everything from perplexity to terror over dreams they have had. And just as often, I've seen consternation turn to fascination when they discover what their dreams may really mean. The difference is simple: Their first response is infused with personal attachment to the scary or confusing elements of the dream itself. However, when a dream is interpreted through the universal meaning—the Universal Landscape—and is associated with dream symbols, an entirely new experience is available to the dreamer—one that is revealing, sparks curiosity, and fosters insight.

Dream Sight is more than a dream dictionary; it is an approach to interpreting dreams in a new way. The unconscious speaks to us in a language all its own—the language of symbols. The meaning of those symbols is rooted in the concept of universality. When we come from this place, there is nothing about working with our dreams that will elude us. I encourage people to pay attention to their dreams and share them with others. This will instigate the dynamic experience of the conscious and unconscious mind interacting with each other. There is nothing to lose and much to be gained as our level of self-awareness increases and enriches our lives now and into the future.

Continuums of Meaning

Throughout the Dream Dictionary, there are many instances when the Personal Focus will present two opposite interpretations for the same symbol. While these juxtapositions may appear contradictory, this is not the case. All of life occurs on continuums. Every human experience exists as a function of its opposite. In the physical world, we understand this in the relationship between night and day, cold and hot, up and down. It is the same with our thought processes and the realm of emotional experience. Joy and sadness are opposites, and any given mood can be identified as falling somewhere on the line that connects them both. Anger and rage are on the same plane as grace and serenity; the way an individual reacts to an evocative situation will be found somewhere in between.

This is particularly evident in the way an image in a dream might be interpreted. As an example, a wallet containing a large sum of money might connect to feelings of abundance. Conversely, it could be compensating for a sense of lack. A flying dream can indicate a moment of overwhelming bliss. It could just as easily be telling the dreamer that the challenges they face on the ground are being avoided.

At any given moment in life, the personal meaning we might most resonate with on such a continuum could be different. It is our job, as effective interpreters, to diligently assess which side of a particular continuum is most reflective of our own self at the time we dream. The content of the Dreaming Lens will be a helpful guide. However, a fearless and honest appraisal of personal beliefs, behaviors, and life experience is the ingredient needed to arrive at an authentic and accurate interpretation that will bring the most value.

Dream Sight Structure

There are over three hundred terms defined in the Dream Dictionary. Each term is listed in alphabetical order and is presented in three sections. These correspond with the structure of Dream Sight as outlined in the previous pages. This will describe how a particular symbol is expressing unconscious meaning in the dream that contains it.

After working with Dream Sight on a regular basis and grasping the theoretical construct of the Dream Sight approach, the process of working with dream symbols becomes instinctive and can be applied to dream symbols that are not contained within these pages.

Please note that each term is broken down into its Universal Landscape, the Dreaming Lens, and the Personal Focus. These segments are explained in the section that follows.

The Sections Explained

Universal Landscape

The Universal Landscape is a singular, conceptual definition of what a symbol represents at its most basic, universal level. This reflects a meaning that should have the most resonance with the most people, no matter what their background or personal history. The Universal Landscape attempts to be devoid of any personal projections based on opinion, cultural biases, and other qualitative perspectives of any kind. It is the first step in approaching a symbol, so that the interpretation has a foundation that is based on universal ideas.

Dreaming Lens

The Dreaming Lens refers to the context of the specific dream in which the symbol appears. This section is written as a series of questions. These are random suggestions that are designed to assist in the use of events from the dream itself to begin narrowing the investigation from the broad-based universal perspective to how that is impacted by the setting and events of a particular dream. These questions are not intended to be absolute or finite. They are guideposts and a starting point to encourage an inquiry based directly on the dream itself.

Personal Focus

It is in the Personal Focus that all other considerations are to be brought into the process. It is the last step of Dream Sight so that our particular responses to any symbol do not obscure our view to what is universal. In this way, conscious, personal associations are free to add texture and depth to the universal information that has its roots in our unconscious minds. This section makes up the bulk of each term in the Dream Dictionary. In addition to what is in the pages that follow, there may be additional specific and personal associations that are not presented here. These can be based on cultural and historical information, family dynamics, strongly held opinions and convictions of any kind. Any thoughts about a symbol are important to consider, as long as they are added *after* the Universal Landscape is used as the foundation to the meaning being expressed. In this way, any Personal Focus provides nuance and texture to the process of Dream Sight, while leaving an effective, powerful, and accurate understanding of the message hidden within the complexity and mystery of the dream.

Part 2

THE DREAM
DICTIONARY

Abandonment

Universal Landscape: Fears around self-worth.

Dreaming Lens: Who abandoned you in your dream? What were the circumstances around the abandonment? Were there legitimate reasons for being left? What was your emotional reaction to being abandoned? What did you do as a result? Did you collapse? Did you take action? Were you the one doing the abandoning?

Personal Focus: The concept of abandonment is a fear-based illusion. The feelings that come up when someone has left us are personal and rarely about the one doing the leaving. The fear of being left alone is primitive and has its roots in infancy. If the loss resonates deeply enough, the emotional reaction taps into a deep reservoir of historical injuries and is experienced as a painful abandonment. The *essence* of this experience is connecting to what it feels like to be alone with ourselves in moments of vulnerability. Thinking that you do not have the ability to face life on your own, especially in moments of adversity, is a falsehood born out of fear. Overwhelming emotions are often accompanied by irrational thoughts that are focused on our weaknesses and invalidate our strengths.

Dreaming of a circumstance in which abandonment is a primary theme is likely to be compensating for something in waking life that is triggering the thoughts, whether consciously or unconsciously. By processing these feelings in the dream state, we are better prepared to face the world when we wake. Pay close attention to who is doing the abandoning as this will factor powerfully into the interpretation.

In a dream, we may be examining ways in which we abandon ourselves. Even if the dream mirrors a life situation where someone you know is not available to you, use the concept of the Character Aspect as a mirror. It may be that part of you is currently inaccessible to your sense of self. For example, being abandoned by a boss might indicate a lack of inner authority available to handle a difficult situation.

The value of any abandonment, in life or in a dream, is that it forces us to see how we can survive when stripped of what we perceive as necessary for our existence. To feel abandoned is to accept a myth that we are not okay without the assistance of others. A dream that allows you to suffer an abandonment and find the strength to continue on that journey may be helping you see where you are not trusting your own instincts and resources.

Age Differences

Universal Landscape: Consciousness that is rooted in earlier times in life.

Dreaming Lens: What age were you in your dream? Were you watching yourself at a different age? Were other people in your dream the same age as you? Was the setting of your dream related to your life at the age you were?

Personal Focus: Dreams often return us to our past. In some cases, a past setting is witnessed from the current life perspective. Other dreams of this type may transform us into the person we were at the earlier time and to the specific surroundings we visited in the dream. No matter what the actual structure of the dream, any time we return to earlier moments in life, we are exploring who we are today as a result of our past.

Our personal history lives forever inside our memory and, in many ways, who we are today is a function of what occurred in the past. Maturity and wisdom can be seen as a function of how well we call forth lessons learned from past mistakes and simultaneously leave behind outmoded ways of being. This cycle of change and growth is a lifelong process from birth to death. The fundamental ways in which we are impacted by the past fall into two categories: experiential and developmental.

The experiential realm contains all the external elements of life: who our parents were and how they raised us, our social environments, our relationship to school and other institutions to which we are connected. This includes *all of the events* that transpired throughout our own personal histories.

Developmental issues reflect the internal side of life, and how we relate to the world changes significantly as we pass from one developmental stage to another. Emotional development and cognitive functioning also follow specific and predictable patterns that are based on our age as we pass from infancy into adulthood. What we understand at ten years old is too abstract for a seven-year-old's mind. These differences exist regardless of outer circumstances.

Knowing what age and level of development you have returned to in a dream can play a key role in your interpretation of it. A perfect example of this is the very common anxiety dream of being back in high school or college completely unprepared for an exam. It was in these settings that we were, for the first time in our lives, faced with the pressure to perform at very high-stake levels. Most adults would agree that as life progresses, the stakes get even higher and the pressure to perform far exceeds the demands of high school. However, since this is where this type of stress is first experienced, our minds contain a powerful imprinting that will forever associate fears of inadequacy and unpreparedness with the origin of these emotions. It would be unusual for an adult to consciously relate a major presentation at work with what it felt like to face a test in math class. In the unconscious mind, however, it is a perfect depiction of such feelings. As a result, moments in our adult lives that have the capacity to inspire similar reactions will often invoke a dream setting that is similar to the time in life where such responses originated.

Often, a dreamer returns to a particular setting and time in their past when they are stuck in some developmental issue. This can last for weeks or years, depending on how much inner work is required to free them from the grips of the past. When an earlier age or setting is prominent in a dream, ask yourself what was going on in your life at that time. How did you respond to such peak moments as moving to a new town, a parent's divorce, getting or losing a pet, the onset of puberty, or the death of a loved one? Any one of these major events can usher us into a new level of emotional awareness. Identifying the theme of the particular time frame will clarify exactly what underlying issue is being stirred up by current events. (See also Taking a Test, High School).

Airplane

Universal Landscape: A very fast transition.

Dreaming Lens: Did the flight take off or land effectively, or were there problems? Did the plane crash? Did you feel safe on the plane? Were you attempting to catch a plane? Were you successful, or did you miss it? What size plane was it?

Personal Focus: Any means of transportation in a dream is synonymous with the way we move through our lives. Because of the dramatic way an airplane leaves the ground and speeds toward a destination, it is connected with any sudden transition in life. In a dream, changes of this nature can connect either to something that is taking place in your life at the moment, or to change that is needed or wished for. As a plane is our world's fastest mode of public transportation, it connects symbolically to those moments in life where change is rapid and total.

When dreaming of plane travel, the first consideration is to look to where you are making a dramatic shift in your waking life. When you have identified this, use the Dreaming Lens to discover how you feel about the change that is afoot. If the movement of the plane makes you very anxious, you might be expressing fear over sudden changes that you perceive to be dangerous. A more relaxed or passive response to a plane in your dreams could indicate a level of acceptance, but could also signal issues of avoidance. Be vigilant in your investigation.

Missing your plane in a dream could indicate a sense that something is passing you by and may illuminate a need to take stock of how aware you are of the opportunities in your current situation. Being stuck on a plane might connect to feelings of impatience and the need to accept external limitations. Take a look at the areas in your life that are stagnant or erupting—you may need to fasten your seat belt and take off.

Alien

Universal Landscape: A Character Aspect that is utterly foreign to you.

Dreaming Lens: Were you in a familiar environment with alien beings? Was the environment alien as well? Were you abducted? Was there danger involved in the encounter? Were you curious about the alien's origin? Were they here to teach or to conquer?

Personal Focus: The foundational meaning to this image connects to the word itself. An alien originally meant an individual who was from a foreign country. While this definition is still in use today, it is usually paired with the term "illegal" and has lost its general meaning. With the UFO phenomenon that emerged in the last century, the word now tends to conjure thoughts of beings from outer space.

The media initially created two distinctly different versions of what aliens look like. There is the short one with the large head and the tall, willowy one. It is not clear why this duality emerged, but a generalized interpretation might assign lower functioning aspects such as aggression to the short one, and gentler, more ethereal qualities to the tall one. More recently, the creative community has produced a wide array of alien creatures. There is an overall association with aliens from outer space that projects onto them violent and destructive intentions. This quality should be considered when you interpret this symbol.

As you would do with any person who appears in your dreams, use the Character Aspect approach, which recognizes a character (or alien) as a part of your personality. If the alien has human features, it may represent a part of your personality or psychic makeup that is new to you and, therefore, feels strange or alien to your nature. In such a case, it is crucial to uncover your meaning from the contextual images surrounding the alien in your dream. Its form and actions, and your feelings about the alien, will give you a sense of what is being brought to light.

Abduction by aliens might be revealing fears about unfamiliar territory or new environments in which you find yourself. The more fear you feel in the dream, the more frightened you may be of the changes that are occurring. On the other side of this equation, feeling an affinity toward an alien and actually wanting to make a connection may indicate a desire to break out of a constricting mold of sameness.

Alternate Universe

Universal Landscape: Alternate Universe.

Dreaming Lens: Were you in an alternate universe in your dream? Did you have an understanding of where this alternate universe existed? Did you move back and forth between more than one set of realities? Was the experience comfortable or did it inspire fear?

Personal Focus: This is one of those enigmatic dream symbols where the universal meaning is literal. The idea that outside of our own existence there may be other planes of a simultaneous but separate reality has fascinated the imagination of men and women for centuries. Modern science and the opening up of space exploration have only fueled this passion for what lies beyond and beneath our world.

At the heart of this image, from a symbolic perspective, is our human ability to imagine worlds that are essentially the same as the one we inhabit, but at the same time so completely new and different that they have the possibility of containing anything we might desire. In other words, if this universe is a disappointment, an alternate universe might provide you with all that you need and expect, but also magically offer you something you covet.

The landscape of any dream is an alternate universe of sorts. If you have the sense that your dream is taking place in some other reality than the one you reside in, the first consideration will be to take in the theme and interpretation you assign to the entire dream as a whole. If the dream has a positive and uplifting feel to it, the alternate universe may simply be a function of the creativity and expansiveness of your unconscious self. However, there also may be an element of wish fulfillment or denial being expressed. Creating an alternative universe might be a simplistic and convenient way to escape the challenges present in the universe that you call home.

Amputations/Missing Limbs

Universal Landscape: Diminished capacity or ability.

Dreaming Lens: What part of the body was amputated or missing? Was it missing from your body? Was the dream about someone you know? What was the impact of the missing limb? How was the limb lost? Did the amputation occur in the dream itself?

Personal Focus: Our limbs are what give us mobility and the dexterity with which to create, all of which are impacted in some way when we lose one of them. Whether it is as significant as an entire arm or leg, or just the smallest finger or toe, the appearance of a missing limb or amputation in a dream is reflecting some sort of invasion of your ability to navigate through life.

The organic usage of the limb is the key to the beginning of your interpretation. Something disconnected from the lower half of your body relates to mobility, while amputation on the upper half has to do with creativity. Arms can also connect to protection and aggression and the inability to defend yourself in some area of life. Hands are the most creative element, and a missing one—especially your dominant one—is about limitations in expression and productivity. Fingers provide us with dexterity, and missing one relates to limitations of skill. As feet transport us, missing one or both relates to an inability to be grounded on your path, whereas missing an entire leg or both legs connects to being completely stopped on your path. A missing toe could point to an impediment to balance. Losing your head could point to an eradication of a thought process, or to your sense of identity.

All of these interpretations shift slightly if you are witnessing someone else in the dream lose a limb. If this is the case, you must apply the limitation to the Character Aspect of that person, as they live within you.

Animals

Universal Landscape: Human instincts.

Dreaming Lens: What animal was appearing in your dream? Were you the animal? Was there more than one type of animal? What were the animals doing? Were you in danger?

Personal Focus: In the spirit of everything in a dream being a reflection of the consciousness of the dreamer, any animal that appears in a dream represents some element of the human experience and the personality of the dreamer. What sets us apart from other animals is our capacity to think. However, animals connect to the opposite of thoughtful navigation through life. They represent the instinctive drives and the deep intuitive knowing that allow a person to feel guided toward right action without intellectually knowing what to do.

Most aboriginal cultures are very connected to the animals that inhabit their worlds. In fact, animals are thought to possess spiritual powers, and these powers are directly related to how each animal behaves in the world. The qualities of the animal that appears in your dream offer clues to the interpretation you make.

For example, bears connect to fierce power. Large cats represent stealth and strategic hunting ability. High-flying birds, such as an eagle or hawk, are expressions of the ability to see from the great vantage point of the sky. When in doubt, think about the facts you know about the animal. The Internet makes this kind of research very easy. Read a little about the animal and you will easily understand what your unconscious mind is trying to communicate.

The second facet of your interpretation will come from what the animal is doing in your dream. The activity they are engaged in will correlate with some type of movement (or obstacle to movement) in your waking life. The dream may be asking you to stop trying to think your way through a situation and turn instead toward your instinctive nature for an answer.

Attic

Universal Landscape: Thoughts, intellect, and memories.

Dreaming Lens: Were you in an attic? Did you know the house to which it was attached? Was it from your childhood? Were you alone? What was in the space? What were you doing there?

Personal Focus: Any house or home connects to your sense of self. The highest floor of the house corresponds to intellect and thoughts.

Attics are often used for storage. In this way, they represent memories, information, and knowledge that accumulate over the course of your life.

The state of the attic in your dream will illuminate your current relationship with your thoughts and memories. A musty, dirty atmosphere means you are in realms that you haven't visited in a while. This can indicate anything from appropriate nostalgia to unhealthy avoidance. The emotional reaction to your dream will help you come to an accurate interpretation if this is the case. An attic that has been decorated and finished indicates that old material has been cleared out. Your job will be to decide whether this has been the result of a healthy inventory or glossing over of older issues that may have needed more consideration. Since things you are not quite finished with are often stored in an attic, going there in a dream may connect to going more deeply into something that you stored away for another time.

Exploring any part of a house symbolizes an exploration of yourself. An attic indicates that your journey is taking you back to thoughts based on your past. These can include generational influences if the attic contains items that originally belonged to your ancestors. Being trapped in an attic might point to being held hostage by old thought patterns. Someone living in your attic is helping you identify a Character Aspect that has a great deal of power in terms of your thoughts. These could be conscious thoughts as well as the more hidden thoughts that tend to have significant influence over our choices in life.

Disarray in your dream attic, and any feelings of being overwhelmed by what you find there, could indicate how you are currently responding to the chaos in your thought process. In such a dream, your psyche may be giving you a message to start cleaning up the junk that's taking up space in your mind to make room for something new.

Baby

Universal Landscape: A new idea, relationship, or event.

Dreaming Lens: Were you in physical proximity to the baby? Was your relationship to the baby intimate or estranged? Was the baby vibrant and expressive? Was it passive, ill, or dead? Were you the baby in the dream? Did you know the parents of the baby? Were the parents present?

Personal Focus: The essential meaning of a baby as a symbol connects to the new life it represents. Babies grow up to become adult human beings, but in their infancy, they embody all the potential that has yet to be expressed. In this way, a baby in a dream is likely to be expressing some new chapter in your life that is just beginning and has yet to unfold into full manifestation. There are intense responsibilities associated with the helplessness of a baby that are key in this particular image. In the dream world, a baby's dependency relates to the fragility of new ideas as they mature into actual life choices and/or options.

Men and women have different relationships to babies, which are biological in nature. A woman who dreams of a baby needs to consider how literally to take the image. Depending upon life circumstances, there may be issues of concern arising out of parenting or pending childbirth. Additionally, this image in a dream may connect to the unconscious expression of feelings around the ticking of a woman's biological clock, both prior to and advancing away from the time frame of fertility. If having a baby is not a realistic proposition in your waking life, there may be elements of wish fulfillment connected to this dream. Also to be considered are frustrations, obstacles, or possible unconscious expressions of futility in whatever creative expression is struggling to become conscious when the dream occurs.

The same meaning of new beginnings will apply to a man having a dream that features a baby as a primary image. The life event inspiring such a dream may require a level of nurturing and atten-tion worthy of this symbol. However, a male dreamer may have to consider the limitations to being biologically unable to create an actual baby as part of an accurate interpretation.

The health of a dream baby might correlate with the vibrancy and strength—or their lack—involved in a new venture. Being sur-prised by the appearance of a baby may equate to sudden changes in direction that are being inspired by new life events. Adoption of a baby could indicate that the new thing in your life may have its origin in someone else's domain. Examine all the information you can remember about the baby and apply what you notice to your interpretation.

Bank

Universal Landscape: Money as power; financial security.

Dreaming Lens: What feelings were evoked by the dream? Was the bank austere and intimidating? What occurred in the bank? Who was there in the dream? Was actual money involved? Did you feel safe about the bank's involvement in your finances?

Personal Focus: Money is a complicated issue for most people, mak-ing any image that relates to money difficult to interpret. There are many contradictions in the way with which this symbol can be as-sociated. Rife with paradox, your own personal relationship with money must be part of arriving at an accurate interpretation. This can be challenging, as most people operate in varying levels of un-consciousness where wealth is concerned.

A bank is a construct of modern society created around the con-cept of protecting the abundance of the average individual. When ex-amined more closely under the scrutiny of symbolic meaning, a bank connects more to fears around money and the desire to hoard abun-dance to gain a sense of security about future needs. Additionally, the institution of banking is founded on the greed principal: those who have more tend to profit from those who have less. While perhaps a necessary function in today's modern world, the essence of a bank connects more to lack than to prosperity.

A bank is where money will be safely guarded while increasing in value over time. Yet in the world of finance, it is the least risky forum for investing and, therefore, represents caution where abundance is concerned. It is also the primary cultural institution connected to expanding lifestyle choices through the borrowing of money. However, this is more likely to connect to living beyond personal means than actual expansion. The reality of being unable to meet a bank's demands include foreclosure, which represents loss and the consequences of overspending.

On a surface level, banks represent stability, longevity and bedrock of foundation, both personally and communally. Consider your relationship to banks and banking, both in the dream and in waking life, and include your thoughts about money, credit, debt, and financial insecurity when interpreting this dream symbol.

Bar

Universal Landscape: Collective escapism.

Dreaming Lens: What kind of bar were you in? Was it a place known to you? Were there other people there? If so, did you know who they were? Were you drinking? What were you drinking? What else was happening in the bar?

Personal Focus: The primary focus of a bar is to consume alcohol, therefore, this symbol connects primarily to escapism. Because it is a public place and rooted in the spirit of socializing, there is a second layer of meaning that connects with how people interact in social environments in a spirited and uninhibited way. Your own personal relationship to alcohol and bars in your waking life will play a prominent role in how you interpret a dream that took place in one.

A dream that takes place in a bar could just as easily be expressing a need to relax, lighten up, and party as it could be a warning against the impact of choosing escapism over dealing with things with a clear head. Your reason for being in the bar comes into play with this part of your interpretation. Since one of the primary reasons why people go to bars is to meet people, a dream about a bar may be pointing to a search for some aspect of yourself that feels as if it is missing. If this is the case, the quality in question may be connected to issues that relate to your social life or public persona.

The atmosphere in a bar can run the gamut, from classy to seedy, from subdued to chaotic. Use this information from your dream to add a shade of meaning to your interpretation. The darker the feeling about the place, the more likely you are investigating Shadow material. If you are familiar with the bar from your waking life, consider that the dream is speaking directly to elements of your current experience that center around your relationship with it.

Why you were in the bar will also be a part of your interpretation. Most reasons for going to a bar fall into two categories: to meet people or drink alcohol, or both. If drinking is what is most prominent, then the theme of the dream is definitely about escapism. If connecting with others was part of your storyline, then there are some other things to consider. Any person you are with or looking to meet up with should be interpreted as a Character Aspect of yourself. If this is a stranger, then your unconscious is expressing a message about connecting with some part of you that is not yet clear. That the dream takes place where people are often drunk, may be indicating a need for you to explore why it might be necessary to bring the freedom that alcohol provides into this interaction. Are you too inhibited, or perhaps not reserved enough? (See also Restaurant.)

Barefoot

Universal Landscape: Vulnerability around immediate choices in life.

Dreaming Lens: Were you barefoot in the dream, or was someone else's feet exposed? Was there a reason you didn't have shoes on, or were you searching for them? Was there danger in being barefoot, or did it feel good and give you a sense of freedom?

Personal Focus: Feet connect to how grounded you feel. They can also indicate issues around how you are maneuvering through your current life choices. There is a direct connection between where you put your feet and where you go. If they are exposed to the elements, it leaves them vulnerable to injury. This can have a great impact on your journey and how you get to where you intend to go. It is important to remember that vulnerability implies easy access to impact and not whether that impact is "good" or "bad." A person walking barefoot on broken glass is vulnerable to being cut, whereas a person walking barefoot on grass is vulnerable to the ticklish sensations that might result and can be considered pleasurable.

Consider all the possible cultural and societal nuances that might affect how this image when it is interpreted. There are many people for whom having the foot visible is an erotic turn-on. Additionally, many yogic traditions require bare feet in order for the body to effectively process energy. In many cultures, it is customary to remove shoes when indoors as a sign of respect. Removing shoes can also be a symbol of freedom and liberation. The same liberation, however, can connect a person to a self-conscious awareness of odor that builds up from prolonged confinement of the feet in shoes, reflecting a resistance to feeling more free.

Bare feet are more connected to the ground. In a dream, this can indicate being more grounded, or that a more grounded approach to some life situation is necessary. This image also connotes feeling more "down to Earth" and implies being laid back and relaxed.

Basement

Universal Landscape: Deep secrets. Hidden or unconscious thoughts.

Dreaming Lens: Were you in the basement? Were you considering a trip to the basement? If so, were you frightened at the prospect? Was there enough light to see? Did you know what was down there? Were you familiar with the basement? Was it finished, or unfinished space?

Personal Focus: Houses represent the Self. Therefore, the basement would be the *Self below the Self*. As such, any dream of a basement connects with unconscious material and anything that lurks below the surface of the psyche. Since many basements are dark and gloomy, they can have an aura of menace about them. This notion is exploited in the media, such as scary basements in films where no one escapes unharmed, making the symbolic meaning of this image connect to the Shadow and those things we are afraid of in life.

Avoiding the basement in a dream indicates a fear of exploring the unknown. If you know what is down there and that makes you feel ill at ease, your dream is letting you know that you are aware of what hidden issues are being avoided. If you are in the basement and filled with fear, you may be going through a process that is scary, but perhaps unavoidable. Trying to leave a basement might parallel the waking mind's desire to be finished with a dark period in life. If the person who is trapped is not you, use the Character Aspect technique to examine what hidden traits within yourself are beginning to emerge and need attention.

If you dream of a basement that is not dark and scary, you are still in the realm of things that are hidden or private, but perhaps not frightening. While this could symbolize previous conflicts that have been resolved, it could also point to Shadow material that is being covered up. Be vigilant in your investigation, for whatever happens below the surface will eventually impact what appears above.

Bathroom/Restroom

Universal Landscape: Individuation and privacy.

Dreaming Lens: Were you in a bathroom? Were you trying to get to one? Was it a private bathroom, or a public restroom? Did you know the bathroom from your waking life? Was it from your past or present? What was your connection to the privacy available to you in the dream? Was anyone else there with you, or waiting for you to finish?

Personal Focus: Somewhere around two years of age in our culture, we come to the most challenging obstacle of our development: toilet training. After sometimes months and months of intense public focus on fecal production, a child gets to do something for the very first time—he or she gets to shut the door. This burgeoning sense of privacy and personal space is the first time we experience control over our immediate environment. The impact of this is so powerful that it remains imprinted on our psyche for the rest of our lives.

In our dreams, we return to this place again and again throughout our entire lives when entertaining issues of individuation, separateness, and privacy. A bathroom inside a home connects with personal issues, whereas one that is more public is revealing information about your outside interactions. Not being in the appropriate bathroom for your gender might be inviting you to explore or discover your own inner feminine or inner masculine. Not being able to get to your destination in time could indicate a pressing need for individuation to occur in your life. Hiding out in the bathroom could mean you are not complete with your self-discovery and are unprepared to face life as your new individuated self. Having to go to the bathroom and not being able to find one may be a call to action about how important it is to find some private reevaluation time. Decorating your bathroom may mean you are updating your sense of individual self to match your current life. The toilet is located in a bathroom. As such, it can relate to relieving yourself of the "shit" in your life that you no longer need.

Beach

Universal Landscape: Where the unconscious and conscious meet.

Dreaming Lens: What was the energy of the beach? Was it turbulent or calm? Was there anyone else on the beach with you? Did you meet anyone on the beach? Were the seas stormy or still? How close did you allow yourself to go toward the water? Were you attracted to swimming in it or repelled? Was it day or night? Was the scene serene or ominous or something in between?

Personal Focus: The ocean represents the deep unconscious mind. Land represents our conscious mind. Our planet is divided into these two distinctly different surfaces. Where they meet is symbolic of the place in the human mind where what we are conscious of and the depths of that which lies below the surface of our awareness exist side by side. Consider the fact that the ocean covers most of the planet with water, with only relatively small masses of land rising above its surface. The same is true for the human psyche. Most of who we are is unknown to us, hidden in the depths of the unconscious.

As a symbol, a beach can be explored through the perspective of either or both of its two components. The quality of the water connects to your current emotional expression. The land that meets it represents your conscious thoughts. The fact that this is where these distinctly different terrains meet, gives this image a mysterious and magical quality, much like our experience of beaches in life. A dream about being on a beach signifies that new levels of understanding are available to you by virtue of the unconscious and conscious minds communing.

Ceaseless ocean waves exert enormous impact over the shape, contour, and boundaries of the shorelines that receive their constant pounding. The same is true of the mind, which is under a constant barrage of thoughts and feelings that burst out of the unconscious. They often spill violently onto the edge of our minds, influencing our moods, behaviors, and choices. This can be experienced positively as creative expression or flashes of insight. However, just like the tides, powerful emotions can feel dangerous, as they sweep everything in their wake back into the depths of unknown territory.

What occurs on the beach in your dream, whom you are with, the time of day and all other factors must be examined when interpreting this image. Additionally, your Personal Focus around the ocean and swimming in deep water is key to an accurate interpretation. Some people thrive in the water and find the act of swimming in the ocean exhilarating. Others feel naturally safe on land and fear deep waters, which can be filled with predators, forceful tides, and the possibility of drowning. There is just as much fear about surrendering to our feelings in our human experience as there is about drowning in the sea. What happens and who appears on a beach in your dreams offers crucial insight into what emotional needs the unconscious wants you to examine.

Beams of Light

Universal Landscape: Focused thought; penetrating energy.

Dreaming Lens: What was the source of the light? From what direction did it come? Was there visible machinery/technology connected to the light? What was the purpose of the light?

Personal Focus: Light is energy in motion. We generally think of it in terms of that which illuminates and makes things visible. However, light is actually a wave of energy, only a small fraction of which is visible to the human eye. In this way, the light we can see represents conscious thoughts. Various forms of light can represent different levels and intensities of thought. A beam is a focus of light that has the ability to illuminate a particular area or object and is, therefore, symbolic of concentrated thought. The concept of "thought" itself is understandably very vague and ambiguous. Therefore, it is important to consider the entire context of the beam(s) of light that appear in your dream in order to begin an effective interpretation.

The beams from the headlights of a car represent the thoughts about the direction the car is traveling and perhaps also its destination. Witnessing headlights from another car represents thoughts about unknown or outside influences that are just becoming conscious. Consider the source of the light: headlights from a police car evoke different reactions than those of a large truck. Add these Personal Focus elements to your interpretation if they are known to you in the dream.

There are many other forms of light beams that could appear in your dreams. In each case, the source and purpose of the beam, as well as its intensity and reach, will lead you to your interpretation. The beam from a lighthouse implies guidance through emotional issues that may be fogging your ability to navigate. A search light from a police helicopter might imply imminent danger or authority issues. A laser beam used as a pointer for presentations could be signaling a need to focus your ideas and gain clarity. A beam from outer space might suggest information from a higher source is becoming available to you.

Beast/Human

Universal Landscape: Integration of primitive traits and consciousness.

Dreaming Lens: What animal was involved in your dream? What part of the human body was present? Were you the human? Did you witness the beast in the dream? What was the beast doing? Was it friendly or harmful?

Personal Focus: Mythology is filled with creatures that combine physical attributes of various animals and the human body. These magical man-beasts appear in many cultural histories, and even the most bizarre dream-related combination may actually have a predecessor in the mythology of an ancient civilization.

The interpretation of this symbol should start with the energy associated with the animal that appeared in the dream. The mermaid is half-fish and half-woman. Its symbolic meaning is the connection between the unconscious and the conscious mind through the feminine principle of receptivity and creativity. As fish, they can swim deep into the unconscious as represented by the ocean. As women, they can surface and introduce into consciousness ideas of integration that emanate from otherwise hidden emotional resources.

The centaur is known for having the head, torso, and arms of a man and the body of a horse. This combines the archetypal meaning of powerful, masculine energy with the intellect and reasoning capacity of a human being. A creature that attaches the legs of a goat to a male torso brings dark, sexual energy together with the masculine principle. One example is Pan, the mythical God of fields and flocks, known for his mischievous nature and predatory sexual practices.

Any time a beast/human appears in a dream, it may signal a need to do some research. Examining historical references that match your dream image can yield a treasure trove of information that your unconscious mind is attempting to convey to you. If no actual data is available to you, simply make an association with the animal in your dream and combine it with the power of masculine intellect or feminine creativity.

Bedroom

Universal Landscape: Part of the self; privacy and intimacy.

Dreaming Lens: Whose bedroom was it? Yours or another's, known or unknown to you? Who was present in the room? What was occurring? How did you feel about the room, or what was going on in the room? Were you trapped there, or free to go? Were you hiding? Were you safe? Did you explore the room?

Personal Focus: A house represents the Self, and each part of a home is symbolic of particular elements of the human personality. The significance of a bedroom connects to privacy and intimacy. A bedroom is usually the most private room in the home, and a place where intimate acts occur. Because of the association with nakedness, sex, and the vulnerability that comes with being asleep, the bedroom represents the part of ourselves that we are aware of, but generally keep hidden and separate from our social and public life. On a primal level, the bedroom is the one room in a home where an individual's scent is most prevalent. Human beings are the only member of the animal kingdom that will compulsively remove their own scent. This deepens the personal nature of this symbol.

If the bedroom is your own, your dream may be revealing issues about your private sense of identity around intimacy. Your feelings around the dream can be a barometer for how these unconscious emotions may be impacting you. For example, a dream where a traumatic event unfolds in your bedroom could point to a sense of private danger, whereas a joyful or pleasant event might relate to positive experiences in this area.

If the bedroom is known to you, but is not your own, your interpretation should incorporate the qualities of the actual resident. When there is no waking life connection to the bedroom, utilize any details that you remember to discover the deeper meaning of the dream. A luxurious room might lead you to consider issues around personal abundance. Similarly, a room that is stark or dilapidated suggests personal issues around lack and limitation. A large room could indicate a sense of expansion, but also a feeling of being overwhelmed, depending on how it felt to be in it. A small room could indicate anything from coziness to claustrophobia. The emotional content of the Dreaming Lens will help you clarify your interpretation. Remember to consider associations from your childhood and what role your bedroom played for you within the dynamic of your family.

Being Chased

Universal Landscape: Fear-based response to threat.

Dreaming Lens: Did you see your pursuer? Did you know the pursuer? Was there more than one? Were you being chased by a person or something inhuman? Were you in real danger, or were you making an assumption of danger based on the heightened anxiety? Did you elude your pursuer, or did he/she/it catch up with you?

Personal Focus: When a person feels threatened at a very primal level, the built-in survival mechanism of the fight or flight response occurs. While most people's routine lives do not provide them with chances to test how they might react to such a threat, the dream world is filled with many such opportunities. Being chased is perhaps the most common dream image shared by all people across cultures and history.

Since this is a frequent dream experience, yet an infrequent life experience, it is important to recognize that the unconscious mind is using a very intense image to express waking life stressors that are not as life threatening as the dreams they provoke. The mind is very economical—it will use the fantastical experience of surviving danger in order to allow us to wake up the next day, ready to face the mundane challenges that may be troubling us. The fact that these are often recurring dreams further illustrates their capacity to balance out the unconscious fears and anxieties that we accumulate during the day. Look to where you may be feeling threatened or anxious in your life when this dream appears.

There is an alternate perspective that is important to consider when dreaming of being chased. Sometimes, it is part of human nature to be afraid of success. This unconscious sabotage can be very difficult to identify. You may be running in terror without knowing that the secret enemy you are running from is yourself. If you do not know your assailant, it may simply be that someone is trying to catch up to you with something important that, if embraced, would allow you to feel more complete. If you know who chases you, the person may have more to offer you if you let him/her catch you. Even if being caught ends in being killed, that death could be a symbolic transformation of such significance as to be the very thing needed to bring your greatest heart's desires into reality. That is, of course, if you have the courage to stop running and turn around.

Birds

Universal Landscape: Messengers; messages.

Dreaming Lens: What kind of bird was in your dream? Was it a bird that exists in nature or some strange aberration? What size was the bird in relation to you or other elements of the dream? Was the bird friendly or menacing? Was it free or caged?

Personal Focus: All animals represent some aspect of the universal mind in the collective unconscious. Birds can fly through the air, and this ability connects them symbolically to the notion of intellect and higher thoughts. Historically, certain birds have been used as messengers because of their innate homing skills. While this practice is considered archaic today, this function remains powerfully imbedded in the human psyche and connects the image of birds to the symbolic meaning of the carrier of messages.

In Nordic mythology, Odin, the ruler of Valhalla, was blessed by the presence of two ravens—Hugin and Munin—that sat on each of his shoulders. Hugin was the ruler of thought and Munin was the ruler of memory. Each day, these messengers would travel through the world of men and bring back important information to this mythological king. The expression "a bird's eye view" further illuminates that the high vantage point and speed with which birds move through the skies and provides powerful insight to those capable of interpreting their messages.

It is crucial to identify the type of bird that appears in your dreams and what associations arise as a result. A fearsome bird of prey could indicate messages of fear or danger. A songbird may relate to more positive meaning, though direct interpretation may be elusive without words to clarify the message. A caged bird may connect to messages about feelings of limitation whereas a bird in free-flight may indicate a desire for freedom. A flock of birds relates to the power of the group mentality and your reaction to the movement of the flock can illuminate whether this conformity is comforting or restrictive. If a specific species of bird appears in your dreams, doing some research may connect you to information available in the collective unconscious.

Blind, Blindness

Universal Landscape: Inability to see; fear of losing sight.

Dreaming Lens: Were you blind, or was there a blind character in your dream? Did the blindness interfere with your intent? Were other senses heightened? Were you fearful or panicked? If someone in your dream was blind, how did you interact with them?

Personal Focus: When blindness appears in a dream it takes on an almost literal connotation. Vision is our primary sense, and as sighted individuals, we experience the world primarily through what we see and rely very little on our other senses. More accurately, we use our other senses to guide our eyes to take in more information. As an example, upon hearing a noise, a typical response would be to turn toward it in order to see what produced it, rather than processing all of what our hearing could tell us. Given the importance we place upon vision, the loss or lack of it is considered catastrophic for most people. However, most blind persons will confirm that their other senses offer a very full picture of the world in which they live.

By dreaming of the inability to see, you may be expressing areas in your life that you may be *blind* to. If a Character Aspect in your dream is blind, you must first determine what part of you they represent. Different parts of us connect to different ways in which we operate in the world. If one of these areas is lacking vision, you may need to rely on your intuition in order to be successful in that area. If the blind person is someone you know, what they represent in your own personality may be the part of you that is not seeing the truth in some matter. You may be dreaming of a situation in your life, or your personality, where you have a *blind spot*. You may have to go beyond what the eyes can see in a situation to determine how to respond authentically.

We also use the term *vision* to express where we see our lives heading in terms of goals and desires. If you are experiencing a loss of vision in your dream, you may be expressing unconscious fears of being unable to see what is coming next in your life.

Consider that the blind person represents limited sight but also the increase of other senses, especially intuition. Being unable to see exactly how things are going to manifest is often the very ingredient necessary for them to do so. Blind faith is one of the most powerful energies there is.

Blood

Universal Landscape: Life force. Passion for living.

Dreaming Lens: What color was the blood? Was it a healthy red, or a depleted blue? Was it a strange and unnatural color? Was it flowing from a wound? If so, was it being lost slowly or rapidly? Was it in a container of some kind? Was blood being removed from or added to the physical body? Did you find it repulsive, or a source of fascination?

Personal Focus: The elixir of life, blood courses through our veins and keep our bodies alive and healthy. Lose enough of it and life slips away. If your dream includes receiving or losing blood, this may reflect a message that you are either in need of more energy or are being depleted by some situation. How this occurs in your dream will add texture to your interpretation. A wound inflicted by another may reflect an external struggle, whereas a medical procedure connects more to an internal process necessary for healing.

Science tells us that there are different kinds of blood and that certain types are incompatible with others. In fact, disparate types between a mother and her fetus can be life threatening. Therefore, dreaming of blood types could connect to conflicts about compatibility that are deeply rooted and may be impacting you in areas of life that you are passionate about. When blood type and compatibility are being examined, the stakes can be as high as life and death. HIV brings a whole new view of blood as something that is potentially dangerous, because it transmits this disease, effectively shifting our collective conscious view of blood as a substance to be potentially feared as contagious on a life-threatening level. Incorporate the Dreaming Lens into whatever issues of compatibility may be surfacing in your waking life.

Bloodlines have figured prominently as coveted evidence of ancestry throughout history. While this perspective may appear to be an archaic form of class-consciousness, we are now aware that blood typology is an effective tool to establish biological ties between family members. If this idea is expressed in your dream, your interpretation should reflect blood as connected to primal feelings about your family connections. Your dream may be expressing this as powerfully passionate, or energetically depleting, depending on the Dreaming Lens.

The color of blood is significant in a number of ways. If this is thematic in your dream, your interpretation must examine the meaning behind it. Oxygen-rich and healthy blood has a distinctive color of deep red that is found nowhere else in nature. If tapped out of nutrients, it turns blue. In the world of science fiction, the blood of alien beings can be anything from green to colorless chemical compounds made up of deadly acids.

There are also many culturally-based meanings associated with blood. The term "red-blooded" is synonymous with virility and strength. Conversely, to be "blue-blooded" connotes a passivity and lethargy related to wealth or privilege. Issues of racial prejudice often included erroneous beliefs that blood differed significantly between people of different cultural background or skin color. The mixing of bloodlines was considered by many as likely to have disastrous results. While that level of ignorance is not as prevalent today as in our past, the foundation of these beliefs still resides in the collective unconscious and can appear in your dreams and is worth considering.

Your personal reaction to blood is also a factor in interpreting this dream symbol. Some people are squeamish and the sight of blood can be very upsetting. For others, curiosity or a sense of eroticism may be stimulated. There are those, too, who are unaffected by the sight of blood by being accustomed to it if their profession frequently brings them in contact with it. Any of these responses can reveal your relationship to the levels of passion and life force you are currently experiencing.

Board Game

Universal Landscape: Solving conflict through structure and control.

Dreaming Lens: What was the game being played? Did you know the rules of the game? Was it an actual game you know from life, or was it an imaginary game? Who was playing the game in your dream? What were your feelings about the players? What level of skill and ability was being expressed? Were you winning, or losing?

Personal Focus: A board game is a civilized approach to expressing competitive impulses and conflict-solving skills. In a dream, it may be an analogy for the "game" in life it is designed to represent. Popular board games are created to convey certain themes of life experience through the process of playing them.

Your first clue to investigating this symbol begins with the game itself. If it is known in the dream, the theme of the game is central to your interpretation. For example, the game of Risk would symbolize the risks we take in life that can lead to power and control. Another is Monopoly: the way we deal with acquiring and managing material abundance. Consider the game you encounter in your dream and determine the theme it expresses. If you do not know the game being played, the meaning you assign your dream should reflect this uncertainty. Your daily life may be reflecting a game plan and strategy that feels unfamiliar.

If you are winning in your dream, you may be expressing recent experiences of successful negotiation of life's complexities. If you are losing, the dream may be reflecting back to you where you are blocked or challenged. If the surreal environment of the game is the dreamscape itself, an overwhelming situation may literally be enveloping you. If the environment is more a source of fascination, your dream may be illuminating a sense of awe that some moments can inspire. With any game in a dream, there may be unconscious feelings that are demanding a strategic approach to understanding and ultimately, winning.

Boat

Universal Landscape: Your emotional journey.

Dreaming Lens: Were you on a boat? Were you seeing a boat, but not on board? What type of boat was it? Was it moving or docked? Was the boat out of water for building or service? Were you seasick or comfortable?

Personal Focus: Any vehicle in a dream refers to our paths in life. A boat travels over water, the universal symbol for anything that deals with the emotions. The size and type of boat in your dream will illuminate your current ability to navigate emotional issues based on resources and levels of skill. The water itself connects with the nature of the emotional territory in which you currently find yourself. The destination of your trip will offer insight into what may be causing an upsurge of emotion and what you hope the outcome will be if you are successful in arriving at your intended destination.

A slow-moving cruise ship denotes the slow, steady pace of emotional unfolding. However, it travels over the deep waters of the ocean, connecting to a need to exert enormous control over what might be underlying fears about the depths of your emotional unconscious. A speedboat indicates faster processing of emotional turmoil as well as a desire to get through an emotional encounter as quickly as possible. A sailboat connects to the merging of emotion and intellect. The boat itself rides on the water of the emotions, while the sail catches the wind of the intellect and uses that as the power that propels one forward. A canoe might hearken back to more primitive emotions. A rowboat indicates that the emotional issues you are facing require direct effort to get through.

The state the boat is in has great meaning with regard to your effectiveness and the safety of your journey. One that is in disrepair or in danger of sinking indicates overwhelm in your current situation. A boat that is docked represents emotional journeys that are yet to be taken. Consider how protected you feel by the boat. Feelings of danger may indicate resistance about diving into the depths of your unconscious feelings.

Body Parts

Universal Landscape: Various functionality or physical abilities.

Dreaming Lens: What part of the body were you dreaming of? Was it your own body or someone else's? Was it separate and disembodied? Did the image involve a loss of functioning? Was there an element of horror to the image? Did the dream have a medical theme?

Personal Focus: The interpretation you give to a body part in a dream correlates directly with its function. The head connects to thoughts and intellect. The neck usually represents issues surrounding communication and the ability to assess a situation. Arms represent activity and strength whereas the hands connect to creativity (fingers can usually be associated with skill and dexterity). The lower body involves issues of being grounded and secure. The legs connect specifically to being in (or out) of control of your movement through life. The direction in which you are heading is often represented by the feet. They also symbolize your relationship to the things for which you are willing (or unwilling) to take a stand.

The Dreaming Lens will provide the perspective with which you should view the meaning you assign to the body part. Most dream scenarios involving the body will fall into one of two categories: decrease or increase. The loss of, or injury to, a body part indicates some sort of hindrance or limitation. The augmentation or expansion of a body part indicates the opposite. Both perspectives can be viewed as positive or negative, depending on the sensation of the dream and/or the residual feelings generated by the dream upon waking.

If the image in your dream is simply a part of the body being highlighted or focused upon, your interpretation need only consider the meaning you assign it. However, if the dream includes a change in the body, you must add this to the mix. Amputation, for example, indicates a drastic loss of functioning, but implies necessity, as a limb is usually only removed to preserve the integrity and healthy functioning of the rest of the body. This shows that choice is involved as well as the need to sacrifice something for the survival of the Self. When in doubt, researching the biology or kinesiology of a part of the body will yield vast resources of information to inform your interpretation.

Bombs

Universal Landscape: Sudden bursts of new ideas for change.

Dreaming Lens: Were you being bombed in the dream? Were you the bomber? Did the bombs actually explode? Did they reach their target? What was the result of the explosion? Were you in possession of a bomb? Was it capable of exploding?

Personal Focus: Bombs generate an instantaneous force that has the power to significantly alter physical structures wherever they explode. Their impact includes the eradication of the current landscape, laying bare whatever was previously standing.

While we usually think of bombs as exclusively destructive and a tool of war, in the world of symbols, no destructive force exists without its constructive opposite. In the war of the unconscious mind, you are both sides: the dropper of the bomb and its victims.

This symbol should be considered for the suddenness of the appearance of its power and the thoroughness with which it manifests its intention, rather than any associations with the realities of battle.

In war, the target of a bomb is perhaps the most important element associated with it. Consider what was being targeted by the bomb in your dream and the efficiency with which it accomplished its goal. Whatever or whomever was hunted or destroyed will supply you with the meaning you should assign this symbol. The area of life that is suggested by the target is the area of your life that needs a drastic change. So drastic, in fact, that only an explosion will provide the necessary momentum.

Having an actual bomb that is not being deployed in your possession is akin to having the means and readiness for a future shift. If this is the case in your dream, look to areas in your life that are calling out for transformation.

Books

Universal Landscape: Knowledge and wisdom. Permanent thought.

Dreaming Lens: Were you reading a book? Was someone else reading? Was the book unopened? Were there many books? Were you in a bookstore or a library? Were the books identifiable or known to you? Were they in your native language? What was the content of the book(s)?

Personal Focus: Our societal perception of books and their value has changed drastically in recent times. Electronic media has already begun a process of rendering them obsolete. However, their rich heritage through the collective unconscious makes them a powerful symbol, despite the shift in how we perceive them.

As Western culture developed, only a very small minority of the population was able to read. Therefore, books became a highly valued commodity reserved only for the very wealthy, or members of religious hierarchy. In this way, books represent wisdom and knowledge. Their tangible, physical structure embodies a sense of permanence of thought as the printed word has come to be synonymous with truth and fact, whether accurate or not.

Books, as a symbol, connect to the accumulation and availability of knowledge. On a personal level, they can represent the measurement of someone's intelligence. Many books appearing in a dream connect to higher level of intellect as expressed by the unconscious. One volume connects to a single area of information whereas a bookstore or library filled with books might symbolize abundant levels of knowledge available to those who seek it out.

Consider your relation to books and reading in life and apply it to your dream. Reading a book in a dream could indicate a need to slow down your mental processes so that you can hear your own thoughts. The printed permanence of books could indicate a need for you to be more exacting in your communication or illuminate areas where you are being held accountable for your words. Books on a shelf can mean wisdom not being utilized in some situation. Reading in a library or bookstore may mean you have tapped in to the collective unconscious where profound information is available to us all. Certain books, such as novels, can represent a desire to lose yourself in another world.

Boulders/Rocks

Universal Landscape: Primitive memory.

Dreaming Lens: Were you dreaming of pebbles, rocks, stones, boulders, or even larger formations? Were these helpful objects, such as tools or building materials? Were they obstacles, such as a block in your path or an impediment to reaching a desired destination? Were they an annoyance, or actually in a position to cause harm?

Personal Focus: Rocks act as the memory for our planet. By examining their elemental makeup and physical structure, scientists can
understand the history of the Earth. The fossil records left in rock
formations literally describe our planet's journey through time.
Seen in this light, even the stones and pebbles you find in your back
yard are symbolic of the ancient past and the secrets of how we
came to be in this vast universe.

At the beginning of civilization, early man made tools out of
stone. This same material was used later by more sophisticated cultures to create buildings. The remains of these objects and structures
serve as symbols of the memory of the evolution of the human race.

Whenever stones, rocks, or boulders are prominent in a dream,
you may be connecting on some level to a primal image rooted in
the distant past. On a more mundane level, the past that is being
represented by this image may be your own personal history. To
begin your interpretation, examine the role or function the rock(s)
or boulder(s) are playing in your dream. If you are using a rock as
a tool or a weapon, your activity should be interpreted on its own
merit, with the added element of history, memory, or a sense of the
primitive. This same perspective should be added to a dream image of constructing something with stone, with the primary meaning being that which you associate with the thing itself: Something
made of stone is built to last forever.

Rocks or boulders can represent obstacles or challenges if they
obstruct your way or present you with some amount of danger. If
this is the case, what may be blocking you in your waking life could
be material that is deeply imbedded in your unconscious. Examine
areas where you may be holding fast to old ideas that no longer
serve you. Painful memories can often seem like insurmountable
obstacles or enormous boulders that appear to be immovable. If
this describes your dream experience, it may be time to let go of

outdated notions that still have the power to hold you back from fuller self-expression.

Breaking Up

Universal Landscape: Sacrifice and transformation of an aspect of personality.

Dreaming Lens: Were you breaking up with someone? Were they breaking up with you? Was it in person or on the phone? Was it a marriage, or was it a more casual relationship? Was it painful?

Personal Focus: When two people are joined as an intimate couple, the way they identify with each other psychologically is the glue that holds them together. It is almost as if their individual sense of wholeness depends on how each partner lives inside the psyche of the other as a projected "other half." When a breakup occurs, each person moves on to their next expression of Self. Neither will be quite the same for having connected.

In a dream, one party (or both, if neither of the couple breaking up is the dreamer) represents a Character Aspect of the dreamer that is being sacrificed in the cycle of death and rebirth in order to make way for a new way of being. While this can hurt intensely, letting someone go is an intrinsic part of growing and expanding our self-identity as we mature, and a necessary step in the evolution of the human psyche.

Viewed in this light, a breakup in a dream signals that this crucial process is underway. People frequently dream of the partner they have parted with in life while grieving the loss. The symbolic meaning of the ex in a dream connects to the qualities in the dreamer that were most brought out by them. If a breakup is occurring to a couple in the dream that is not you, then the Character Aspects represented by one or both of them will provide clues for the qualities that are being discarded, or need to be let go of.

Violence or conflict surrounding a breakup may illuminate elevated levels of resistance or perhaps higher emotional stakes. Con-
soling someone after a breakup may point to being further along in
the process of change. Advising someone or seeking advice around
the issue of a breakup (convincing or being convinced as well) could
represent an unconscious attempt to battle resistance to change. The
varying levels of emotional content in such a dream will reveal the
depth of the shift that is taking place.

Breasts

Universal Landscape: Feminine resource; nurturance.

Dreaming Lens: Whose breasts were featured in the dream? Were they
yours? Were they anatomically appropriate to the person who had
them in the dream? What size and shape were they? Were they real
or augmented? How did you feel about them? Was there a sexual
connotation in the dream? Was nursing a baby involved?

Personal Focus: Breasts are perhaps the most confounding parts of
the human body. In essence, they are practical and functional, providing sustenance and nutrition for the young of all mammals. In
this way, they connect symbolically to the feminine principle of
nurturance. However, they are also a powerful erogenous zone and
are, therefore, part of sexual expression and physical pleasure. This
dichotomy has allowed our society to imbue them with complicated levels of projection that run the gamut from objectification,
shame, judgment, covetousness, and more.

Dreams can reflect this abundance of Personal Focus, depending on the gender, sexual orientation, curiosity, and proclivity of
the dreamer. For an accurate interpretation, it is important to begin
with the Universal Landscape of nurturance and filter any other
meaning through that perspective. Augmenting breasts to make
them larger represents a need to increase one's capacity for care

giving, even if the form it takes is sexual generosity. A dream in which the breasts are reduced or removed may be reflecting a loss of feminine power, or a drain of over-giving in a relationship or life circumstance.

Dreaming of breasts often connects to the level of self-care of the dreamer, whether they are male or female. Even erotic dreams involving this symbol should be viewed through this concept. Breasts that are not real might indicate that the nurturing you give yourself as an adult is somehow false and not truly nutritious. Older or sagging breasts would indicate a resource that is no longer full. Breasts on a man could indicate a need to cultivate more sensitive and nurturing qualities.

Breathless

Universal Landscape: Diminished life force. Panic.

Dreaming Lens: Were you breathless or gasping? Was someone else having difficulty breathing? What was the cause of the breathlessness? Was it connected to anxiety or physical exertion? Was the environment lacking oxygen? Were you in dangerous circumstances? Were you being helped or assisted?

Personal Focus: The breath of life is also the physical representation of our level of serenity. When breath is slow and nourishing, we are at ease. Any elevation of breath indicates that we are either in fear, emotional reactivity, or intense physical activity. Each of these has very distinct differentiations. A fear response is internal and is generated by chemical reactions in the brain. These moments of anxiety usually have more to do with irrational thoughts than what is actually occurring in your world. A moment of emotional reactivity is more likely to connect to another individual or outside situation that is contrary to your expectations, therefore, resulting in disappointment and feeling out of control. Physical activity that impacts the breath is visceral and is frequently connected to exercise and, therefore, to self-care. On the opposite side of this is becoming winded by virtue of a physically exertive effort to escape from danger. While this is still in the realm of caring for one's self, it adds the element of threat to the mix.

The essence of any meditative discipline is the control of the breath. Furthermore, all high-performance athletes, from dancers to football players, understand that channeling their movement through their breathing is what produces excellence and mastery. In this way, it is clear that your personal relationship to breathing is a direct barometer for your level of mastery, serenity, and effectiveness. The loss of breath, therefore, is symbolically connected to a diminishment in your ability to master life itself.

If a physical activity is making you breathless in a dream, it could indicate that burdens in your life are overwhelming you. If there is no clear explanation for your lack of breath, your unconscious mind may want you to know that your inner equilibrium is off. If this is the case, you must investigate and find the cause of the disharmony. Whatever challenges life is bringing you, your unconscious mind may simply be reminding you to not forget to breathe.

Bridge

Universal Landscape: Connections; a transition or solution.

Dreaming Lens: Were you on the bridge? Were you considering crossing or were you already on the other side? Did the bridge seem safe to cross? What was the bridge connecting? What was it going over? What type of bridge was it? How big was it? Was it from a location you know from life?

Personal Focus: A bridge is essentially that which makes a connection between two separate entities. It can offer a solution to the problem of getting across an obstacle of some kind. Since it takes you from one place to another, it also carries the meaning of a transition in life. Man-made constructions that require a high level of sophisticated engineering to create, they express the complicated ways in which we often approach solving problems in life. They also represent the ability to expand into new territory previously unavailable for exploration. The primary meaning, however, relates to the connections we make in life, hence the warning in the phrase *don't burn your bridges*.

Since many bridges are suspended over water, an emotional issue is often the underlying conflict being expressed by this symbol. The intensity of the water below will indicate the level of emotions being stirred up. Some bridges, however, are used to traverse difficult terrain over land. In a dream, this might point to some construct or obstacle in your life that you'd rather avoid by somehow rising above it. If there is a conflict in your life that you can easily identify, a bridge in a dream may be symbolic of bringing together opposite sides of an issue. The integrity of the construction of a bridge could illuminate how effectively you are approaching the situation.

Broken Bones

Universal Landscape: Loss of foundational integrity.

Dreaming Lens: Were your bones broken in your dream? Was it someone else who was suffering? Was it happening present time in your dream or had it already occurred? Was there pain involved? What bones were broken and how did the injuries occur?

Personal Focus: The skeleton at the core of our bodies is the foundation on which the whole system is built. Since most of the human body is soft and moist, we rely on the solid, durable, calcium-based bone structure for what little solidity we feel. Nothing can be any stronger than the foundation that supports it. And when that foundation is compromised, we are rendered immobile and vulnerable.

Bones as foundational indicate that the essence of the stressor that is being expressed has to do with how something is structured or being supported. If you dream of a bone being broken, it tells you that some area of your life is on shaky ground. The solidity and strength beneath that which is creative or expressive is what is compromised.

To get more specific, look to the bone that was broken. Consider the use and purpose of the body part that is supported by the bone in question and add that to your interpretation.

What follows are generalized starting points for your consideration. Each distinction could relate to many different areas of your life. The feet represent feeling grounded, while the toes are about maintaining balance. The legs connect with freedom, choice and movement. The knees are the symbolic home of humility, subservience and/or surrender. They are also the place where we hold our fears. The hips are the center of the core and, therefore, represent the integration of systems and all the elements of your life that have to interact with one another in order to function. The ribs are about vulnerability and protecting ones self from emotional pain. The ability to withstand pressure and the needs of others is associated with the shoulders. The arms are the structures that allow us to take action and accomplish our goals and desires, while the hands give us the creative ability to do so. The individual fingers are how we relate to details and life's complexities. The spine is our moral center and where our values are located. The neck, though a part of the spine, has the distinction of providing us with discernment and choice. The skull is related to our beliefs, ideals, and opinions; and the bones that support our faces connect with community and the desire to connect with others.

If your dream included the injury itself, add the means by which your bones were broken to your interpretation, including if there was another person responsible. The more facile and creative you can be with your rumination of these symbolic meanings, the more successful your interpretation will be.

Bus

Universal Landscape: Movement on life's path that is public or shared.

Dreaming Lens: Were you riding a bus? Were you driving one? What type of bus was it? Were you waiting for a bus? Had you missed your bus? Did the bus crash? Who else was on the bus with you? How did you feel about riding the bus?

Personal Focus: As with any mode of transportation, a bus connects with one's path through life. When you ride a bus, you turn the reins of control over to another, take a seat and go along for the ride. Relinquishing the driver's seat is an important point to examine, as your comfort level in the dream will help deepen your interpretation. Positive reactions to riding a bus may point to the well-being that can accompany letting go of control. A negative experience may point to resistance to such surrender.

Given that most bus rides are associated with public transportation, the symbolic meaning of your dream may connect to paths in your life that you share with others in your community. Consider who else was on your dream bus for clues to what area of your life is being illuminated.

The type of bus offers shades of meaning. A school bus may indicate regression to an earlier mentality, whereas a public transit bus could point to a need to follow a course that requires being patient with the paths of others. A private bus, such as a tour bus, may indicate levels of abundance and the need to gather large creative resources for future use. However, if the bus was used in place of a car, feelings of lack and limitation may be indicated. If you were not actually riding the bus in your dream, the meaning you give your interpretation should explore this. If this is a bus you should have been on, you might want to consider what obstacle or resistant thought is keeping you from moving more effectively on your life path.

Candle

Universal Landscape: Creative spark. Harnessed power.

Dreaming Lens: Were you lighting a candle or was it lit? Was this the only source of light? Were there many candles, as on a birthday cake? What color was the candle or its light? What was the intended mood produced by the candlelight: romantic, spiritual, or celebratory? Did you have a resource for lighting the candle? Was the candle posing the danger of starting a fire?

Personal Focus: When we light a candle, we are committing an act of creation. Fire has an enormous amount of power. When it is restrained in such a benevolent and gentle manner, it symbolizes the dominion that human beings can have over the elements to bring light to a dark place.

There is a magical glow to candlelight, perhaps even more so in modern times, because of how subtle it is compared to artificial light. Lighting a candle is a mainstay in various rituals that symbolize the beginning of something sacred, as if it represents the point of contact with our Creator. In this way, lighting a candle can be an indication of the beginning of some important event, phase, or relationship in life. The amount, color, quality, and other information from the Dreaming Lens will provide you with an accurate interpretation.

The connection of candlelight to romance is crucial and could indicate the desire or readiness for love and intimacy. Conversely, blowing a candle out might mean the end of such a phase. Dream candles might also symbolize creative impulses. The association of candles on a cake and birthdays could reflect a moment of taking stock of where you are in your life at this time. Candles can easily start a destructive fire, so consider the potential for danger if the flame you are burning should get out of control.

The structure of a candle itself represents the spiritual perspective to creativity and change. The candle is the idea you are having, while the flame is the power of focusing your intention, and the wax that melts and burns away is the transformation that results.

Candy

Universal Landscape: Instant gratification.

Dreaming Lens: Were you eating candy in the dream? Was someone else? Was candy being exchanged as a gift? Were there children eating candy or being refused candy? What kind of candy was it? How did you feel about eating it or avoiding it?

Personal Focus: Candy is a food substance that delivers an enormous amount of sugar into the body, significantly altering its chemistry in rapid fashion. The brain responds almost immediately, and while there is an initial surge of energy, it is then followed by a rebound effect shortly thereafter. Much of the symbolic meaning of this symbol connects to this physical phenomenon, as there is an addictive quality to the experience of eating it. Have a little and the body will want more.

There is a romantic element to candy as it is considered an appropriate gift for a man to give when courting a woman, though this may be an old-fashioned sentiment. However, considering the enormous connection between candy and Valentine's Day, there is still great power in candy as a symbol for expressing affection.

Children and parents have an intense relationship with candy. This can manifest in a variety of ways, from parents who forbid their children to have it to others that use it as a reward in behavior modification. No matter what the chosen perspective is, there is no avoiding the candy issue when you are the parent of a small child.

Candy in a dream could be as simple as an expressed desire for more sweetness in life. Since it is high in calories, many people associate it as a guilty pleasure if they are concerned about their weight. If this is the case, then candy could be representing something that you feel you are doing in your life because it feels good, but may not be in your best interest. If there is a romantic connotation to candy in a dream, you may want to examine ways in which you are attempting to achieve certain results with sweetness. There may be nothing wrong with that course of action, unless the sweet behavior is inauthentic and, therefore, a manipulation.

Car

Universal Landscape: Traveling the path through life.

Dreaming Lens: What was the condition of the car in the dream? Was it drivable? Were you able to drive it? Were you in control or out of control? Were you in the driver's seat? Was someone else in control of the car's destination? Was it a car from your own life? Was it a fantasy car for you?

Personal Focus: Since we rely so much on our automobiles to get where we're going, a car represents the connection we have to our path through life. Its speed, working status, style, and so forth, represent our feelings about our movement on that path. Any time you dream of a car, your unconscious is expressing thoughts and feelings about where your life is going at that moment. The best interpretation will combine this basic definition with shades of meaning based on the Dreaming Lens.

For example, an old car may point to an old way of maneuvering whereas a new car may indicate you are moving through life in a new way. A car from your past indicates that part of your history is under investigation. A fantasy car may mean the path you wish you were on. Driving someone else's car might indicate a path that has been abandoned for the sake of another's wishes, or even another's path that you wish to emulate. A parent's car could indicate the path taken by virtue of the wishes of the parents. A dirty car might indicate something that needs to be cleaned up. A crashed car could be calling you to examine the choices you are making on your path through life—are you paying attention to the danger signals?

The color of the car might have significance as well. A blue car may indicate your path toward more effective communication. A red car could point to issues of security or aggression (See also Colors). People have every different relationships with their cars, so your Personal Focus in this area should be considered when making your interpretation.

Cat

Universal Landscape: Powerful energy in the feminine principle.

Dreaming Lens: What kind of cat appeared in your dream? How many were there? Were they domesticated or wild? Was there a sense of danger involved? What was the setting? What activity was the cat(s) involved in?

Personal Focus: Cats of all types represent powerful feminine energy, which includes receptivity, creativity, sensuality, and stillness. They are hunters by nature, and their nocturnal behavior associates them with the feminine aspect of night. While their masculine counterpart, the dog, embodies a pack mentality, the cat is the symbol of self-reliance. First domesticated about three thousand years ago, cats were revered for their ability to control rodent populations that would have beleaguered the stores of grain that were so crucial to the emergence of civilization.

Cats have long been associated with magic and witchcraft, with the classic black cat as the carrier of the most superstition. There is a very pungent odor to their urine, correlating this smell with the dark side of the powerful feminine energy that this symbol represents. If your dream held any of these elements, you may be expressing unconscious thoughts about mysticism or spirituality.

Wild cats come in many sizes and are formidable hunters. If the cat in your dreams is one of the many species of cats found in nature, the meaning is the same, but with two additional distinctions. The prowess associated with predatory aggression comes into play with the largest of these beasts, the tiger. The lion is often linked with maternity due to the behavior of the lioness with her cubs. Cheetahs and leopards are symbolically correlated with speed and agility. The panther's sleek black coloring brings even more sensuality and Shadow material into the symbolic picture. For a truly accurate interpretation, doing some research on your dream cat will provide you with a wealth of information.

Celebrities

Universal Landscape: Archetypal Character Aspect; heightened expressions of human traits or qualities.

Dreaming Lens: Were you with a celebrity intimately, or was it a celebrity sighting? Did you know each other? What was the connection between you? Were there other people around? Did you have sex? Were you comfortable with the connection that you had? Did you want more? Did you want less?

Personal Focus: Celebrities are the gods and goddesses of modern life and represent archetypal human qualities with which we all identify. The essence of a particular celebrity's image can be distilled into a Character Aspect, based on our perceptions. Millions of people hold the same projected image of celebrities. The power of all that magnified perception endows them with superhuman status and removes any sense of who these people are underneath their personas.

Celebrities show up in our dreams when the stakes are a little higher in terms of what we're dreaming about. By providing a more powerful image, the unconscious is telling you to pay more attention. Approach the interpretation of a celebrity the same way you would anyone else who is in your dreams. When considering the qualities of the person you are dreaming about, remember to look at everything about him or her. Take into account how you perceive the person, including if you are a fan or not, or whether he or she is currently in or out of public favor. When interpreting a celebrity from a dream, first consider what this person embodies on the universal level. Then, and only then, add your personal feelings about the person. When you have done this, you will be clear about what Character Aspect of yourself you are dreaming of.

In the way that people in our dreams represent Character Aspects of ourselves, celebrities represent Character Aspects of the global consciousness as reflected by the idea of archetypes. Celebrities are our modern-day gods and goddesses. Dreaming about one of these elite individuals represents a need for you to explore their qualities as a Character Aspect that is embodied by you, but in a much more powerful way. In a process identical to working with a Character Aspect of someone at the pedestrian level, a celebrity's fame elevates the significance of the meaning you assign to them. Your unconscious is using the notoriety associated with their public visibility to get your attention. It is, in effect, providing you with an image that has a chance of making the dream memorable upon waking so that you might more readily take notice of the guidance available to you in the dream.

Sexual dreams with celebrities are common. Most dreamers assume this is so because of how attractive most of them are. Additionally, what they do puts them in a position to carry the sexual fantasies of their fans. However, in dream work, sexual dreams with celebrities are common because the drive to integrate archetypal energy is integral to the evolution of our souls. When the unconscious is encouraging you to own the more powerful parts of your psychic makeup, there is no better way for it to get your attention than through highly charged, sexual imagery.

It is natural for us to need larger-than-life representations of the human experience to motivate us through the various challenges we face while managing the stressors and disappointments that are a part of life's journey. Our culture's fascination with the life of celebrities provides us with hope that our own lives have the potential for excitement and glamour, even if this is just a fantasy. In fact, such fantasies can function as survival mechanisms for many people.

Discovering what a dream that involves a celebrity might be telling you is the same as with any Character Aspect. Since we are in the realm of archetypal energy when dealing with celebrities, the quality that your dream is inviting you to explore may be very obvious. A sports figure may be asking you to examine your willingness to play the game of life with more confidence whereas a pop singer may be suggesting that more self-expression is crying out for release. If you get stuck on how to interpret the meaning of a celebrity's presence, the technique of using three adjectives to describe them works just as well with the famous as with the ordinary.

Cell Phone

Universal Landscape: Instant connection and communication of thought.

Dreaming Lens: Were you using your phone? Was someone else using a cell phone? Did you have a clear connection, or was there interference? Did you lose your cell phone? Did the cell phone feel like a helpful tool or a burdensome necessity? Was the cell phone user being responsible?

Personal Focus: In a matter of a few decades, the relatively new phenomenon of cell phones have become so commonplace as to be taken for granted in the Western world. They provide an instant connection from one person to another no matter where either party is located. On the mundane level, they represent the accelerating speed of the world in which we live. Symbolically, they embody a concept that might be called supra-conscious: the connection between human beings across the planet through technology that provides the instantaneous exchange of ideas almost at the speed of thought.

When considering the symbolic meaning of this particular device, we cannot overlook the limitations that are currently part of the experience of using them. Static interference, abrupt disconnection, and accidental dialing are all part of the pitfalls of the current technological development. If any of these experiences play a role in your dream, your interpretation must include such challenges. If the object itself holds the meaning of instant connection and higher levels of thought, then a frustrating cell phone interaction symbolizes disconnect instead. Static could indicate that communication is blocked and you are feeling misunderstood or misunderstanding some life event. If there is a stigma of pretentiousness attached to cell phones, it could represent a move toward or away from conformity. A cell phone that cannot make a connection could mean your quick fix thinking may be failing you. A smooth connection could be telling you the answer to your communication problems is right there in your pocket.

Choking

Universal Landscape: An overwhelming or dangerous block to effective communication.

Dreaming Lens: Were you choking in the dream? Was someone else? Were they choking on something they swallowed? Was the choking the result of a violent act perpetrated on one person by another. Were you choking someone? If so, who was it? If you or someone else was choking on food, was the choker rescued?

Personal Focus: Any experience that connects with the neck and throat places us in the realm of communication. When someone is choking, their ability to speak is limited or even eradicated. Someone choking or being choked in a dream is dealing with communication issues that are intense enough to be, at least symbolically, a matter of life and death.

If there is some thought or idea that you need to express in your life right now, a dream with this image indicates that there is some sort of block to that expression. This image is so violent that it is likely pointing to something that is very intense, to say the least. When exploring your interpretation, look to where issues of communication are connected to people, places, or things, and where the stakes feel very high.

There are two categories that the idea of choking will fall into. You can choke on something you have ingested, such as food, beverage, or a small object. Or, the choking can be the aggressive act of another person attempting to stifle the breath and perhaps life out of the victim by stopping the flow of breath from passing into the lungs. Whatever the case, the key factor involved is the breakdown of the ability to communicate where the cost and impact could be so great as to cause death.

In the first construct, where there is an object that is being choked in, the object itself needs to be considered as part of your interpretation. If it is food or drink, then some aspect of nurturance and self-care is not being acclimated properly. If it is any other type of object, what it is must be interpreted and that meaning should be incorporated into your perspective of why you are feeling blocked. If you are being attacked by someone, use the Character Aspect technique to identify what part of your personality is choking off your ability to express yourself. If you are choking someone else, consider that you may be trying to stifle a particular way of communicating in the world that may be out of control or not serving you in some way. (See also Strangling.)

Church/Temple

Universal Landscape: The spiritual self.

Dreaming Lens: What kind of church was in your dream? What was the denomination or religion being practiced there? What state was the church in? Was this a church or temple from your daily life? Why were you there?

Personal Focus: Churches, temples, and mosques are the center of spiritual life for any community. Just like a house in a dream, any building can be interpreted as representing one's current sense of self. In this way, any place of worship ultimately points to your relationship with spirituality and religion. Because this element of life can be particularly controversial, it is very important that you make a clear distinction between the universal meaning of church as connecting to matters of spirituality and whatever personal feelings you harbor about organized religion.

The state the building is in is an important part of your interpretation. A church or temple that is in disrepair is likely pointing to your spiritual life suffering through neglect. A more modern building may connect to newer spiritual perspectives whereas an older structure may correlate with a more traditional viewpoint.

What is happening within the church or temple in your dream is something to consider as well. If the event in your dream is in alignment with the typical uses of such a place, a more literal interpretation may be in order. However, if there is a contradiction taking place, your own sense of spiritual confusion or inconsistency may be what is being expressed.

A church has long been synonymous with safety from worldly dangers in the form of protective sanctuary. A person could be considered safe within the confines of a church from all enemies, political and spiritual. Once inside, an individual cannot be harmed by the enemy, whether that enemy is the government or a legion of demons. Consider the possibility that this dream image is suggesting a need to receive the ultimate level of protection from unseen dangers.

Circus

Universal Landscape: Escapism of enormous proportion.

Dreaming Lens: Were you at a circus as an audience member? Were you performing? Were you backstage? What kind of circus was it? Was there a sideshow? What was your enjoyment level of the circus atmosphere? Did you run away with the circus or have the desire to do so?

Personal Focus: The circus has its origins in ancient Rome and the massive spectacles such as chariot races and gladiator fights. Since then, any large entertainment venue in the shape of a circle that contains a variety of acts of pageantry or feats of skill may be referred to as a circus. From its first days to modern times, one theme has remained the same: the size and scope must be massive and the performance must thrill its audience.

Any form of entertainment must be considered symbolically connected to escapism. With a circus, the additional texture of enormity must be added. This symbol contains a surreal element as well, as exemplified by the strangeness of clowns and the oddities of the sideshow.

Additionally, the circus has a reputation of catering to the fringes of society; a closed community that is secularized from the rest of the world. The mythology that surrounds the circus is that it is a place where freaks, outsiders, and loners can find a home. In this way, the meaning of escapism also includes a fantasy element in which someone can literally escape their mundane world by running away with the circus.

There is also a familial element to the circus in that many acts involve generations of family members participating in the exhibition of some skill. A child born into such a family is often expected to keep with tradition and join the troupe. You may need to ask yourself what generational peculiarities from your family of origin such a dream might be expressing.

If you were an audience member, then escapism should be the main theme of your interpretation. If you were performing in a circus, you may be expressing some inner pulls toward grandiose expressions of your sense of individuality and originality. If you were more connected to what was going on behind the scenes and the community of performers, look to where in your life you may be seeking agreement from like-minded people in a realm that is off the beaten path.

Depending on the size and scope of the circus in your dreams, there may be an unconscious expression of chaos represented by the simultaneous appearance of more than one set of stimuli. Ask yourself if your life is feeling like a three-ring circus. If this resonates, the dream may have some insight for you about how you are helping to create an atmosphere of disorder in some area.

Climbing

Universal Landscape: Growth and expansion through great effort.

Dreaming Lens: What were you climbing? Was the climb doable, or was it an impossible task? Was it enjoyable? Was it treacherous? Were you invigorated by it, or depleted? Did you know your way? Was the path clear? Were you alone, or with others, being led or leading others?

Personal Focus: A climb is the effort that must be expended to reach a particular goal. All goals require effort; many can involve struggle. As you identify what struggle in your life might be represented by the climb, the feelings and images in the dream can inform how you are approaching the current challenge in your life.

A dramatic shift is akin to embarking on a journey of some kind, whether it is emotional, financial, spiritual, or dealing with a health challenge. It may show up in a dream as a climb as your psyche tries to show you that you have the resources to make it to the top, despite the fear or intensity of the effort involved. By the same token, the dream may be telling you that you may be overemphasizing the struggles in your life and that you are applying more effort than is required. If this is the case, consider the lack of balance between effort and expectations you are currently experiencing. Your job is to define the journey and find the balance between intent and effort. This way, the ascent to your destination can be met with joy and enthusiasm.

Climbing Stairs

Universal Landscape: Transition to higher or lower consciousness.

Dreaming Lens: How many flights of stairs did you traverse? Were they in a home? Were you moving up or down, or standing on one step? Did you know your destination on the floor above or below? What was the focus—your destination or what you were leaving behind? Were the steps clean, dusty, or covered with obstacles?

Personal Focus: A staircase allows you to move from one place to a destination that is located above or below you. They are symbolic of your ability to raise your consciousness to a higher plane, or explore deeper territory beneath you. Any set of stairs or steps in a dream is an indication of examining a higher or lower level of your psyche, depending on which direction you are moving.

If the stairs are in a home, it is your sense of self that is being examined. Social issues and how you operate in the world are connected to a stairway that is located in a building or public place. Moving upward could indicate an increase in awareness and a readiness to elevate your thought process. Moving downward might connect to reexamining your past or considering something more deeply.

The rooms connected by a stairway should be factored into your interpretation. After you assign a meaning to each location, consider the stairway as the pathway between the knowledge you take from where you started and the ability to use it when dealing with the issues you may find at your new destination.

It is also important to consider the sensations and feelings around this image. If you were expending a lot of effort in your dream-climb, you may be in a burdensome transition. Falling down stairs may be about the risks you are taking to get to a new level in your life. Tripping on the stairs might be an indication that you are not quite ready to move further. A broken stair reveals an obstacle in your life that requires mending before you go further. A spiral staircase could connect to feeling that you are going around in circles while trying to ascend through some area of your life.

The floor you are moving to or from could have some significance if you were aware of what story you were on. For example, the second floor might indicate a progression in and around sexuality, whereas the third floor could connect to following your gut instincts and self-esteem. The stairs that connect these two floors would represent the transition that occurs when you become more instinctual or intuitive around your sexuality. The same approach can be applied to how many steps were on the staircase. This is especially significant if you were stopped or stuck on a particular stair. See Numbers for more details about working with numerology.

Cloaked or Hidden Figure

Universal Landscape: Archetypal Character Aspect: messenger from the unconscious; the Archetype of Death.

Dreaming Lens: Did you know who this figure was? Were they silent or did they speak to you? Were they showing you something? Were you aware of what message they had for you? Did you have a sense of menace or ease?

Personal Focus: This image has its essence in anonymity and may, therefore, never be clearly known to you. As a Character Aspect, it is a figure from your unconscious mind that has the capacity to visit you in the dream state and deliver a message. The Dreaming Lens will tell you what the message is, or at least where to begin looking for it. However, if they closely resemble the commonly held visage of Death in your dream—the cloaked figure without a visible face that roams the world snatching the living into the world of the hereafter—you are definitely experiencing an archetypal dream.

Deciding whether this figure was a personal Character Aspect or the Archetype of Death should be based directly on your experience of the dream. If you had the sense that you were in the presence of Death within the context of the dream, your instinct is probably correct. If your dream portends a death, it is almost certain to be a symbolic one, such as dying to an old behavior or relationship in order to make way for something new.

More clarity about whether to consider this dream as archetypal can be discovered in the structure of the dream itself. Archetypal dreams are usually very simple in their imagery, often with just one setting and rarely containing any spoken words. If your dream was more typical with shifting perspectives, changes in location, and the exchange of words, then you are in the realm of the personal. If the dream feels archetypal, the message will reveal itself to you over time. And like all archetypal dreams, it connects to your journey toward integration of Self. If the dream feels personal, the Dreaming

Lens should offer you clues as to what this hidden or cloaked figure is trying to express. If this is not obvious to you, your work will be to ruminate on what you can glean from the emotional residue of the dream. Eventually, your intuition will help you identify the true nature and intention of this figure and of the dream.

Closet

Universal Landscape: Hidden agenda. Avoidance.

Dreaming Lens: Were you inside a closet? Were you locked in the closet? Were you contemplating going into the closet? Were you looking for something inside a closet? Was the closet empty or filled to the brim with stuff?

Personal Focus: A closet is a place used for storage. The items found in a closet usually fall into one of three categories: frequently used items kept out of sight for the sake of organization, things stored for later use, and forgotten objects that we continue to hold on to even though they have lost their purpose. A dream that features a closet as a primary image or location may need to be considered through one of these themes.

Many objects found in a dream closet connect to shame. The level of this will correspond to how hidden something is and/or how much fear there is around it. Keep in mind, however, that a closet is also a storage space where we file away things we no longer need on a regular basis. There may be old thoughts, feelings, or ways of being that need to be recognized and discarded in order to make room for new growth that is on the horizon.

The phrase "in the closet" has come to be linked almost exclusively to an individual who is hiding their homosexuality. However, in a dream, this can refer to any hidden sides of the Self. What you discover in a closet should be viewed through the focus of something you are hiding from or not wanting to face. If it is a person you find, use the Character Aspect technique to explore what part of your personality you have been neglecting. If what you find in there is an object, the same meaning applies based on the interpretation you give it.

The type of closet has meaning. A linen closet may connect to feelings of comfort or protection whereas a janitorial closet might relate to the need for a major mental cleanup. An empty closet may be indicating the need to abandon a current course of action or situation in your life—there may be things you need to store away for the time being and return to at a future date. A full or overstuffed closet may point to avoidance issues that need attention.

Clothes

Universal Landscape: Personal expression, connected with the persona.

Dreaming Lens: What articles of clothing were in your dream? Were you wearing them? Did they belong to you or to someone else? Were you shopping? Were there many articles of clothing, or just a few? Where were they being kept, or thrown away? What time period were they from? Were they old or new? Were they costumes or street clothes?

Personal Focus: What we choose to wear has enormous implications for how we feel about ourselves and how we would like the world to perceive us. Symbolically, they represent creative personal expression. However, clothes can also represent the ways in which we cover up who we really are and alter what the world sees. Additionally, the clothing we wear at any given time can reveal things about our moods and emotional states that might otherwise go unnoticed.

The quality and style of clothing in a dream will provide you with different shades of meaning for your interpretation. Old clothes might represent old ways of being that are resurfacing. New clothes could indicate a desire or need to match your inner growth and shifts with your outer presentation. A costume might illuminate roles you are playing in your life that are false, whereas your own clothes indicate that the issue at hand is with your present sense of Self. Being inappropriately dressed represents your concern about fitting in with others. Wearing too many clothes can sometimes indicate a lack of comfort with your sexuality or body image. Having to deal with many layers of clothing denotes that there are obstacles between where you are and a deeper level of authentic expression. A desire to take clothes off may mean a need to break out of the stereotype you find yourself in; while adding more clothes could mean putting on a few more layers in order to protect yourself from perceived outside harm. No clothes usually reflects feeling very open and, therefore, vulnerable.

Clowns

Universal Landscape: Subversive, untrustworthy expressions of playful energy.

Dreaming Lens: Was there a clown in your dream? Were you the clown? Was there more than one clown? What was the setting? Was the clown happy or sad? Was the clown performing? Was the image of the clown delightful or creepy?

Personal Focus: Clowns are a fascinating image and have an ironic ability to contain enormous contradictions. They are playful and childlike, but also grotesque. There is a subversive quality to the concept of the clown: They are seemingly innocuous, but with something possibly darker lurking just below the surface. Their expressions are permanently fixed and, therefore, not to be trusted. However, the entertainment they provide can be masterful and absolutely delightful, when done right.

If you are someone for whom clowns are just fun and delightful, then consider the humorous side of this meaning for your interpretation. Is there some aspect of life in which you are clowning around? This symbol in a dream could mean a need to rein in your buffoonery, or it could mean the opposite view and be a push to lighten up and be more playful.

On the other hand, if either the dream itself had sinister overtones, or if you are someone who, in life, finds clowns to be creepy by nature, you may want to consider the darker side of this interpretation. Look to where there may be some mistrust in how a lighthearted situation may be hiding something more sinister underneath.

Coffin

Universal Landscape: Death of a Character Aspect.

Dreaming Lens: What was your relation to the dead person? Was he/she known to you or a stranger? Did you experience grief? Were other feelings evoked by the knowledge of who was in the coffin? Was the coffin empty? Were you in the coffin? Was the coffin prepared for someone who was not yet dead?

Personal Focus: A coffin is made to hold a person after death. As a dream symbol, it should be interpreted by examining the individual inside the coffin as a Character Aspect of the dreamer. This applies whether you know who is inside the coffin or not. Any death is symbolic of change. When examined as a Character Aspect, the death represents sacrificing a portion of the personality that is no longer a useful part of the whole. An effective shift requires clearing out old ways of being in order to make way for new, more evolved functioning. Death is always followed by rebirth, but when a coffin is present, it signifies being at the beginning of the transformation process.

If you know the person in the coffin, consider their personality. It will tell you what traits of your own are dying away. For example, if the coffin contains a friend or relative who is demanding and overbearing, that quality may be dying in you, or you may need to let go of it as a way of being in the world. If you don't know the inhabitant you may need to investigate what element of your life *needs* to change. If the coffin is empty and ready for use, you may not know what is getting ready to be sacrificed in you, but the dream may be a wake-up call to find out. Death in dreams means change of a powerful magnitude. If any of the trappings of death appear as symbols, such as funerals, urns, etc., you can be assured that big change is afoot.

Colors

Universal Landscape: Universal creative, energetic, and spiritual expression.

Dreaming Lens: Dreaming in color is often viewed as a particular phenomenon that sets a dream apart from others you have. There is an implication here that if a memorable dream is thought of as vibrantly filled with color, other dreams must be in black and white by comparison. However, all dreams are likely to be experienced with various intensities of color and the memory of vibrant color is just one more way the unconscious is speaking to you.

This section deals specifically with the general meaning of colors as universally accepted in reference to the spectrum of visible white light. Use this information to add texture to the meaning of a symbol if a specific color was indicated in your memory of a dream. This can refer to anything, from the quality of light to the color of an object.

Personal Focus: Light is experienced as white, but if refracted into separate wave lengths, the naked eye can perceive the seven distinct bands of color that make it up. Seven is an important number in numerology, as it represents spirituality and higher thought. One of the applications of this significance is the chakras, or energy points on the body that corresponds to a gland in the endocrine system. By aligning the colors of the spectrum and the seven chakras, the foundational and universal meaning to colors is generated.

This is only a starting place, as many permutations and personal associations will alter the meaning of colors as you interpret your dreams. However, consider the logic of even some of those permutations. For example, green is the color of the heart center, but is also associated with jealousy or being green with envy. Though these are very different emotions, love and jealousy are both products of the heart. Yellow represents the emotions, but has come to signal caution in the Western world. Again, very different life experiences actually have the same origins when examined closely. It is in paying attention to our gut feelings that we are made aware of when to exhibit caution. The following guide is meant as a foundation and starting place for symbolic interpretation.

For specifics on the seven spectrum colors, see below:

1. Red	Base of spine	Security, grounding	Testicles
2. Orange	Genitals	Sexuality/creativity	Ovaries
3. Yellow	Belly	Feelings	Adrenal gland
4. Green	Heart	Love/healing/center	Thymus gland
5. Blue	Throat	Communication	Thyroid gland
6. Indigo	Third eye	Intuition	Pineal/pituitary
7. Violet	Top of head	Spirituality	Above the body

Red: The first color of the spectrum, red is associated with security and grounding. This energy is connected with the base of the spine and the testicles in men. Often thought of as a color of passion, red aligns with aggression and sexual expression in the masculine principle. We stop at red lights, creating security for ourselves by avoiding the danger of oncoming traffic. Blood is the essence of life force itself and, therefore, related to being grounded in our physical body.

Orange: The next color of the spectrum corresponds to the area near the ovaries in woman and the lower belly in men. Orange is also related to sexuality, but through the feminine principle of intimacy and transformation. It is the color most associated with creativity.

Yellow: Yellow is the color of emotions and gut feelings and is appropriately centered in the solar plexus, creating a relationship with this area of the body and the color of the Sun. This is where we experience our feelings and the rapid shift from one state to another. Associated with the adrenal gland, yellow connects to adrenaline, the chemical manufactured by the brain that creates anxiety, sudden bursts of energy, and the fight-or-flight response. This is reflected in the use of yellow to indicate caution in signage and traffic management. Of course, many emotional states are very pleasant, which is embodied by our experience of sunlight as warm and comforting. This chakra is also associated with self-worth and how one relates in the world.

Green: Green is the color of the heart center, which can be confusing due to the representation of the heart as red, made especially prominent in Western culture with Valentine's Day. However, green is the central color of the spectrum and the heart is considered the center of both our physical and our emotional bodies. This connects the color green to love, healing, and all matters of the heart. It may be easier to understand the meaning of this color if you consider the Earth and Mother Nature's love affair with the color green. Keeping with traffic signal analogies, if you go when the light is green, that is like following your heart's desire to move forward. When the heart is soured by hurt, green can turn to the menace of envy.

Blue: Blue is the color of communication and connects to the body through the throat and the thyroid gland. There is a connection between our metabolic activity, which is regulated by the thyroid, and the effectiveness of our communication. Through our voice, we communicate with others, but it is through our energy levels that we commune with our immediate environments. Other communication concepts associated with this color are the blueprints that communicate the structure of something not yet created. The call of a hospital emergency is known as a Code Blue. Before a brochure or magazine page is printed, the early version used to finalize the design and layout is known as the blue line. When blood circulation diminishes due to a drop in body temperature, the lips will turn blue and communication is hindered. These are but a few examples that may not relate to a specific image; however, when the color blue is prominent in your dream, incorporate issues of communication into your interpretation.

Indigo: Indigo is an elusive color—many people would be hard pressed to describe it or identify it upon sight. Since intuition shares some of these same indefinable characteristics, it is ironic that the two are linked. Somewhere between blue and violet, indigo is the sixth color of the spectrum and vibrates with what is known as the third eye, the point behind the forehead that is the seat of inner vision. The pineal and pituitary glands correlate with this color, which contains yet another irony: the first regulates all of our body's rhythmic cycles and the latter stimulates growth and incites the onset of puberty. They perform these functions at the right and perfect time, as if guided by intuition.

Violet: Violet is the final color of the spectrum and is considered the most spiritual. It is connected to the crown of the head and, therefore, not encumbered by the demands of the body. In this way, it is the vibration that is connected to us, but reaches upward into higher realms of energy. There are many examples of violet— more commonly referred to as purple—being associated with spirituality and high levels of consciousness. Merlin, the wizard from the King Arthur tales, is often depicted as wearing a purple hat; the Purple Heart represents ultimate bravery; and in Catholicism, during the holiday of Lent, all images of the Christ are covered with purple.

People who meditate with discipline report seeing violet light as part of the trance experience.

Black: Thought of as the absence of color to some, in the world of physics, black is actually the presence of all colors in the object that embodies it. It is the color that absorbs the most light, retains heat and is associated with death as it is the opposite of life affirming white. As the color of mourning, black clothing represents the social construct of receiving consolation. When we are in mourning, we are surrounded by people who share in our sadness. In the same way that a black shirt will absorb all wavelengths of sunlight, a person in mourning wears black in order to absorb the light from those who surround them. In the world of fashion, black has a connotation of being trendy and sophisticated. Nighttime is when blackness reigns, bringing secrecy and the ability to hide into this color's symbolic meaning.

White: Purity and wholeness is represented by white, as this is the unification of all the colors of light that are visible to the human eye. For some, white is the color of highest spirituality. For others it connects to the perfection that arises out of the absence of contamination as in virginity and chastity. An object that appears white reflects the light back outward, absorbing none of the individual colors of the spectrum. It is in this concept of reflecting the light that shines onto you back out into the world that embodies the high consciousness associated with the color white.

Commerce (Buying, Selling, Renting)

Universal Landscape: Equitable contribution.

Dreaming Lens: Were you the buyer or the seller? What was being purchased? Was the transaction a final sale or an agreement to rent or lease? Were you comfortable with the details of the transaction? Were you in control?

Personal Focus: Commerce and the concept of fair trade are the feminine principle in action. While the masculine principle demands that we simply take what we want or need, the balancing energy of giving something in order to get something in return relates to the feminine. In this way, a commitment to integrity is established and the character trait of fairness is created.

Because buying implies permanence, purchasing holds more weight than renting. You will also have to consider which of the two sides of the transaction you are on. If you are selling, you are letting go. If buying, you are choosing to pick something up or discovering a need. If you feel that you are being fairly treated, then a balance is likely being struck. If you are unhappy with the settlement, then there may be a message that equity is lacking in some area of your life. And finally, what price are you paying or getting? The dream transaction is inviting you to look at how much you value or undervalue yourself in your waking life.

Computer

Universal Landscape: Organization of thought; memory. The brain.

Dreaming Lens: Were you using a computer? Were you inside a computer? Was it a PC or laptop? Mac? Mainframe? Older? Newer? What were you trying to accomplish on the computer? How was it functioning? Did your hard drive crash?

Personal Focus: A computer is structured very much like the human brain. There is an operating system that allows other software programs to run. This is like the network of nerve cells that make up the majority of brain tissue. There is also a hard drive, which stores everything that has ever been input into it. This is akin to the neural pathways created by the brain's recording of sensory data it receives in the form of memory and knowledge. There is RAM, or desktop memory, that is like your conscious mind. This includes your daily production of short-term memory that is processed each night when you dream. The process that occurs during REM sleep is much like backing up your computer files for protection on a daily basis.

When a computer features prominently in your dreams, you are considering how your mind is working. The state of affairs in your dream computer may very well be mirroring the state of affairs in your current thought patterns. If you experience a computer crash in your dream, the same overload is likely to be happening in your experience of some chaotic element of life. Backing up your hard drive may be a signal to retain new information that has recently been integrated into your sense of self. Writing code or installing new software could connect to changing or upgrading your thought patterns and perceptions in life, or a need to do so. A network of more than one computer may point to a life situation that requires interaction with others on an intellectual or academic level.

How readily you understand and comprehend the computer's functioning in your dream will mirror your waking life ability to operate in the realm of intelligence or learning.

Concealed Identity/Stranger

Universal Landscape: An unknown Character Aspect; unconscious drives.

Dreaming Lens: What was your relationship with the unknown person? Was the stranger an assailant or attacker? Was the stranger physically hidden from you in some way? Did the stranger reveal their identity to you in some way? Were you aware of whom they really were? Were they pretending to be someone else? Were they simply an unknown person?

Personal Focus: A person unknown to you is still representing a Character Aspect of your personality, even if his or her identity is concealed or if it is a stranger. When making an interpretation about a person you don't know, you must put your focus on what you actually *do* know. What the person is doing in your dream and how you feel about that will give you the essence of your interpretation. That it comes from a stranger or person with a concealed identity indicates that the unconscious is not quite ready to reveal some aspect of your personality that is being called into action in your current situation.

We learn in stages and increments and often resist change, so be prepared for initial levels of fear to come up around this type of imagery. The unknown assailant who chases us may simply be trying to give us our forgotten lunch money or an umbrella because it is raining. When there are clear personality traits and the identity is unknown to you, it likely points to an area of development within your own personal makeup.

An angry or aggressive stranger may point to an integration of that energy into consciousness. A more helpful or gentle stranger indicates that softer elements are being called into prominence. Whatever end of the continuum your dream stranger is on, be prepared to consider the necessity and power of the energy he or she is embodying in the dream. A deliberate deceit of identity can also indicate a matter of the unconscious tricking the conscious into hearing a difficult piece of information; for just as in life it is sometimes easier to hear impactful news from a stranger than from someone we love.

Cookie

Universal Landscape: Reward and pleasure; nurturing.

Dreaming Lens: Were you eating the cookies or was someone else? Were they uneaten? Were there limits or obstacles to getting the cookies? Were you being generous with the cookies and giving them away? Did they taste good? Were they homemade, or a favorite brand? Were the dream cookies in a plausible environment (kitchen, school, store), or in a strange setting?

Personal Focus: Cookies take their universal meaning from the child's perspective, for it is as children that most of us were introduced to these potentially irresistible sweets. Cookies are intrinsically bound to the nurturing energy of mother, grandmother, or female caretaker. And while not all mothers bake cookies for their children, this notion is reinforced through literature and the media. Mother and child baking cookies together is a television staple for representing healthy bonding in the home.

Cookies connect to early lessons of reward and punishment. They might be offered as a prize for good behavior, or a prescription for lifting the spirits in a sad moment. However, they are to be limited before meals for fear of spoiling the appetite. And beware the wrath that might befall the child who got his or her hand "caught in the cookie jar." This construct of a highly sought after object under the firm control of the adult imbues cookies with a combination of desire and guilt, as well as the meaning associated with reward and pleasure.

Your own life experience around this brand of nurturing should play a large part in your interpretation. The type of cookie in your dream and your personal tastes should be factored in as well. A disagreeable taste might indicate something askew in your sense of personal reward. Eating too many or feeling sick might represent a pattern of overdoing the reward in life and the refusal of responsibility. Baking them yourself may suggest a regressive need to be comforted in some way.

Cowboy

Universal Landscape: Individualistic spirit of expansion.

Dreaming Lens: Was there a cowboy in your dream? Who was the cowboy? Were you the cowboy? What was the cowboy doing? Was there more than one? Where did the dream take place?

Personal Focus: Cowboys represent the rugged individualism that is intrinsically bound up with the mythology of the American tradition of expansion and cultivation. The cowboy is often considered a lone figure; connecting with a sense of isolation that is no less capable for his solitude. The media has turned the cowboy into an icon of enormous proportions. They represent the silent strength of the masculine principle at its absolute best. Any dream that features a cowboy is likely connecting to this spirit of independence.

Are there new frontiers in your life that need exploring? Perhaps there is something to be done that must be done on your own. After all, the cowboy is ever riding off into the sunset, propelled by the belief that there is always something new just over the horizon.

Criminal

Universal Landscape: Character Aspect; disregard for consequences.

Dreaming Lens: Was the criminal in your dream a stranger to you? Was it someone you know in waking life? Were there more than one? Were they male or female? How dangerous or menacing did they feel in your dream? What criminal act was being perpetrated? Were you the criminal in your dream?

Personal Focus: When a criminal appears in a dream, he or she should be considered as a Character Aspect of your sense of Self. While criminal behavior is varied and can cover a wide array of activities, there is one common denominator for all crimes whether mundane or heinous: there are consequences for breaking the law. From this perspective, any choice that ignores this societal agreement indicates a lack of regard for these consequences.

Since crime is essentially antisocial in nature, the Character Aspect of a criminal in the world of dreams is Shadow material. By examining the fundamental nature of the criminal in your dream, you will discover what part of your unconscious is being expressed.

The severity of the act or intent reveals the extent of the darkness of your current emotional state.

Theft of any kind connects with feelings of a limitation of resources. The thief is the part of your psyche that embodies this sense of lack and the need to rob another to compensate. Violence from one human being toward another is acting out underlying aggression that might indicate serious levels of frustration or anger over some life circumstance. If murder is the theme in your dream, then some aspect of your personality may be undergoing a sacrifice in the process of transformation. If this is the case, closely examine the Character Aspect of who is doing the killing and who is being killed. If the victim is you, it is more important to focus on the killer as the aspect that is revealing something unconscious. If the victim is someone else, look to them for answers about what part of your psyche is being impacted by a disregard of consequences in your current state of affairs.

A dream that involves elements of organized crime could point to a structured way of thinking or feeling that is not supporting your higher nature. This may involve a lack of awareness on your part of negative thoughts that are just below the surface and seemingly innocuous. When examined more closely, they may actually be insidious and dangerous to your well-being.

Cross-Dressing

Universal Landscape: Opposing expressions of gender to the outside world.

Dreaming Lens: Were you cross-dressing in the dream? Was someone in your dream cross-dressing? What gender was being contradicted? Was it sexual or erotic in nature? Was it connected to gender identity? Was there a spirit of fun, as in a costume? Was there any shame or humiliation involved?

Personal Focus: The clothes we wear relate to the persona, the part of our self that we show to the world. When gender lines are crossed, the main theme of your interpretation will be the integration of the masculine principle or the feminine principle, depending upon the direction of the switch. Taking on the garb of the opposite sex could mean a desire to incorporate more of those traits into the way people see you.

This can be a confusing area for people, because there are several categories of cross-dressing in the world; each is different and almost entirely misunderstood. Unless you personally fall into one of the categories of people who cross-dress, a dream about being in the clothing of the opposite sex is more connected to embodying principles of energy and expression that are an appropriate and natural part of the journey toward a more integrated Self.

A woman in male drag could be expressing a desire to be seen as more aggressive or powerful. A man in drag might be considering what it would be like to be more receptive in the world and be perceived as more sensitive. Be willing to make sure your cross-dressing dream doesn't expose a level of inauthenticity in your presentation. Is your sensitivity for real? Is flexing your power really genuine? The context of the dream should give you all the data you need to make an accurate determination.

Crying

Universal Landscape: Emotional expression and cleansing.

Dreaming Lens: Were you crying in the dream, or were you watching someone cry? If it was someone else, did you know the person? Did you comfort him or her? Did anyone (or anything) comfort you? Could you feel yourself crying?

Personal Focus: It is said that the eyes are the windows of the soul. In the spirit of that saying, crying washes the windows of our souls. It cleans and lubricates them so they can see more clearly and easily. Water represents emotion, and tears are the fluid expression of our deepest emotions as squeezed out by the body. Just as crying in life is an involuntary expression of deep feelings, the same can be said about crying in a dream.

Often people report the sensations of crying when dreaming; that it is felt as acutely as it is in the waking state. The interpretation is generally very literal, though the Dreaming Lens will provide some focus for how to understand and utilize the emotionality that is being expressed.

If you are crying in a dream, then you are likely in some sort of mourning or expression of grief. If someone else is crying, then a Character Aspect that lives within you is involved in a powerful emotional process. If this is the case, then use the character who is crying to have a deeper understanding about what part of your personality is undergoing a shift. Tears of sadness connect to loss. Tears of joy connect with gain and could indicate getting to the other side of a challenging transition.

The more acutely you can feel the physicality of crying upon waking, the closer to consciousness the wound is. The level of disconsolation you feel may give you an idea of the intensity of the hurt you are cleansing. Remember that in your dreams, just as in life, crying is a healthy and powerful way of processing grief and facilitating transition and transformation.

Cut(s), Cutting

Universal Landscape: Evidence of wounding; protection that is instinctive.

Dreaming Lens: Did you sustain a cut in your dream? Was there evidence of a cut after the fact? Were you cutting someone else? Was someone else cutting you? Were you cutting yourself? What was the implement or tool used? How badly were you hurt? Was there bleeding?

Personal Focus: The skin is the largest organ of the human body. Comprised of three layers, its primary function is to separate the outside and inside of the body, offering a mildly protective shell for the tissue beneath it. Cuts in the skin hinder the effectiveness of that protection and the body quickly responds to any injury it may sustain.

While a cut opens the body to risk, the healing response is powerful and immediate. As the brain releases chemicals that block pain and ease stress, the blood begins to clot, closing the opening made by the cut. The immune system responds with protective mechanisms that fight off infection. Seen in this light, the larger portion of the experience of a cut is on the healing side of the equation. It is this response that becomes the essence of this symbol's meaning.

A cut leaves a mark that is the evidence of the wound. Depending on whether the wound occurs in the dream, or appears to have happened in the past, indicates where you are in the process of responding to some hurtful moment in life. Additionally, your interpretation will vary depending on the part of the body that is affected. The arms relate to strength and action, the legs connect to movement and motivation. The hands represent creativity, and the face connects to the persona one shows to the world. See "Body Parts" for more thoughts to augment the meaning you assign this symbol. Additionally, consider that a cut on an exposed part of the body means your wound is visible to others. An area that is generally covered by clothing may connect to the ability or desire to hide your wounds.

The phenomenon of "cutting" is a ritualized addiction where a person deliberately cuts their body as a stress-relief mechanism. People who cut will describe a satisfaction in having an interior experience of emotional pain expressed physically on the body. Being cut in a dream, whether self-inflicted or otherwise, is a similar action by the unconscious mind to express inward pain in an outward manner.

Dancing

Universal Landscape: The contemplation of merging. Sensual expression.

Dreaming Lens: Were you dancing? Was someone else dancing? If you were dancing, were you dancing with anyone else? Who were you dancing with? Did you know the person? What kind of dance were you doing? Was it couples dancing, or was it a group dancing? What kind of music was involved, if any?

Personal Focus: Dancing is an elaborate mating ritual. It is a socially acceptable behavior that is designed to escalate toward intimacy and sex. Even dancing alone is a sensual experience that celebrates the ability to move in space. This results in a sensual experience of one's body, signaling a readiness for sexual expression. Dancing in a dream relates to this need for connection to the celebratory experience of bodily desire.

When dancing, each partner responds to the other in an opposing manner. This is most apparent in ballroom dancing where the actual steps taken will be done in reverse by each. The same could be said of free-form dancing, in that a vibrant dance experience often relates to how well the two dancers play off one another. In group dancing, such as ballet or modern dance troupes, the symbolic conversation expands to the idea of poetry in motion.

If you are one of the dancers, you may need to masterfully integrate the energetic qualities of the person with whom you are dancing. If you are watching others dance, then you may need to incorporate the qualities of the pair that is dancing. A modern dance club atmosphere is likely a call for abandon or a cry for freedom of expression. Partner dancing indicates a demand for the working together of the disparate elements represented by the two who are dancing. A more free-form style of dance may point to a need to let go of control whereas more precise movement may indicate that a level of discipline is required. Watching a dance performance likely connects to a need to be more expressive with your body and/or your relationship to sensuality.

Death

Universal Landscape: Change at a transformational level.

Dreaming Lens: Who died in your dream? Was it you? Was it someone known to you or a stranger? If known, were they alive or dead in life? What was your reaction to their death? Was it sudden? Was there violence? Was there illness? Were you responsible for the death?

Personal Focus: Death is about change. All change involves the cycle of something dying to be reborn again. This applies to all of life, from the changing of the seasons to the coming and going of relationships and the process of birth and death itself. Death in a dream signifies that an enormous shift is occurring in your life. An accurate interpretation depends on exploring who died in your dream and how and why it occurred.

Begin with the person who died in your dream. If you know this person from life, decide what Character Aspect of yourself he or she represents. How they operate in life is what is changing within your own psyche. The change is so great that it is being expressed by the ultimate of changes—death. If the person is a stranger, then use whatever information you can remember about them from the dream to explore what elements of your personality are undergoing a transformation. The quality that is being shifted could be about behaviors, habits, or character traits. It will always be illuminated by the person who dies and what he or she represents to you. Very often, we are not aware of what needs to die in order for something new to emerge. If your dream offers you very little information to work with, it is very likely that dreams with the same theme will appear in the near future.

The manner of the death can provide additional information to add to your interpretation. The more violent and sudden the death, the more combustive and intense the process that you are going through is likely to be. A death that has already occurred could signal that you are in a later phase of change, rather than at the beginning.

Certain people dying in dreams can also carry specific themes. Death of a parent, for example, could be about needing to let go of ways you parent yourself that no longer serve you. Death of a friend could mean the letting go of their energetic quality as it lives in you or even a behavior that doesn't serve you that is carried by that person. If it is you who dies, the transformation may be so complete that it involves your entire life or lifestyle (i.e., a move, changing jobs, a breakup, a new relationship, an end to destructive behaviors). Before wonderful new life experiences can be fully embraced, a death of the past is required.

There is an amusing myth that you can never die in a dream, because if you did, you would simultaneously die in the real world as well. Obviously this can never truly be substantiated due to the fact that anyone who could actually prove the point would be dead. I have heard many dreams of death, dying, and rebirth over the years. Death is an ending, which must always be followed by a new beginning. This is symbolic and never literal. As a dreamer, trust that you are safe from dying a dream-related death. But, of course, we'll never know for sure.

Defecation/Feces

Universal Landscape: Personal creativity.

Dreaming Lens: Was it your feces in the dream? Was it someone else's? Were you in the process of moving your bowels, needing to, or was it after the fact? What were you doing with the feces? Was the experience repulsive? Was it matter-of-fact and free of judgment?

Personal Focus: While the elimination of waste might be the first thought that comes to mind when thinking of feces, at the heart of it, bowel movements are our first connection to us as creative beings. Consider the power and intensity associated with potty training and all the effort that goes into guiding a child toward controlling this bodily function. This period in a child's life has a profound impact on how they operate in the world.

Often the most effective method of this training involves helping a child make a creative connection to what comes out in the toilet. For the young mind, this is quite an impressive feat. When taken in this perspective, defecation or feces in a dream is always going to connect *first* to personal creative power. Then and only then, the Personal Focus should be added to inform you what your unconscious is trying to communicate. Whatever that turns out to be, it is likely going to be about the state of your individual, creative affairs.

Notice whether the experience in your dream is repulsive or not. Often in such a dream, there may not be an association to feces as dirty. If the experience is indeed repugnant, then you may be in some form of resistance to a deeper process that is going on that may require getting "down and dirty" with Shadow material. Eating feces points to needing to integrate your own creativity into some aspect of your life. Playing with or handling feces (and how you felt about doing so) may indicate your level of comfort with a transition in your life that may be requiring you to go deeper into your "own shit" in order to find a new sense of self.

Deserted Place

Universal Landscape: Unmet needs; the risk of death.

Dreaming Lens: Where were you that was deserted? Was it a familiar place? Was it from your past or present? Were you aware of who should be present but was missing? Did you know why the location was deserted? How did you feel about being alone? Were you at risk or in danger? Were you happy in your isolation?

Personal Focus: Human beings are social animals. We have lived in community with one another since our earliest arrival on the planet. This close proximity has only increased with the passage of time and the advancement of civilization, because while individual personality types may prefer a solitary existence, for the most part, humankind is a race of communal beings. We are so conditioned to the interpersonal structure of the societies in which we live that it is easy to take for granted how much we depend on the countless denizens who, even anonymously, provide for most of our daily needs.

To find yourself in a place that is deserted and devoid of the presence of other human beings would leave you helpless in many ways. The severity of this vulnerability would depend greatly on where you were, what resources you had access to, as well as your own fortitude and courage. Even in the best of circumstances, your very survival would be at risk; hence, the primary symbolic meaning connected to risk and death. While loneliness might be thought of as the underlying emotional content of such an event, it is the absence of human resources that carries the interpretable weight of this symbol. Even if you found the absence of other people comforting, this meaning still applies. You may want to consider how relying on others for getting your needs met may be the root cause of the anxiety that sparked this dream.

The Dreaming Lens will be essential to complete your interpretation, for it is in the environment in which you find yourself deserted that will provide the message that your unconscious is attempting to communicate. When you have assigned an interpretation to that environment, introduce the element of risk. This should inform you of the area of your waking life that feels vulnerable and may require an effort on your part to seek outside contribution in order to restore balance.

If the deserted setting is from your childhood or any earlier time in your life, you may be experiencing a current crisis that had its first appearance at that point in time or that period of your emotional development. If your past or present workplace is the scene, you may want to examine how supported you feel by your colleagues or superiors.

Some deserted environments will connect to specific circles of friends or family units that would normally populate them. If this is the case, you will want to investigate issues emerging about contributions you feel you receive from these groups, and notice where your emotional and psychic needs may not be being met.

When towns or cities reflect emptiness of this nature, the symbol is expressing a more generalized unconscious anxiety around helplessness. As a general rule, the larger the location, the greater the anxiety is likely to be. A familiar location may indicate a specific and identifiable loss of support. If the location is fictional, the underlying fears being expressed by your unconscious may not yet be clear. Whatever the scenario, this image in a dream is a wake up call to discover ways in which your current lifestyle is not supplying you with the psychological resources you need to feel comfortable and safe.

Devil

Universal Landscape: Bondage to an ideology; restriction. Shame. Temptation.

Dreaming Lens: Was it a devilish being in your dream, or was it actually Satan? Were you the devil? Were you in danger? Were you fearful or nonchalant? What was the devil doing in the dream? Were you a witness or a victim? Were you being tempted by the devil? Were you being asked to sell your soul?

Personal Focus: Most people will fall into two categories regarding the Devil: the religious and the non-believers. There is a third category of people who don't necessarily believe in the Devil, but were raised in environments that embedded certain beliefs that they may have consciously rejected, but still have great power in the unconscious mind.

The origins of the Devil as Satan or Lucifer come from the Old Testament. One would have to be a religious scholar to identify all the different references to this character; however, there is one basic story line that most people recognize—Lucifer was a beloved angel who challenged God on his love for his human creations. God punished Lucifer by banishing him out of heaven and casting him into the lower realms of hell, where he reigns supreme over everything that is not God-like.

The first and foremost quality of the Devil is temptation. The ultimate motivation for the temptation is for ownership of a person's soul. In the world of psychology and dream work, the soul is akin to your spiritual nature and the totality of your experience as a human being. The presence of God and the Devil in our world offers each of us a choice: with whom will you align yourself and on what will you base your life choices? Your higher nature through the choice of love, or your lower nature through the choice of fear? The presence of the Devil in a dream indicates that powerful degrees of fear are being expressed.

Bondage is another important element associated with the Devil. The contract he offers is permanent, with severe consequences. In symbolic terms, the Devil could illuminate areas in your life where you feel you have sold out. Look for situations in which you feel stuck for reasons of obligation, financial insecurity, or outmoded satisfaction. Often, we make choices that initially provide us with something we desire, only to discover that we pay a price we hadn't counted on.

Real soul searching may be called for when the Devil appears in a dream. What thoughts or old ways of being must be cast aside for your greater good? From a lighter perspective, what devil-may-care attitude might be inviting you to discover that which your inner critic won't give you permission to explore? Friend or foe, the term "the devil made me do it" can be either a misguided excuse for bad choices, or a call toward letting go of judgment.

Dog

Universal Landscape: Boundless masculine energy.

Dreaming Lens: Was the dog known to you? Was it your own dog? Did it belong to someone else? If so, were they in the dream as well? Was the dog dangerous or loving? Was the dog connected to you by a leash, or was it free to move about on its own? Did the dog respond to your authority or resist it? Were there other dogs?

Personal Focus: In the case of the adage *dog is man's best friend*, gender plays a significant role with regard to energy. Dogs are a masculine symbol whereas cats are the feminine version of domesticated animals. Both connect to unconditional love and people keep pets as an expression of this. Particular to dogs is an unbridled expression of enthusiasm as evidenced by the excitement they embody every time their human returns home.

How you personally react to dogs will play a significant factor in how to interpret a dream in which this image appears. Most people will fall into one of two categories: either you love dogs or fear them. First, consider the Universal Landscape of the symbol of a dog. Then factor in the Dreaming Lens to deepen your interpretation. The final step is to add the Personal Focus of love or fear and you will have an accurate interpretation.

There are undertones of meaning to this symbol that also connect to the masculine principle. Dogs are by nature dedicated to the person who cares for them. In this way, they represent loyalty and stead-fastness. In the arena of socialization, they are very direct in how they evaluate another dog or a person that is new to them. Using their powerful sense of smell, they will sniff each other without hesitation and very quickly establish an order of dominance. This corresponds to the masculine principle of straightforwardness and confidence.

A dog in your dream connects to loyalty and love, which can in-dicate that issues of commitment and intimacy are being triggered by some event or circumstance. A positive dream experience could be pointing to places in your life that are sparking enthusiasm, or requiring you to become more enthusiastic and joyful. Frightening images involving dogs may be inviting you to investigate uncon-scious fears around love and connection. A rabid dog represents inner fears of danger that may befall you if you get to close to an intimate situation. An actual dog bite represents the misuse of kindness or consideration. An obedient dog may point to a sense of control in areas of friendship and trust.

Dogs can embody a variety of qualities, from the one that res-cues a person in danger, to the harrowing attacker. They range in shape from something tiny enough to put in your pocket to large breeds that resemble small bears. The size and attributes of the dog in your dream will inform you of the scope of the unconscious no-tions being expressed.

Door

Universal Landscape: An opportunity or choice to venture into the unknown.

Dreaming Lens: What was the status of the door in the dream: closed, open, locked, or ajar? How many doors were there? What was the size, shape, color of the door(s)? Was there any heightened emo-tional sense as you approached it? What knowledge did you have, if any, of what might be beyond the door?

Personal Focus: A door is the obstacle that separates a person from accessing whatever is in the room to which it marks the entrance. It represents both opportunity and choice. What is on the other side connects with opportunity. The volition required to open it and cross the threshold connects with choice. Additionally, we are taught in childhood that when one door closes, another one opens, suggesting a correlation with transitions in life.

Even if you think you know what it on the other side, a closed door creates mystery and uncertainty and usually refers to something that is unknown. A door that is ajar or open is an invitation from the unconscious to check out what's beyond it. The more doors there are, the more complex the choice at hand may be. The size and weight of the door may indicate the importance of the issue being expressed. Shutting a door indicates the will to end something or the ability to set a boundary with certainty and clarity. A door being shut on the dreamer is an obstacle created by another person or a set of circumstances in the dreamer's waking life. The person creating the obstacle may, in fact, be yourself. If you are not in control of whether the door is open or closed, issues of forced choice or lack of choice could be indicated.

The color of the door can represent the area in life that is referring to the choice at hand. For example, red could mean a survival issue, while purple might be more of a spiritual or soul decision (see Colors). More than one door indicates the complexity of the issue at hand and can be interpreted through numerology (see Numbers).

Dragon

Universal Landscape: Greed, avarice, and overprotection. Also charisma and good luck.

Dreaming Lens: What was the dragon doing in your dream? Is it a dragon from the Eastern tradition or Western lore? Were you or someone else in battle with the dragon? Was a battle likely to occur or about to start? Were you fearful or courageous? What size and color was the dragon? What were you battling over? Was the fight winnable? How did it turn out?

Personal Focus: According to Western mythology, dragons are the guardians of treasure and virgins. These things are of no use to a dragon, a creature that does not need money to get what it wants; and a dragon cannot safely consummate a relationship with a woman. Despite this, it will face all comers with a mighty ferocity, challenging the courage of the most able warriors. In this way, we can say that dragons are a symbolic representation of a fight for something that is of no use to you.

The dragon in your dream may represent the battles you fight in life that either you cannot win or do not need to be fought at all. By the same token, you may have to fight an inner battle and face the part of you that is in the way of you getting what you want in life. Is it possible that your inner dragon may be keeping you from receiving the love you deserve and the abundance you desire? There is also an implied theme of confrontation in battle when a dragon appears in your dreams. What are the battles in your current life? Are you fighting for something that you do not need or cannot use?

This cross-cultural symbol may have other meanings depending on the Personal Lens you look through. In contrast to the symbolic meaning of the Western dragon, consider that the Chinese dragon carries the connotation of luck and charisma. This interpretation will apply if you have any connection to Eastern philosophy or culture, or if the Dreaming Lens contains this type of dragon. Additionally, through the power of the collective unconscious, no matter what your background is, if this interpretation resonates for you, it could be meaningful.

Driving

Universal Landscape: Your movement on your path in life.

Dreaming Lens: Were you driving or was someone else? Were you in control of the car? Were you in the proper seat? Were you speeding, slowing, or stopped? Were you comfortable or was panic setting in? Were you responsible for anyone else, such as passengers or pedestrians?

Personal Focus: As a culture, we are dependent upon our cars. They take us where we need to go in our lives with such regularity that they hold the symbolic meaning of how we are moving on our paths through life. The circumstances around the car and the driving experience will identify for you what emotional and psychic challenges are surrounding you at this time.

If you are driving out of control in the dream, you must consider what area of your life might be beyond your ability to regulate. If you are in the back seat and need to gain control of the car, look for ways in which you haven't yet stepped up to the plate. You may not be able to do so yet because of circumstances beyond your control. If your car isn't responding to you, you may be feeling ineffectual about taking charge of some path you are traversing. Varying speeds might be reflecting movement in life that feels either too fast or too slow for your comfort.

A vehicle other than a car might point to being in foreign territory. You may not be feeling confident in your ability to work with the circumstances you have been handed. Causing an accident could be an invitation to look at the consequences of your choices. Being an accident victim might encourage you to look at ways in which you have abandoned your own direction because of another person or outside force beyond your control. Driving in the rain connects emotional issues to your current route. Icy conditions indicate that emotions are being frozen over, making your way treacherous. Down or up a hill would illustrate the sense of effort or ease involved in your life movement.

Drowning

Universal Landscape: Surrender to emotional processing.

Dreaming Lens: Were you drowning in your dream or was someone else drowning? Were you saved? Did you save another? Did you die? Did someone in your dream die? Was it frightening? Was there frantic desperation involved or was it peaceful?

Personal Focus: This image must be carefully considered through the Universal Landscape before adding the Personal Lens. Many people have free-floating anxiety associated with the fantasy of drowning. When this is the case, the universal meaning of peaceful surrender will often be overlooked when considering this as a dream image. No matter how deep your level of fear is around the frightening possibility of an actual drowning, the return to our watery roots and turning one's self over to the gentle embrace of the weightlessness of water implies a very serene experience from the symbolic perspective.

Water, as a symbol, always connects to the world of emotions. To drown is to die. To die is to sacrifice part of the Self in order to be reborn again. Therefore to drown in a dream is a beautiful transformation that occurs by virtue of giving one's self over to inevitable emotional processes that lead you to a new way of being in the world. The presence of panic in a dream of drowning is a signal of resistance to the emotional change that is afoot. The more intense the panic, the greater the resistance being expressed. Being able to breathe or, at least, function normally under water is a common dream image. While this is not generally experienced by the dreamer as a drowning dream, the meaning connects to the same concept of grace and ease with emotional overwhelm.

Drugs

Universal Landscape: Instant, but temporary shift of consciousness.

Dreaming Lens: Were you using drugs in your dream? Was someone else? What types of drugs were involved? Were they legal or illegal substances? Were you transporting drugs? Were you in search of them? Were you in danger? Was the experience pleasurable? How much self-control did you exhibit?

Personal Focus: All drugs dramatically alter the experience of the individual taking them. Hence, they represent a shift in consciousness that is controlled by the user and is instantaneous. Also inherent in considering this symbol is the matter of consequences. When many substances are abused, especially recreational drugs, there is a disregard of the potential harm they can cause and the often-challenging aftereffects of their use. The desire for the high outweighs the difficulties that result from the overindulgence. When this appears as a theme in a dream, there may be a life situation where you are looking for the quick fix rather than the more difficult path of meeting things with authenticity and conscious awareness.

Mood and mind-altering drugs fall into different classes, and each is responsible for different sensations. Your interpretation should reflect these distinctions. Narcotics create euphoria and imply an aversion to pain and a desire to numb the emotions. Stimulants amplify energy and correlate with a need for increased focus, attentiveness, and a sense of personal power. Sedatives relieve anxiety and are a symbolic buffer to life's stresses. Marijuana and other organic psychedelics connect to expansion of consciousness and alcohol represents a desire to release inhibitions. If any of these substances appear in a dream, focus your interpretation on the symbolic effects rather than the sensations they produce.

Examine your personal relationship with substances when considering the meaning of them in your dream. The person who uses drugs in waking life has a very different perspective than someone who does not. Therefore, drugs can be a symbol that has a moral dilemma attached to it, or not, depending on this personal perspective. Permissiveness aside, the legal status of most abused drugs implies strong consequences that go above and beyond the personal experience of using them.

Not all drugs are mind or mood altering, so the meaning you assign this symbol must reflect the desired shift the drug in your dream promises to deliver. Health issues in your waking life may be sparking unconscious desires for quick and instant healing. If the drug is pharmaceutical in nature, look to a circumstance that is in need of healing and consider if your dream is expressing a desire for a fast process of change.

Dungeon

Universal Landscape: Unconscious negative beliefs.

Dreaming Lens: Were you in a dungeon? Were you under threat of being taken to a dungeon? Was the dungeon yours? Did you know to whom the dungeon belonged? Were you working in the dungeon? Was anyone being tortured?

Personal Focus: Dungeons are a place of torture and imprisonment. Originally, they were part of a castle or fortress that belonged to the nobility of the land, so at the heart of this symbol lays the fact that a dungeon was initially part of a home. As such, they represent an element of the Self (see Houses). Because dungeons are located at the lowest level of the building that houses them, they correlate with deeply hidden and unconscious thoughts and fears. They were a place where people were kept locked up and tortured; therefore, a dungeon is the part of the Shadow where our most frightening ideas and thoughts create ongoing and imaginable levels of suffering and pain.

Within the societal structure, the essential and historical use of a dungeon was to keep the safety of the community in tact by capturing and sequestering enemies who might do harm. Torture itself was implemented to extract information that would lead to the capture of more enemies and increase the safety and well being of the world above. The mere thought of such a place was so terrifying that the threat of ever being taken there essentially kept order and harmony among the common people.

There is a sexual element to this image that connects to the fetishism dominating or submitting in sexual role-play. A dungeon, in this case, need not be a fear-inspiring dark and dreary place; it can be private and possess the appropriate equipment to facilitate the activities associated with such sex play. If you are in this scene in your waking life, then your dream may be a reflection of the people and emotional experiences associated with that corner of your environment. If the dungeon in your dream is sexual in nature and this lifestyle is foreign to you, consider ways in which your sexuality and thoughts about physical intimacy may be holding you hostage or, conversely, may need an avenue of healthy, playful expression.

The Dreaming Lens will offer important information for your interpretation. The setting accounts for the part of our unconscious we are dealing with; the Shadow and fear being fully expressed. The type of action a dungeon is known for also figures prominently into the symbolic meaning associated with it. The threat of being taken to one is the more powerful element to consider. If you were being tortured, the Character Aspect of your captor will illuminate what parts of you are holding you back through fear. If you were the torturer, than your prisoner(s) will shed light on what aspects you feel the need to punish. Also be willing to look at your sense of justification for your actions or lack there of. We often imprison parts of who we are, torturing them (and ourselves) for elements of our humanity that we don't understand or that frighten us.

Earphones/iPods

Universal Landscape: Control exerted over incoming data; escapism.

Dreaming Lens: Were you wearing earphones? Was someone else? If it was you, what were you listening to? Were they operating properly? If someone else was wearing them, did you feel impacted by this fact? Were others wearing earphones collectively?

Personal Focus: The five physical senses are the mechanisms by which we perceive our immediate environment. Our sense organs receive a continual flow of information and we use that information to guide us step by step, from choice to choice every moment of our lives. Symbolically, our collective senses can be seen as the tracks over which the vehicle that is our body moves through time and space. While we experience the senses separately, they operate as a system, with each of them representing a particular component of the sensorial experience.

Our ears are the sense organ over which we are able to exert the least amount of control. In our daily lives, we can avert or close our eyes, avoid taking air into our nostrils, choose not to put something into our mouths, and avoid touching objects—all this to minimize incoming data. However, sound enters the ears from all angles, even though they are constructed for directional optimization. The ears are open and vulnerable to all outside stimuli unless impacted by an external object. While people often use various items to minimize incoming sound, the purpose of the earphone is to replace the naturally occurring inflow of data with something of the individual's choosing, usually music. This is where the element of escapism becomes an important consideration of the meaning attached to this symbol.

Music is a powerful phenomenon, capable of creating a myriad of alterations in mood and emotionality. By substituting what your ears would naturally be experiencing in any given moment with such a transformational stimulus, the presence of earphones will connect both with controlling and escaping from your environment. The emotional content surrounding this symbol will be crucial to your interpretation. Look to the Dreaming Lens to inform you as to your level of enjoyment in escapism, as well as the possibility of fear inspired by a sense of isolation or separation from the experience of others.

Earthquake

Universal Landscape: Disruptive change of great magnitude.

Dreaming Lens: Where was the earthquake? Were you in an earthquake, or was your dream after the event? Was it your home or someplace else? How much danger was present? What was the duration of the earthquake? Was there any death? What was the level of the damage? Were you prepared?

Personal Focus: When the tectonic plates of the Earth shift and collide, the result is an upheaval of colossal magnitude. The energetic source of these violent alterations of the ground is deep below the Earth's surface. The shift of landscape is the result of changes that originate in the subterranean world. This is representative of how unconscious thoughts and feelings can have an enormous impact when they suddenly become conscious. Earthquakes themselves are of relatively short duration, so the life event this image may be reflecting is likely something that occurred quickly or appeared suddenly.

The symbolic meaning of an earthquake is comprised of three elements, which are: A great change has *already taken place*. The onset of the change originated from a deep and unconscious place. And things will never be the same.

The enormity of an earthquake renders its victims helpless to avoid the consequences of the changes taking place. Look to situations in your current life that are, or seem to be, inevitable or unavoidable. If a shift in your life is knocking you off balance, an earthquake may reflect a level of vulnerability and a lack of security. The real danger of earthquakes arrive in the aftermath: more people die in fires and post hoc structural damage. A dream earthquake could be a warning about danger that is pending due to recent dramatic changes in your waking life.

Egg

Universal Landscape: New beginnings; possibility.

Dreaming Lens: How is the egg presented in the dream: as food or as a dormant life waiting to be hatched? What are you doing with the egg(s)? Are you in the egg? Do you know what is in the egg? What are your feelings about what is in the egg? Does the egg hatch in your dream?

Personal Focus: An egg symbolizes the potential for life that lies within it. From this perspective, this symbol always connects to new possibilities and new life. The type of egg in your dream and what it might hatch should provide the foundation of your exploration. The subtleties of your interpretation bring other meanings into the picture, including the context of the Dreaming Lens and your Personal Focus.

Any egg will fall into one of two categories: fertile or infertile. We are so used to consuming eggs in the Western world that it is easy to forget that if fertilized, our breakfast might well have become a chicken. Examine your dream egg to determine whether you perceived it as food or not. If so, your dream may point out issues of nurturing and self-care that are in the embryonic stage and waiting for birth and new life. If the egg is not for consumption, the meaning is more likely to fall on the side of creative possibilities on the horizon.

There are a number of other associations bound up with the image of the egg. The most prominent of these is the age-old question of which came first. There is no answer to this adage. Since either the idea in mind (egg) or the resulting manifestation (chicken) can be born *without the other*, an egg can represent the spontaneous manifestation of something new, whether the new idea has visible *parents* or not.

A person who is considered basic and decent is sometimes called a *good egg*. In this fashion, an egg can symbolize basic values and a sense of goodness. Additionally, the fragility of the shell of an egg prompts us to use the phrase *walking on eggshells* to refer to situations where we hold ourselves back, usually to hinder a reaction in others. This may be reflecting the care and consideration you direct toward what is new in your life so as to protect the delicacy of life unfolding. Conversely, you may be so careful that you stop yourself from moving toward your goals with certainty and power.

Electricity

Universal Landscape: The energy of manifestation. Faith.

Dreaming Lens: Were you witnessing the activities of electricity or simply acknowledging its presence? Were you out of power? Was the sense of electric flow contained or uncontrolled? Were you attempting to control the power, or was it controlling you? Did you get shocked?

Personal Focus: Electricity is an invisible force that is present in our lives for most of us in the Western world on a daily basis. We generally take it for granted, but trust it to be there when we flick a switch. In this regard, it symbolizes faith and the power to manifest your thoughts into reality. We don't necessarily know how it works, only that it does indeed work. We are completely dependent upon it for smooth functioning of our lives. In this way it is like faith; it is most apparent when we lose it.

Electricity is the basis for many forms of energy. From the outside world of machinery to the inner world of the brain and central nervous system, it is this mysterious force that is exemplified in the relationship between cause and effect. When harnessed properly, it can work miracles. By the same token, it is deadly when we connect to more of it than our bodies can handle. It represents the power we yield as human beings to create our own destiny, and the responsibility to use that power wisely.

When electricity is the theme in a dream, you are considering your relationship to the flow of creative energy that infuses life with possibility. The Dreaming Lens and your emotional response to the dream can inform you of how much faith you have that something is possible even when there is no evidence of it in your current circumstances.

If the electricity is out, you may be experiencing a spiritual crises or a dark night of the soul—a time in which you cannot clearly see where you are going. The successful harnessing of electricity toward a particular aim could be expressing a move into your power to create. Being electrocuted might point to being overwhelmed by your own power to manifest your desires. It could also represent the feeling of shock associated with being presented by something unexpected in life that you are actually responsible for creating. The conduits of electricity—switches, outlets, power chords, and so forth—represent the tools with which you tap into the endless supply of creative energy needed to fill your life with abundance.

Elevator

Universal Landscape: Rapid transition between levels of awareness.

Dreaming Lens: Were you waiting for the elevator or already riding it? Were you reaching your intended destination? Were you frightened or in danger? Were you going sideways? Were you stuck in an elevator? Were you moving faster than what felt safe? Who were you with? Were you pushing the buttons or was someone else?

Personal Focus: Elevators carry us from one floor to another at the push of a button. The different levels they transport us to connect to various perspectives of our awareness. We decide our destination on an elevator, aligning this symbol with the choices we make about what areas of our consciousness we are willing to investigate. What happens in the elevator of our dreams may reveal how well this process is going in our daily lives.

The floors involved in a dream can hold significance. In a general way, moving upward connects with higher, more sophisticated levels of thinking, while moving downward indicates investigation of lower levels, past issues, and behavior patterns. Moving downward can also align with visiting hidden or Shadow material.

The actual floor number or numbers, if remembered, can be examined through the concepts of numerology for additional meaning (see Numbers). If there are specific associations with the floors you visit or the building where the elevator is located, this should be factored strongly into your interpretation.

To go up when down is desired may indicate a pressing need to operate with higher insight than that with which you are currently engaged. Going down when up is anticipated may point to the need to uncover additional material hidden in the lower depths of your consciousness or your past. Being stuck on an elevator is to be midway through a process or shift. Your response to the lack of movement may reveal levels of impatience with your progress in some area of growth.

An elevator out of control is similar to a falling dream, but the added component of transition and choice must be considered. While you may be falling, you have chosen to take the elevator in search of new information. Going sideways is to be confused about the direction in which a current transformational shift may be taking you. If the elevator is out of service, you may be stuck in some issue in your life. Another possibility with a broken elevator is a need to stay where you are and not try and escape your current situation by rising above it or sinking to a lower level.

E-mail

Universal Landscape: Instant communication that can be controlled.

Dreaming Lens: Were you writing an e-mail in your dream? Were you reading one? Were you in anticipation of receiving an e-mail? Was your e-mail sent successfully, or were you getting error messages? Were there problems with your computer? Were you receiving spam? Were there attachments, such as photos or video?

Personal Focus: E-mail is a communication venue of the new world order. We are simultaneously brought closer together and further isolated by this almost instantaneous way of connecting our thoughts to the minds of other people. The realm of the intellect is represented by this image. The newness of Internet technology imbues the symbolic meaning with a sense of uncharted territory in the world of thought and interpersonal expression. We live in a time where the technology has evolved faster than our ability to formulate a universal sense of etiquette and propriety. Its speed implies spontaneity. However, the ability to edit and alter our words prior to sending the finished product adds a dimension of control that should not be overlooked when arriving at an accurate interpretation.

Words typically account for about twenty percent of any verbal interaction. Absent from the e-mail experience are the crucial elements of tone and body language. Despite this enormous limitation, most people approach e-mail as if they are clear and accurate when they are, in fact, subject to projection and presumption. In this way, an e-mail in a dream connects to communication that is assumed to be lucid, but may not be received with the same intention with which it was sent.

The immediacy of the writer and the keyboard allows for an enormous amount of editing. We read as we type and retype as we read, changing our words till we are satisfied with the final product. This can insert a subtle lack of authenticity and spontaneity that did not exist with handwritten or typed letters. This image invites you to consider what role restraint or manipulation may be playing in your thought process. Writing an e-mail might represent a need to figure something out that needs direct and immediate attention. Anticipating a reply may represent wanting an answer to a question you are seeking.

Who you write to or receive e-mail from will help you uncover what areas of your psyche need to be interacted with. An e-mail from supervisors at work might point to a search for inner authority. A reply from a beloved might connect to decisions around romance and relationship that require fast consideration. Junk mail and spam might point to undeveloped thoughts or ideas that are routinely cast aside as valueless. They can also represent a general sense of overwhelm with sensory input that may not feel important to you.

Executions

Universal Landscape: Sacrifice of a way of being or thinking that no longer serves you.

Dreaming Lens: Were you witness to an execution? Were you the one being executed? Were you the executioner? What was the method of the kill? Was the execution thorough and completed successfully? Was there fear present?

Personal Focus: Death is always an indicator of the rebirth that inevitably follows. As we execute our undesirables, death by execu-

tion adds the elements of purpose or intent. Often, the undesirable qualities within ourselves are what we hold on to the most.
The execution of a Character Aspect in a dream indicates that a
moment of reckoning has come. A particular way of being in the
world as represented by the character being executed is no longer
necessary. If it is you who is being executed, then your whole sense
of identity is being confronted with drastic change. If you are the
executioner, then your ego mind is getting ready for some dynamic
housecleaning. If neither of these scenarios is the case, consider
what you know about the person being executed. It is in the Character Aspect that they embody where you will find what is currently
up for transformation.

Death by gunshot might indicate that the force of change is
rapid and deeply penetrating. Hanging might indicate a change in
the area of how you communicate since hanging impacts the neck,
throat, and voice. Electrocution points to a more organic and neurological alteration of thoughts, as the brain is an electrically run
organ. When someone is burned to death, a total transmutation is
implied by virtue of bringing the physical body back to the carbon-
based material that makes it up. Death by lethal injection or poison
may connect to the toxic effect of some life experience or individual
surrounding you at the time of the dream.

Whatever your feelings around a dream execution, never forget
that as we grow and mature, we must discard old ways of being that
no longer serve us. This allows us to take up new paths and fresh
ways of being. This ongoing process keeps us in a sort of psychic
balance, much as balancing of the scales implies justice in the image
of an execution.

Faceless

Universal Landscape: Lack of persona. Limited perception.

Dreaming Lens: Was it you that had no face, or someone you encounter? Did you know the person? How did it feel to see the lack of face? Were there many faceless people?

Personal Focus: The face connects to the concept of the persona; the part of who we are that we readily show to the world. We hide our true self behind our face and choose what we want to present to others. This process can be oppressive, and a dream image of being faceless may indicate either the consequences of holding back too much authenticity or, conversely, of exposing more than we feel is comfortable. While your actions identify what you are committed to, it is through your face that you reveal your motivations. Without a face, the assimilation of an identity is impossible.

An aspect of your personality that has no face may connect to a new way of being in the world. Lacking a face may indicate that it is not yet fully formed as an active part of your outward persona. Three of the five visceral senses are located here, so being faceless represents extreme restrictions in your ability to perceive the world around you. If the faceless person in your dream is someone else, consider that Character Aspect as limiting you in some arena in your life. This may be a call to face the world in a new, more enlightened way.

Face-lift/Plastic Surgery

Universal Landscape: Superficial shift in persona.

Dreaming Lens: Did you have surgery in your dream? Were you contemplating it? Was the surgery successful? Was it unsuccessful or disappointing? Were you performing the surgery? Were you adding to or subtracting from your actual physical appearance? Was there a sense of before and after?

Personal Focus: How others see us is a function of what is known as the persona. The symbolic representation of this is the face. Any alteration to the face is akin to exerting some measure of control over the mask we show to the world. When this alteration is reflected as surgical in nature, the resulting change is manipulated and inorganic. When plastic surgery is being considered in real life, the choice to do so is best if one's expectations are realistic and the motivation is not based on shame. If the choice is bound up with unconscious feelings of inadequacy, disaster can result.

A dream with this image should be interpreted with all of these considerations in mind. Your personal relationship with the idea of plastic surgery must guide you as well. Filter all of these complex issues through the notion of a desire to shift how you appear to others in a radical way. Plastic surgery is usually chosen in an effort to appear more attractive, desirable, or acceptable than one already feels. Ask yourself how authentic you are being in your interactions with others. This dream could point to something out of balance with how you feel and what you project.

The procedure itself will offer shades of meaning. Any plastic surgery will fall into one of two categories, either adding to or subtracting from one's natural appearance. Either way, the underlying issue is a sense of inadequacy and a need to cover that up.

Falling

Universal Landscape: Loss of control.

Dreaming Lens: Were you falling or watching someone fall? How fast was the fall? How long did it go on? What fears came up while you were falling? Did you have a sense of surrender to the falling? What incited the fall? Were you pushed? Did you trip? Did you jump? Did you land in the dream, or wake up first?

Personal Focus: One of the most frequently occurring dream images, all human beings have experienced falling in a dream. A fall can be very frightening; however, the real danger is not the fall itself, but the sudden stop that is likely to follow. Therefore, the real source of the fear associated with this symbol is what *may* occur and the anxiety about not being able to directly impact the outcome of a situation.

The deeper meaning of falling dreams is to surrender yourself to the lack of control you are experiencing in a difficult situation. In any situation where there is no control to be had, letting go is the only powerful choice to make. Most dreams of falling do not consummate in landing, further cementing the symbolic connection with surrender when a dream of falling appears.

Where and how you land will be directly tied into the quality of your descent. The more graceful the fall, the more likely you will benefit from where you wind up. The Dreaming Lens will offer you subtleties of meaning by examining the way you are falling in your dream. Falling backward indicates not being able to see the direction you are taking. Facing forward might enable you to see what you are facing, but your fall still indicates lack of control. Spiral twisting is an even stronger loss, as in spiraling out of control. The amount of fear felt in the dream is the barometer of how much unconscious fear is being suppressed. A fall that is easy and flows with a sense of surrender might be telling you that you are ready to let go of control in some situation. It is also possible that falling in a dream could be a compensatory dream, indicating that some inflation is going on in your waking life.

Farm

Universal Landscape: Self-reliant; capacity to nurture.

Dreaming Lens: Were you living on a farm, visiting one, or was your connection to the farm unclear? What season was it? What type of farm? Were animals present? Was it current time, or a past era?

Personal Focus: A farm represents the production of food and the capacity to provide nurturance through abundance on a large scale. Evoking images of serenity and simplicity, they hearken back to a connection to the land that is all but forgotten in our current culture and history. However, they can also connect to the decay of the family-based agrarian culture that once thrived, but has slowly become obsolete in the face of corporate consolidation.

Working on a farm points to a call to action to dig deeper and take responsibility for getting your needs met. Owning a farm connects to how responsible you are to your self-nurturing and perhaps the dependence of others upon you for such needs. If you can eat only that which you plant and tend, then farms connect to taking (or not taking) responsibility for your personal needs and how you get them addressed.

A specific farm crop could afford you some additional texture to your meaning. A dairy farm might connect to emotional matters, maternal concerns, and thoughts around children. A farm that slaughters animals suggests more substantial issues around taking care of sustenance. Slaughter and sacrifice relates to having to let go of something in order to receive something else and, therefore, achieve balance. An organic farm points to radical measures urging you toward a healthier approach to meeting your needs. If you actually live on a farm, or connect to one in some way in your waking life, this will require you see the farm in your dream through the Personal Focus of your specific experience.

Fat

Universal Landscape: Additional protection and provision.

Dreaming Lens: Were you fat? Was someone in your dream fat? Was the fat extracted and separate from a body? Was being fat part of a conversation? What was the emotional content around the issue of fat? Was there an element of amusement? Was there shame involved?

Personal Focus: At its most fundamental level, fat is the mammalian body's way of creating stores of energy to be tapped into during times of lack. The human body can live on its own fat cells for quite a long time. It is for this reason that as we age, we carry more of them. This was designed to protect the old who fell low in the pecking order for food in early civilization. Fat also serves the physiological need for warmth as it offers protection from temperatures in colder climates. In this way, the Universal Landscape meaning for fat represents provisions for future needs as well as protective measures that aid in survival.

The conundrum with this symbol comes into play by virtue of our current cultural and social view of excess weight. We are obsessed with impossibly thin body types as ideal and anything falling short of this is considered unattractive. This makes the presence of fat in a dream a potentially highly-charged image to interpret. For most people, being fat is associated with sloth, blame, and shame. The media virulently reinforces this perspective. Therefore, your Personal Focus with regard to fat as a symbol must connect to your own experience of your body shape and size.

Gaining weight in a dream could point out an unconscious need to gain protection from emotional stress. It can also indicate a need to put a protective barrier between yourself and the outside world. Losing weight could represent either a shedding of old defenses or a depletion of resources. Look to areas in your life where you may be feeling a sense of lack or fears of future limitation.

Fence

Universal Landscape: Boundaries.

Dreaming Lens: What was the size and scope of the fence? What side of the fence were you on? Was your desire to get around the fence? Was the fence there for your protection? Was there frustration surrounding the fence's placement in the dream, or a sense of being protected? Could you see through the fence?

Personal Focus: Fences mark the boundaries that we set in the world and any dream that contains this symbol can reveal current issues as they relate to the boundaries in your life, both those that you set and those that are set for you by others. The size of the fence and the material of which it is made adds texture to any interpretation of a fence in a dream. The more impenetrable the material is, the stronger the boundary it represents.

Which side of a fence you are on in a dream will figure heavily in how you examine such a dream. As a general rule, if the fence is protecting you, then the interpretation should focus on boundaries that you have set or should consider setting. If the opposite is the case and you experience the fence as an obstacle, look to areas in your life where your intentions are being hampered by the needs, desires, or resistance of others. If the fence is for protection, then the level of your safety will be measured by the materials from which it is made. A flimsy wooden fence could indicate you are too exposed, while a high concrete wall may indicate shutting the world out for fear of being vulnerable. A break in a chainlink fence could indicate a weak spot in your ability to protect yourself in some area of your life. If the fence contains barbed wire or some other harmful material, this could represent the consequences of taking the risk to shift boundaries in some life situation.

Someone able to get over or around a fence could indicate poor boundaries, such as the inability to say no, so that your needs are ignored by others. Trying to climb a fence indicates a need to take action in the face of obstacles. If you are inside the perimeter of such a fence and climb out, you may be feeling bound by some life constraint and willing to suffer consequences in order to break free of limitation. To climb over barbed wire is to risk being wounded in order to gain access to something or achieve your desires. Setting boundaries is a powerful indication of personal growth, which can require great courage.

Fire

Universal Landscape: Powerful transformation that is rapid and complete.

Dreaming Lens: Were you witnessing a fire? Were you starting a fire, or attempting to put one out? Was the fire manageable and pleasant, or raging out of control? Were you burning, or in danger of being burned? Were you present for the fire, or just the aftermath? What color was the flame? What was being burned?

Personal Focus: Fire is the combustion of some material undergoing a radical increase in temperature that results in a rapid restructuring of its molecular structure. If the material that is burning is organic in nature, the residual compound that remains is carbon, the basic foundation for all life on our planet. This is what makes fire such a powerful symbol for transformation and change. That which has been burned is transmuted back into the substance that is the underlying material from which anything can be created anew.

There can be many different colors present with fire and these can be explored in your interpretation process. Red flames can represent passion, frustration, or aggression, as well as issues of security. Orange connects to sexuality; yellow to emotions; green to healing; and blue to communication issues. Indigo relates to instincts and intuition and violet means that spirituality is the focus of the shift. (See Colors for more on this.)

What is burning is likely the most important focus of your investigation. If it is something you are familiar with, it may indicate that a major transformation is occurring in your life in the arena represented by that thing. A house on fire connects to a transformation in your personal identity. A public building relates more to your social identity. An object that you possess could be explored and the meaning you associate with it can be combined with the idea of radical change in that area. A fire in nature might point to a loss of resources, nurturing, or creativity. If someone dies in a fire, that Character Aspect will inform you of what part of yourself is being sacrificed in order for a new sense of self to emerge.

The size of the fire and your emotional response to it will illuminate issues of overwhelm and loss of control. A large fire that is out of control could indicate broad-based changes are underway, which will result in a total dissolution of the old landscape of your life. A contained fire could indicate the change will be manageable, or even intentional. An outdoor campfire could represent your ability to create powerful change out of limited resources. A fireplace or woodburning stove often relates to harnessing change to your benefit or pleasure.

While fire is dangerous and violent, it has the power to purify and create space for renewal and new growth. When it appears in a dream, be aware that great change is afoot and that the future is likely to bring new life and new possibility.

Fireplace

Universal Landscape: Harnessed power; manageable transformation.

Dreaming Lens: Where was the fireplace? Was it functioning properly? What was it made of? Was there a fire in it? Was there a specific purpose connected to the fire? Were you making the fire? Were you enjoying it?

Personal Focus: A fireplace is a man-made construction designed to take the amazing power offered by a fire and contain it in such a way to provide any number of services. Fire represents change and transformation on an enormous scale. However, when it is enclosed in a safe and durable structure, that force of change becomes both highly effective and specifically focused.

The usable power of fire is in a very small window of the continuum on which it exists. A small fire does little more than look pretty. Just a little too much, though, and the danger is life threatening and enormously destructive. A fireplace is the organizing principle around which great power can be harnessed to accomplish a very specific goal.

The original use of a fireplace was as a household tool. The hearth was the center of a home, providing both protective warmth and facilitating the nurturance of the family through cooking food. If this is the apparent function of the fireplace in your dream, use the Dreaming Lens to examine your current relationship to taking care of your basic needs to ensure that they are being met.

If the fireplace in your dream is clearly just for ambient purposes, then its presence may indicate a desire for being able to manage the changes that are happening in your life. If your dream fireplace is being under utilized, then consider where your life is asking you to step up the power to change. If the fire is overtaking the fireplace's capacity, then you may want to examine your current ability to manage the transformation that is taking place. (See also Fire).

Fish

Universal Landscape: Ideas that swim in the unconscious.

Dreaming Lens: What was the container for the water that housed the fish? Was it natural or man-made? Was it the ocean? Was it clean and clear? Were the fish colorful? Was there one fish or an entire school? Did they feel dangerous or innocuous? Was the fish out of water? Was it dead? Was it being consumed as food?

Personal Focus: Bodies of water represent the unconscious mind. Below the surface and invisible from land is all the material that we are unaware of in our day-to-day lives. Most of the content of the unconscious mind is emotional in nature as symbolized by the ocean. The beings that inhabit these waters are the thoughts that swim freely about their watery habitat. Some are quite close to the surface while others dwell at depths of almost unimaginable darkness. This is also true of our unconscious thoughts. There are thoughts that are accessible from the surface and those that must be fished for, but that can be caught with intention and effort. Still others are completely inaccessible.

The size of the fish correlates to the scope of the idea being represented. Schools of fish are individuals that move in the same direction, so the more fish there are, the more agreement or concurrence of thought is being expressed. Fish that are colorful and interesting might indicate creative ideas that want to be expressed. The food chain of larger fish eating smaller fish is symbolic of the way ideas grow and get bigger in our minds. Fish that are dangerous or poisonous can relate to negative or destructive thinking.

Fish in a tank may be the ideas from your unconscious of which you are actually becoming aware. Containing them in a tank can indicate that you are ready to act on them, but containment could also indicate being stuck in a cycle of limiting your creative expression. A live fish out of water reacts violently. In a dream, this often symbolizes the awkwardness surrounding vulnerable expression. Eating fish is to experience satisfaction from the constructive use of your ideas and thoughts.

If your dream involves the act of fishing, there is an entirely different interpretation to consider. The act of fishing is the search for an idea that matches a particular desire. The process requires the

proper tools, an element of attraction (bait), and the most important ingredient—patience.

Floors (Flooring)

Universal Landscape: The foundation of our self-identification.

Dreaming Lens: Was the floor underneath you solid or was it giving
way? Was it covered up? What was it made of? Was there damage? If
so, what was the cause of the damage? Fire? Water? How solid was
your footing on the floor in your dream?

Personal Focus: Buildings in dreams represent our different perceptions of consciousness. Houses, especially, connect to our sense of
self. As such, the floor represents the foundation on which we stand
as individuals. The quality and integrity of the floor in your dream
informs how grounded you currently feel.

A solid floor with structural integrity points to solidity of identity. Any type of erosion indicates there is change afoot. If there is
fire present, the change is swift and transformational. If water is the
culprit, there is an emotional shift occurring. If the floor in your
dream is in any sort of decay, it might connect to festering issues
that are forcing changes within you of which you have been previously unconscious. The discovery of the decay is akin to a new level
of consciousness on the horizon.

If the floor is carpeted, there may be a desire to hide what is
underneath. The newer the carpet, the more recent the attempt to
gloss over what is below. A new carpet is a sign of abundance, but at
what cost? Abundance that is created by covering over older issues
may be superficial and, therefore, inauthentic. An old or outdated
carpet may point to very old methods of hiding. A glass bottom
or see-through floor indicates an ability to see beneath the current
state of things. A slippery surface may be a warning of the dangers
inherent in not paying attention to the issues at hand. A dirt floor

harkens back to fundamentals and grounded foundation, but may indicate a lack of refinement or finesse.

Buildings other than houses also connect to your sense of self, but may be representing certain parts of your life. For example, a work-related building may indicate who you are in terms of your career. The same interpretation for flooring applies, but you should adjust your view with the interpretation of the environment in the Dreaming Lens. In most cases, the floor is something that becomes most evident when it is changing. If it plays a prominent role in your dream, rest assured there is significant shifting where you tread in your waking life.

Flowers

Universal Landscape: Expressions of love and affection.

Dreaming Lens: What type of flowers appeared in your dream? Were they being given or received as a gift? Were they wildflowers or store bought? Were they indoors or outside and part of nature?

Personal Focus: Flowers are one of nature's delights. They embody the notion of beauty that knows nothing more than to be beautiful. Their attractiveness is designed to ensure their continued survival, so their very existence is tied directly to their beauty. They have come to be relied upon as expressions of love and affection when given as a gift. In fact, there is an entire language of flowers, known as floriography, associated with the meaning of different flowers. Although floriography is long out of fashion, it can be easily re-searched should a particular type of flower appear in a dream.

Wildflowers have a different connotation than those that have been cultivated. Any image that connects with nature is reflecting some expression of unconscious thoughts entering your conscious awareness. However, cultivated flowers connect with a sense of de-liberateness with regard to the presence of beauty. Wildflowers are

evidence of beauty as a natural part of life, and that in the absence
of any attention whatsoever, love will always find a way to express
itself through the veil of beauty for beauty's sake.

Most often, flowers are exchanged as a token of love, thanks, or
apology, so look to areas in your life where one of these themes may
be present. If a person was connected with the flowers in the dream,
use him or her as a Character Aspect to see what elements of your
own personality might be calling for love or reconciliation. (See also
Garden.)

Flying

Universal Landscape: Ascension; rising above mundane life.

Dreaming Lens: Did you attempt to fly in the dream, or were you flying effortlessly through the air? Did you jump off after several steps
or did you simply lift off? Where did you fly to, or from? Were you
alone? Were you with others? What were you flying over? Were you
joyful, or fearful?

Personal Focus: This is one of the most common universal dream
images. One of the most delightful aspects of dreaming, this cross-
cultural symbol means that you are rising above everything that is
on the ground. Since this can be a wonderful sensation, it is often
associated with intense feelings of a positive nature. A flying dream
could indicate strong feelings of freedom and bliss, which can represent moving toward a higher state of awareness or connection
with spirit. It can also provide a broader perspective on your life by
virtue of giving you a higher vantage point.

However, it should not be overlooked that this very experience
can be used as a defense by the unconscious. When this dream appears, it begs the following question: Is there anything that is being
avoided or overlooked by rising above the conflict or simply not
being grounded in reality?

Fog

Universal Landscape: Illusory blend of thoughts and feelings.

Dreaming Lens: Were you in a fog in your dream? How much did it impact your visibility? Was it dangerous or was it pleasant? Did you feel safely hidden? What was the source of the fog? Did it lift?

Personal Focus: One of the interesting things about fog is that it mixes the symbolic meaning of two different elements: air and water. It occurs as a phenomenon in the air, yet it only exists when there is an abundance of moisture in the atmosphere, therefore, connecting it to the emotions. By combining the two elemental aspects of air and water, fog is symbolic of what can happen when unconscious thoughts and hidden emotions combine.

Fog can completely block your vision and impair your ability to navigate safely. It is often prominent near the ocean as a function of high moisture levels and rapid shifts in temperature. Since the symbolic meaning of the ocean connects to deep, unconscious levels of emotion, the presence of fog in a dream should be interpreted through this perspective.

Fog presents a potential danger to those who are traveling through it, whether over water or on land. It may be seen as the blindness that can result when our thoughts and feelings interact with each other in a confusing way. It also indicates a need to slow down and be more careful as you move about your environment.

There is a sensual nature to fog and its presence adds an element that is both mysterious and magical to any landscape. It limits what can be seen, which brings illusion into the interpretive mix. If fog is present in your dream, ask yourself if there is any area in your life that you may not be seeing accurately. Sometimes, the lies we tell ourselves are more acceptable than the truth that lies below. Fog eventually lifts and it is wise to be prepared for how things will look in the harsh light of reality.

Food

Universal Landscape: Sustenance; self-care, nurturance.

Dreaming Lens: Were you eating? Were you not eating? Were you hungry? Was someone else eating? What food was in the dream?

Personal Focus: The relationship that human beings have with food is very complicated. As everyone must eat to survive, there is no exemption from the various issues that can surround food and eating. Food in a dream connects to self-care and nurturing, and the Dreaming Lens will illuminate how this is currently being played out in your unconscious.

For simplicity's sake, approach this symbol from one of two broad perspectives. If you exert rigid control over your eating in life, then you must consider food through the lens of control. If you abandon all discipline in the face of eating, you must consider food through the lens of indulgence. As this is a continuum, place yourself anywhere on the scale between these two extreme opposites.

If you are eating in the dream, combine the quality of that experience with your waking perspective. For control, eating might suggest more nurturance in some area of your life is needed. If indulgent, you may be getting a warning of a need for discipline or a hidden impulse to stuff feelings that need expression. If you experience dream-hunger, then the control perspective could point to the impact some exertion of limitation or lack is having in your life. Ask yourself if you are starving in some way.

Fountain

Universal Landscape: Emotional expressiveness.

Dreaming Lens: Was there a fountain in your dream? Was it flowing with water, or dried up? Was size was it? Was it in a public or private place? Was it from an earlier time period? Did you use it in any way?

Personal Focus: Because a fountain is a water fixture, it is important to work with the symbolic meaning of water when working with a fountain. This is so even if the fountain was devoid of water in your dream (see Water).

At its core, water represents the emotions. How the water behaves gives color and shading to the meaning you discover. A fountain manages and manipulates the water that flows through it. In this way, the fountain represents the ability to manage the emotions. Since many fountains inspire a sense of tranquility, they embody this ability to take an emotional experience and process it in such a way that keeps the integrity of the water and allows it to move with grace and ease. It has no need to make the water disappear and a fountain only does what it is capable of. In the real world of human emotions, this is very difficult to accomplish. A dream with a fountain in it may be compensating for waking life emotions that are a bit overwhelming.

The size and scope of the fountain in your dream, as well as the amount of water involved, should be applied to your interpretations as a barometer of the situations that may be inspiring it. Because they are decorative and are often placed strategically for others to see, a fountain in a dream may be revealing a desire to be more restrained with your emotional expression in social or public settings. From the opposite perspective, it could be your unconscious showing you that your sedate and charming expression of feelings may be too constricted. Look to both the Dreaming Lens and your current life circumstances for a more effective interpretation.

Frog

Universal Landscape: Potential. Malleability. Fast escape.

Dreaming Lens: Was there one frog or many? Was it in a natural setting or appearing in a location unusual for frogs? Was it repulsive to you, or did it interest you? Was it sitting still, or hopping away? How did you respond to the frog? Did you kiss it?

Personal Focus: There is no escaping the fairy tale of the frog that might turn into a prince when kissed by a young maiden. This has implications for both men and women. Through this myth, young girls are taught that if they kiss enough frogs, they are bound to find their prince. This can foster a pattern of being drawn to inappropriate partners in the belief that they can change the frog they've met into the prince they desire. The inverse psychology of this for men connects to the part of the story where the prince was turned into a frog by an angry witch. This can manifest as an unconscious feeling of being a prince trapped inside the shape of a frog, wishing for the right woman to come along to break the spell with a kiss. The essence of this construct is potential, which can be a powerful force for change if it is embraced. On either side of the equation, however, potential that is not met is of no value whatsoever.

There are other meanings associated with frogs because of their amphibious nature. They represent parts of us that can survive in both land and water. Unseen when under the surface of a pond, they can hop out at any moment, just as a strong emotional response can sometimes hop out of the unconscious without warning. However, keep in mind that they cannot go very deep into emotional depths, nor can they reach very high levels of intellectual consideration.

Their ability to avoid capture by propelling themselves back into the pond in an instant represents the elusiveness of these emotions. Ironically, the legs that provide them the ability to jump and suddenly escape danger are the same legs that invite harm to them, as many consider frog's legs a delicacy.

In a way, all the notions connected to a frog symbolize the apparent curses in your life that may well end up being blessings, with a little love and acceptance.

Funeral

Universal Landscape: Processing a major change or transformation.

Dreaming Lens: Were you at a funeral in your dream? Whose was it? Did you know the deceased? What was the mood and atmosphere like? Was it your own funeral? Where was it located? Was there a religious element to the funeral?

Personal Focus: While a funeral centers on someone who has died, the event is designed for the living. A powerful ritual, funerals help people process the death of someone close to them in a collective procedure that acknowledges the loss and marks the beginning of a new chapter in their lives without the deceased.

Funerals are often very somber occasions where people feel they have to behave in an appropriately solemn manner. This restraint can limit the level of authenticity at such events. On the opposite side of the spectrum, there are many cultures in which gregarious expressions of joy are employed to deal with the feelings of grief.

If your dream involves either one of these extremes, consider how a recent life change may be impacting the authenticity of your expression. If your behavior at the funeral in the dream was inappropriately or contrary to the expectations of those in attendance, you might want to investigate areas of your life where the expectations of others are causing you difficulty.

In a dream where you are at a funeral, the identity of the deceased will play an important role in your interpretation. By examining them as a Character Aspect, you can consider what part of your psyche no longer serves you and has been sacrificed. In this case, only half the transformation is complete because funerals mark the death and not the rebirth that inevitably follows.

A common dream with this symbol involves the dreamer discovering that the funeral they are attending is their own. If this is the case, then the transformation that is taking place is more generalized and may connect to a developmental stage in life or a change of large enough magnitude as to imply a death of Self. Another potential interpretation of this dream connects to feeling a lack of passion or life force in your current circumstances. (See also Grave).

Garage

Universal Landscape: The anticipation of movement in life.

Dreaming Lens: Were you in a garage in your dream? Was it your own garage from life? Was it a private garage connected to a home or something larger and more public? Were you in a car? Were you searching for your car?

Personal Focus: The primary purpose of a garage is to keep a car safe and protected when it's not in use. The car is symbolic for how we maneuver through our lives. When a garage is prominent in a dream, some element of how you are moving forward (or not) is being expressed. The essence of a garage connects to being prepared to move out into the world.

If the garage is a private one that is part of a home, then you must use the symbolic sensibility of the house as self to come to a satisfying interpretation. Every room in a home connects to some part of your sense of self. The use or purpose of the room is what illuminates the meaning that should be assigned to it.

The garage represents your potential for movement and direction. If a car or other vehicle is in the garage, a dream that takes place there may be indicating some movement in a new direction is about to occur in your life. No car could mean a limitation on your mobility or motivation in regard to where you would like to be heading. If the garage is being used for some other purpose than storing a vehicle, consider that your ability to move more effectively toward a specific direction in your life may be hampered by choices you made that took you away from your intended goals. Are you being distracted from your life purpose in some way?

A public garage indicates that the dream is reflecting issues that center around your social experience. Since there are many cars being stored in such a setting, it reflects a significant amount of choices available to you. Being unable to locate your car in a garage is indicative of being temporarily stuck in some area of your life. Ask yourself where you would like to be heading and what you have to do to prepare yourself for the journey. (See also House, Car).

Garden

Universal Landscape: Structured and boundaried self-care and nurturance.

Dreaming Lens: Were you in a garden? Were you trying to get to a garden? Were you tending to the plants and soil, or enjoying the fruits of labor? Were you alone or with others? What sort of garden was it? Was it beautifully tended or full of weeds?

Personal Focus: A garden is a planned, deliberate construct that creates growth in a confined area. Whether the growth is for beauty or consumption, it represents the feminine principle of creativity and nurturing. The structure and boundaries of the garden are the expression of the masculine principle in action. In this way, gardens are a microcosm of the act of creation itself. The act of gardening is often reported to produce significant levels of serenity, relaxation, and pleasure for the enthusiast. In a dream, a garden may represent a need or desire to produce an atmosphere of peace, abundance, or nurturance in your life. The type of garden, the state it is in, and what you are doing in relation to it reflects what area is being expressed and your current ability to be effective in it.

Different types of gardens have different distinctions of meaning. A flower garden might represent a desire for beauty and grace for grace's sake, or artistic creativity. A vegetable garden signifies a proactive consideration of self-nurturing and healthy living. An herb garden points to the need to enhance the flavor of your life and connect to more esoteric modes of expression. A rock garden points to structure and memories and beauty that need no attention. Public gardens relate more to issues connected with social structures and your outside life. A botanical reserve calls forth a desire to connect with a personal sense of beauty that is shared with others. A publicly shared garden may indicate primal desires to return to older ways of communal living.

If the garden is overgrown, it may be reflecting a lack of attentiveness to your needs for sustenance or creativity. Weeds are unwanted expressions that have the capacity to strangle that which is held dear. With any dream that contains a peaceful and serene setting, it is important to consider the possibility that there is something outside of the confines of the garden that needs your attention.

Ghost

Universal Landscape: The memory or imprint of a former idea, concept, or person.

Dreaming Lens: Did you see a ghost in your dream? Were you the ghost? Were you in fear? Were you in danger? Was it the ghost of someone you knew? If so, was this someone who has passed or is currently living? What form or shape did the ghost take? Did you face it or run away? Did the ghost have a message for you?

Personal Focus: Most people consider ghosts through the context of whether they believe in them or not. The argument around their existence is irrelevant in the world of symbols. A ghost is defined as a remnant of a person's energy that remains connected to the physical world after he or she has died. Some metaphysicians theorize that a spirit can be stuck here due to unfinished business or an untimely death. There are scientists who explore the possibility of ghosts as bumps in the electromagnetic field of energy that can sometimes be perceived by people who are living. No matter what camp you fall into, a ghost is symbolic of something from your past that continues to have a presence in your consciousness long after the event or person that inspired it has passed. This can include memories, habitual patterns, and even obsessions.

The three things to examine when ghosts appear in a dream is their identity, energetic quality, and their intention, if you know it. Who they are will lead you to the part of your personality that is being highlighted by your unconscious. How they appear reveals the power this experience is having on you. What they want will give you clues about the shift your unconscious mind is guiding you to consider.

If the ghost is someone you know who is not actually dead, use the Character Aspect technique to discover what qualities are traits that you have let go of, but that still arise in your behavior or thought patterns from time to time. Someone who has actually passed away can be considered in the same fashion, but might represent the impact they had on you in life, whether positive or negative.

The influence the ghost in your dream may have can be seen by the form and structure they take. An ethereal and insubstantial energy might point to less of a hold on you than something more grounded and solid. If the dream offers you any clues to the ghost's intention or desire, add that in a literal fashion to expand your interpretation.

In many indigenous cultures, good fortune comes to a dreamer who faces a ghost and doesn't flee. This image in a dream could point to a need to face the ghosts of your past in the form of old choices and behaviors that still haunt you with regret. Accepting the mistakes made earlier in life is crucial to emotional growth, and the ghosts of your youth will let you alone when you take on self-forgiveness.

Running from a ghost in fear may represent unwillingness to face certain inevitabilities. The notion that ghosts are souls who cannot transition to the next level of existence connects with resistance. Consider areas in your life where you are not letting go of something that no longer serves you, or where you are holding on to something or someone that truly may no longer exist in your life in a real way.

Gifts

Universal Landscape: Unknown sources of joy.

Dreaming Lens: Were you given a gift in your dream? Were you the recipient of one? Was there a gift exchange? Was the gift wrapped? Did you know what it was? Did you know the other party in the exchange? How did you feel about what was given to you?

Personal Focus: In most cases, the part of receiving a gift that has the most charge to it is the element of surprise. It is general practice to keep the gift a mystery, even to the extent of putting an obstacle in the path of the recipient in the form of a box and/or wrapping paper. This speaks to the metaphorical gifts that life can bring us. We don't know what the gift from a difficult situation is going to be until after we unwrap it. Examine your current situations to see if there is something new in your life that may not have appeared so initially, but is actually a gift.

While often associated with events that merit them, the giving and receiving of a gift speaks more about the relationship between the two parties than the reason for the giving. If your dream includes another person involved in a gift exchange, examine him or her as a Character Aspect that is highly beneficial to you at this time. This is so whether you are the giver or the receiver in your dream.

Gift exchanges can be so charged with elation that many people are motivated to gift others in order to experience this elevated feeling. If the dream reflects this perspective, look for places in your life that might be in need of an injection of joy.

If there was any mystery surrounding the gift in your dream, the unknown factor points to areas in your life that may be offering you gifts, the value of which is not yet known. Your unconscious mind will always know well in advance of your conscious mind when a seemingly challenging situation is really a gift. This symbol in a dream may be the first sign that something of value is on the horizon, even if it isn't yet apparent.

Glasses

Universal Landscape: Increased effectiveness in navigating life.

Dreaming Lens: Were you wearing glasses in your dream? Was someone else? Were they the right prescription? Had you lost your glasses? Were they broken? Were you avoiding wearing glasses? Were they sunglasses?

Personal Focus: Glasses improve a person's vision by altering how light is received through the eyes. If a person wears glasses, the implication can be made that there is a flaw in the design of their eyes. The glasses themselves are the tool that corrects that flaw.

Human beings are very vision-oriented, as it is our primary navigational sense. Since glasses allow a person with visual limitations to function at a much higher level, the symbolic meaning connects to a person's effectiveness at seeing where they are going in life. Without this ability, it would be impossible to manifest our intentions and desires.

Dreaming of glasses will require a very different interpretation for the person who actually wears them than for someone who does not. For those that do, the presence or absence of them in a dream may have a somewhat literal connotation. This is especially so if the dream is about being unable to locate the glasses, in which case, the dream can be interpreted as representing anxiety about being effective. For someone who does not require them, dreaming of wearing glasses could point to some need to increase the quality of one's metaphorical vision in some area of life. The Dreaming Lens will help inform what that area might be.

If glasses are being worn by someone else in a dream, and they are somehow featured prominently or seem important, this will impact your interpretation of that Character Aspect. Whatever meaning you assign to the person must include the implied limitation of their vision that the glasses represent.

There is also the potential for people to feel less attractive with glasses and some will actually forego improved eyesight for the sake of vanity. If this theme appears in a dream that features glasses as a symbol, it may indicate some choice you are making in your life that is not serving you and is affecting your ability to see the issue clearly.

Gloves

Universal Landscape: Hidden talents, abilities, skills, or expressiveness.

Dreaming Lens: What was the style of glove? Were they dress gloves, leather-driving gloves, insulated mittens? Were they clearly men's or women's gloves? Was there a sexy element to them? Was there a purpose to wearing the gloves? How did they make you feel? Were you wearing the gloves or was someone else?

Personal Focus: Whatever the purpose of a specific kind of glove, the universal thread is that they cover the hands that wear them. The hands represent expressiveness, skills that require dexterity, and the ability to create. If hands are covered in some way, the symbolic meaning connects to limiting the hand's ability. This can be deliberate or imposed; helpful or limiting. The type of glove and how they appear in the dream will give you clues for an accurate interpretation.

The primary meaning associated with the hands relates to expressiveness. Because we gesture with our hands, a dream about gloves may connect to the part of communication that is above our words and part of our body language. Gloves represent the various masks we wear in our communication to present that which we want to, while hiding our true skins underneath.

The style and material of the gloves are an important consideration. Sexy, tight-fitting gloves connect to subtle elements of seduction. Work gloves might help you find areas in your life where you feel you have to work hard to conceal your true meaning. Lace gloves evoke delicate communication that is only thinly veiled or hiding the authentic meaning. Boxing gloves point to a fight brewing from a challenge in your life. They might also be inhibiting your communication because of guardedness—hands inside of boxing gloves may be ready to fight, but they can't be very gentle or expressive. Mittens may connect to a need or desire to be more comfortable, but at the loss of the same expressiveness or effectiveness. Long gloves that extend up one's arms connect to the extensiveness of the hidden issues or the seduction at hand. Rubber gloves may represent projection of underlying messages that reflect a more serious vulnerability to communication that is toxic.

Gorilla

Universal Landscape: The struggle for leadership or domination.

Dreaming Lens: Were you facing the gorilla directly? Were you safely barricaded from harm? Were you in the gorilla's habitat, or was it in yours? Was there more than one? Were you the gorilla? Was your dream gorilla exhibiting human behaviors? Were you or other humans exhibiting gorilla behaviors?

Personal Focus: Animals represent the instinctual part of our human nature. Gorillas are pack animals that live in communities led by a dominant, alpha-male figure, which is usually the biggest and strongest of the clan. The media has perpetuated an image of the chest-beating ape that reinforces this collective view of masculine and aggressive behavior. Initially, any interpretation of a gorilla in a dream is likely to be viewed from this perspective, representing instincts of competition, aggression, and the need for domination.

However, there are other elements to be considered. In the wild, gorillas display a rather shy disposition unless they are unduly disturbed. They also exhibit stable family structure and uncomplicated social interactions that contradict the stereotype often coupled with them. The fearsome outburst associated with an angry gorilla is, in reality, a posturing meant to establish leadership or a reaction to being disturbed. Consider that the appearance of a gorilla in a dream may point to rage that is more a facade than genuine anger. This can reflect a moment where your reaction is greater than the situation merits.

A gorilla in a cage might indicate feelings connected to being imprisoned, such as underlying aggression that is keeping you stuck in issues of anger management. A gorilla on the loose might point to the unsettling consequences of expressing previously locked up emotions. Facing a gorilla in a dream might indicate some readiness to confront your aggressive impulses or receive the expressions of anger from someone in your life.

Since a gorilla's aggression connects to territorial disputes, watching peaceful gorillas in their own habitat might indicate a level of acceptance that your security no longer needs to be aggressively defended. As always, power is something that is most effective when it is silently present and not proven boisterously. Ask yourself about your relationship to your inner gorilla. Are you feeling aligned with your personal power or are you beating your chest to make your point in life?

Graves

Universal Landscape: Generational connection to the past; thoughts of death.

Dreaming Lens: Were you in a graveyard? Were you moving past a graveyard? What was the reason for being where you were? Was there a specific person connected to the grave? Were you being buried?

Personal Focus: The human race has a very powerful and profound relationship with our dead. While the bond is ultimately mysterious, there is no getting around the fact that we must stay connected to those who have passed in order to make meaning of the present. A graveyard's primary purpose is to provide space for the living to make this connection. In this regard, a graveyard in a dream may be calling you to consider how some element of your current life, or your personality traits, may be the result of generations of family that preceded you.

A secondary symbolic meaning has evolved and emerged through the media. A graveyard is also home to all of the dark elements associated with death: ghouls, goblins, vampires, and other creatures of the night (see Vampires). This setting in a dream may be an indication that you are in the realm of Shadow material; it may also represent the fear of death. (See also Death, Coffin).

Gun

Universal Landscape: Power over others.

Dreaming Lens: Were you holding the gun in your dream, or was someone else? Was it laying some place where anyone might be able to pick it up? Was it loaded? Was it being fired? Was it unable to fire? Was it real or fake? Was the gun hidden? Was it being brandished in a threatening manner?

Personal Focus: Whoever has the gun is in charge. Connected to the masculine principle, the gun represents male-oriented power in an extreme form. The key to understanding this symbol is that the power represented by a gun is available to whoever possesses it at any given moment. Even the most timid individual can wind up controlling any interaction if the intimidating power of a firearm is in their hands.

The masculine principle is related to action and the ability to make things happen. A gun of any type connects to this universal energy, but with an over-intensity that indicates a lack of balance or containment. While the presence of a gun may imply a sense of control in a chaotic situation, its deadly and unpredictable nature implies a breakdown of stability and the potential for lethal danger.

The type of firearm is important to consider as this indicates the amount of power being yielded. A handgun relates directly to personal power and should be interpreted as what is available to you as an individual. Something with more firepower, such as an automatic weapon, relates to the ability to express strength at a more social level.

The proximity of the gun in a dream indicates where the power currently resides. Holding the gun puts the dreamer in a position of ownership, but the level of confidence (or lack thereof) should be noted. Having a gun aimed at you indicates that some Character Aspect of your personality is demanding to be heard and dealt with. If this is the case, your interpretation needs to include working with whoever yielded the gun in your dream. Brandishing a weapon could indicate a need to be seen as powerful in some area of your life. A hidden or concealed gun indicates elusive power that is felt, though not flaunted.

Given the role of guns in our culture, how you personally feel about them must figure strongly in how you interpret them as a symbol. The more reticent you are about them, the more power this symbol may have for you. If this is the case, a gun indicates that

Shadow material is being explored. However, do not be misled into thinking that the firing of all guns in dreams is murderous or even harmful—a hunter loves his gun like a trumpeter loves his trumpet. Additionally, something being killed off in a dream can actually be a positive thing, such as an old belief or pattern that no longer suits you.

Being wounded (or wounding someone else) in a dream brings us to the idea of the gun wielding great amounts of power. Where the wounding occurs will provide access to deeper levels of understanding of how this power is impacting you, whether positively or negatively. For example, being shot (or shooting someone) in the chest could be thought of as a destructive act, but this could also indicate the need for your heart to be opened up to receive love. This is especially true if there is a situation in your waking life that includes a level of intimacy that is great enough to be frightening on an unconscious level.

Hair

Universal Landscape: Beauty; strength of persona.

Dreaming Lens: Was your own hair the focus of your dream? Was it someone else's? Was it different from your natural hair? Was there a change in style or color? Were you losing hair? Gaining hair? Was the hair in your dream unconnected to someone's head?

Personal Focus: At the most primal level, hair connects to beauty and to presenting personal attractiveness to the world. In popular culture and the media, changing hairstyles are a source of fascination and imbued with importance. In the mundane world, it is common for people to divide their experience into "good hair days" and "bad hair days." For men, and some women, the loss of hair is often considered tragic and supremely disappointing. This lends credence to hair and hair loss as being directly linked to a sense of personal attractiveness and sexual vitality.

In general terms, hair is a feminine symbol and connects to strength and power as expressed by the feminine principle of creativity and receptivity. However, in Western mythology, the figure of Samson and his divine strength was directly connected to his long hair, the loss of which resulted in his ultimate demise. Therefore, Sampson's strength was only accessible to him while his masculine body was integrated with the feminine principal as represented by his hair.

Another phenomenon to be examined where hair is concerned relates to coveting: those with curly hair wish they had straight hair and those with straight hair wish for curls. Since modern chemistry allows for alteration with alarming precision, the color of hair in dreams can hold powerful symbolic significance. Consider changes in color as connecting with an unconscious desire for a shift in expression in your outward persona. The color that shows up has meaning as well. Blonde hair is most coveted, but is also associated with a lack of intelligence. Intellect is the realm of the brunette. Red hair is correlated with passion and magic.

Given that hair is on the head, this symbol connects to thoughts, both conscious and unconscious. Dreaming of long hair can indicate thoughts based on a desire for beauty to be more fully expressed. Hair that is bound in some fashion might reflect unconscious feelings of constraint in the area of personal expression. Hair being cut, lost, or radically altered can point to the need for a shift in thoughts about attractiveness. A wig represents a desire to actively create a mode of expressiveness that is not organically your own.

Hands

Universal Landscape: Personal creativity and expression.

Dreaming Lens: Whose hands were featured in your dream? Were they your own, or the hands of another? If someone else's hands appeared in your dream, do you know to whom they belonged? How were the hands being used in the dream? Were they normal in appearance or were they exaggerated or disfigured in some way? Were they functional?

Personal Focus: Hands have an enormous capacity for creativity and expression that are the exclusive territory of human beings. On a personal level, one's hands divulge an extraordinary amount of information. The condition and appearance of a person's hands directly reflect what they do with them on a regular basis. A person who does manual labor will have rough and careworn hands. Hands that are soft and smooth indicate a lifestyle that is free from such work.

Some ethnic groups are known to talk with their hands, while others are known for certain levels of reserve and containment. Whatever your personal style is with regard to your hands should be juxtaposed to the Dreaming Lens when interpreting this symbol, especially if body language plays a part in the dream.

Consider whether the presence or prominence of the hands in the dream is empowering or disturbing. Holding on to or hiding one's hands can be an indication of a need to exert a measure of control over personal expression. Overuse of the hands while talking could point to excessive amounts of embellishments in communication that may put a distance between you and others. A disembodied hand can represent actions without conscience. A hand poised in the air could land in a slap or a caress, so there is an element of anticipation of the possible outcome in such an image.

Notice the presence or lack of adornments; a well-adorned hand signifies wealth, whereas a plain hand could mean anything from lack to simplicity. Each of us has a relationship to our hands that is intimate and familiar, as in the expression *I know that like the back of my hand*. The act of making something with your hands could indicate a call do so more often in life. The notion of "getting your hands dirty" can apply to having a richer experience as a result of throwing yourself fully into something.

Hat

Universal Landscape: The containment of thoughts and/or ideas.

Dreaming Lens: Were you wearing the hat or was someone else? Was it a man's hat or a woman's hat? Was the hat related to keeping warm in the cold weather? Was the hat more for the purpose of adornment or fashion? Were you aware of to whom the hat belonged? Why did you have the hat and how did you feel about it?

Personal Focus: The head is the symbolic wellspring of our thoughts and ideas. Hats both adorn and protect the head. As such, a hat can represent specific ideas or thoughts themselves, but also the need or desire to contain them. In terms of adornment, a hat can be the outward expression of an inner idea. In the realm of protection, a hat can connect with keeping such ideas firmly in place.

Wearing someone else's hat could indicate expressing the notion of trying on someone else's ideas. If you can easily make an association between the hat in your dream and a person in your life, use the Character Aspect technique to inform your interpretation. The same would apply if someone in your dream was wearing the hat.

Style should be considered as well. A man wearing a woman's hat may be considering a more flamboyant or expressive thought pattern. An old-fashioned hat might connect to an outdated modality of thought. Something very flashy could represent the creativity of your current way of thinking. How you feel about such a hat would indicate the level of risk associated with the choice to be expressive in such a way. Keep in mind the various ways in which hats have been in and out of fashion. The days of ubiquitous hat-wearing are considerably out of fashion. Ski caps used to be exclusively worn in winter, but are now part of the "gangsta" culture.

The motivation for wearing a hat may play a large part in a dream's interpretation. A hat may be used to hide a loss of hair in which case the meaning takes on a new slant connecting with the authenticity (or lack thereof) of what you are presenting to the world. There are cultural considerations to examine as well: in some cultures, wearing a hat indoors would be considered rude while in others there are religious demands to keep the head covered at all times.

Heart Attack

Universal Landscape: Sudden and destructive impact of a wounded heart.

Dreaming Lens: Did you have a heart attack? Did someone else have a heart attack in your dream? What was the end result of the heart attack? Was it painful? Where did the heart attack take place?

Personal Focus: A heart attack refers to any of a number of different wounds to the heart. Results of a heart attack can range from innocuous discomfort to death. The heart is the symbolic center of love. When love is compromised for too long, the heart may rebel and attack. In this context, when we use the word "love," we aren't necessarily referring to feelings of romantic attachment. Love is the primary principle on which life is based; anything that opposes love, such as anger, resentment, envy or pride, are all qualities that can have an impact on the heart.

Often the causes of a heart attack go unnoticed for a long time before the actual event occurs. In this way, such a dream image may indicate that the underlying cause of your unconscious discontent may have been lingering below the surface for a long while before this time.

If you are the one having a heart attack in your dream, then look to where in your life issues around love may be hurting you on a deep level. If someone else in your dream is the victim, then use them as a Character Aspect of the part of your personality that is suffering due to a matter of love, or the lack thereof.

Heights

Universal Landscape: Higher perspectives of consciousness.

Dreaming Lens: How high were you? What structure was affording you the height? Was there a view? Were you frightened or secure? Was there danger of falling?

Personal Focus: The higher your vantage point, the more expansive view of your environment you will have. This takes on the symbolic meaning of expanded consciousness. The higher your level of thought, the more enlightened you are considered to be. This is so because there is a correlation between expanded consciousness and making positive, life-affirming choices.

In simpler terms, the more you see, the more you know. The more you know, the more informed you can be about your choices. This expansion, however, comes with a caveat. Choosing to live at higher levels of consciousness brings with it a great deal of responsibility. The higher you go, the farther you can fall should you lose your footing. The greatest issue here is whether your fear of falling from a great height is real or imagined. Even the most precarious precipice is safe, as long as you practice stillness. However, stillness is perhaps the greatest challenge in the human experience.

The key to understanding this symbol is relativity. The roof of a small building will afford you a view of everything that is near it. Conversely, being up in space can afford a view of our entire world.

The greater the height, the higher the level of consciousness being expressed. Your emotional experience of that height in your dream must color the interpretation you assign it.

Helicopter

Universal Landscape: Observations of consciousness. Rapid movement between thoughts.

Dreaming Lens: Was the helicopter in flight or on the ground? Were you flying in it or were you watching one from the ground? Was the helicopter crashing as part of your dream? Were you piloting it, or were you a passenger? Was it a private helicopter, or part of law enforcement or the media?

Personal Focus: Like any vehicle or mode of transportation, a helicopter in a dream represents movement on your path in life. However, a helicopter is primarily connected to its ability to move up and down, hover, and move swiftly while staying close to the ground. Because of this, it is often used for observation or transportation across very short distances in a very fast manner. In a dream, it represents these same concepts as they relate to consciousness: the vantage point to observe the lay of the land more effectively and the ability to jump from one place to another with ease and speed.

While similar to an airplane's connection to fast transitions in life, a helicopter gives you a much greater degree of personal control over the different options they offer. In the realm of transitions, they symbolize a shift that is rapid, but not necessarily dramatic. A helicopter cannot travel the far distances that an airplane can, so the transition that is represented is more akin to shifting your perspective within the same landscape as opposed to completely changing your environment. A helicopter leaves you quite exposed to the elements, making the process one of vulnerability and a bit frightening.

A helicopter on the ground may indicate a powerful resource on hand, such that when change does inevitably come, you will be able to handle whatever direction you find yourself needing to go. A crashing helicopter could be pointing to the danger that comes from too much power or too many choices, or a lack of restraint or discipline. If you are traveling in a helicopter, you may be dreaming about some fairly significant shift in perspective going on in your life. Your unconscious mind is telling you to hold on—that although it may be somewhat frightening, you are actually well-armed with lots of choices, power, and possibilities.

Hidden Room

Universal Landscape: Unknown or hidden resources.

Dreaming Lens: Did you find a hidden room, or did you just search for it? Was it difficult to find, or did you come upon it with ease? If you found a hidden room, what did you find in it? Was the room well lit, or dark and mysterious? Were the feelings around the search and discovery of the room scary, friendly, helpful, or dangerous?

Personal Focus: A house or home of any kind represents the dreamer's sense of self. If you discover a room that you didn't know was there, it is like finding a new aspect of yourself that was formerly unknown. This can be interpreted as something that is just becoming available to you, such as new thoughts, resources, or strengths that exist in you but were previously unavailable or untapped.

What you find in a hidden room should figure prominently in your interpretation. Your association with anything you seek or discover should be considered as symbolic of a resource that you already possess, but are just now able to utilize.

Not all hidden room dreams are pleasant; some can be quite disturbing. If this is the case, remember that if you find something troubling within your psyche, accepting and incorporating such Shadow elements are crucial to facilitating integration.

If the room suddenly disappears, consider that the resource you counted on finding within yourself may not be as fully formed as you had thought. No matter what the sensibility of the discovery, this image is always an embodiment of the possibility that at any moment in life, more can be revealed.

High School

Universal Landscape: Passage from adolescence to adulthood.

Dreaming Lens: How did you feel about being back in this time period? Were you experiencing anxiety or nostalgia for days gone by? Were you experiencing yourself as noticed or invisible; stuck or safe? Were you with present-day friends, or your high school circle?

Personal Focus: The primary symbolic meaning for this image is deeply connected to your own personal experience of this period in your life. In a general sense, high school is where most of us learned life lessons of responsibility and sexual identity, as well as where we built the foundation for the directions we took as grownups. However, the overall experience of this turbulent time varies from person to person and can range from fun and joyous to excruciatingly painful. When you dream of high school, your unconscious is expressing emotional issues that have their root at this time in your history.

As a common dream, most people experience this related to performance anxiety. High school represents the first time as individuals that most people are faced with a level of responsibility that is most like what we deal with in the adult world. When our current lives spark insecurity about our readiness to face life's tests, we may express unconscious fears by returning, unprepared, to this time

and suffering the humiliation of being lost, not knowing the sched-
ule, not being ready for an exam, or even finding ourselves naked.

The lessons faced in adolescence were, for some, accompanied
by mistakes being cleared up for us by parents or other authority
figures. As such, this dream image could indicate an unconscious
wish to have the burden of adult responsibilities magically disappear, as if someone else could handle them for us.

If the dream is uncomfortable, look to present stressors that may
feel burdensome in the same way you felt as a teenager. The pressure to perform at certain levels is a major theme of the high school
experience. This may be revealing issues of performance anxiety
in your current life. Inherent in this image is the fear of facing the
expectations that others may have of you. Examine your current
life for issues of this nature and you will be well on your way to an
accurate interpretation.

Hospital

Universal Landscape: The need for healing.

Dreaming Lens: Were you in the hospital? Was someone else? Was
there surgery involved? Illness? Was it an emergency that led you
to the hospital? Were you being helped or hindered in the hospital?
Was it an empty place?

Personal Focus: Hospitals tend to evoke powerful reactions. The discomfort that color associations tend to overshadow the benevo-
lence connected to hospitals as places of healing. It is common for
people to fear hospitals, adding a touch of irony to our relationship
with the healing process. Healing is transformation and the first
step to any major change is the breakdown that precedes the breakthrough.

Since the breakdown is the scary part, we avoid it, just as some
people avoid hospitals in waking life. It is easy to forget that in or-

der for surgeons to heal an illness they must first cut the body open, creating a wound. And since not everyone who checks into a hospital is fortunate enough to check out, they are indelibly connected to the fear of death and dying. However, remember that death is always followed by rebirth.

In this way, being in or near a hospital in a dream is always going to indicate that some healing is either underway or necessary. If you are the patient, then consider that your sense of self is undergoing a significant shift. If you are a visitor, then the healing transformation is connected to a Character Aspect or particular way of being as embodied by the person you are going to see. If you are playing the part of healer, the dream may be helping you step into that role in some area of life that is undergoing a transformation.

The fear or repulsion that is present in the dream will give you an idea of how much resistance you may be unconsciously engaged in. If you are experiencing a health issue in life, the image of a hospital may be literal, in which case your dream relationship to the hospital will inform you of underlying resistance to surrender to your body and its functioning (or lack thereof).

Hotel

Universal Landscape: Transitory self; sense of Self when in transition.

Dreaming Lens: What was the state of the hotel? Was it lavish or dilapidated? Were you a welcome guest and were your needs met? Was the hotel scene central to the dream or only cursory? Was it business or pleasure that took you there? Who was with you?

Personal Focus: Any home-like dwelling in a dream is representative of the Self. A space of transitional living such as a hotel or motel room connects to the Self in a temporary state of being. This symbol usually appears when there is change afoot, indicating that the sense of Self is in transition and not yet fully "home." Given this transitory nature, such a dream may indicate the need for a temporary respite in order to consider being more authentic with regard to your identity.

Look to the Dreaming Lens for an accurate interpretation when a hotel appears in your dream. For example, if the dwelling is dilapidated, as in an inexpensive motel, then you may be experiencing downward movement in the areas of abundance. If the hotel is grand and lavish, you may be preparing yourself for an increase in abundance. Conversely, this same imagery could be compensating for lack as a wish fulfillment. The level and quality of service may help you explore your current relationship to receiving. If the service was bad, you might consider seeing if your needs are being met in life. If you were well taken care of, you may be allowing contribution and assistance in your life, or need to do so in greater measure.

Hotel rooms can also be connected to both sexuality and mortality, as they are often used in life for sexual encounters and suicides. Hotel-room sex could indicate a self-investigation that involves looking at an area of your sexual expression. If the latter image is present, ask yourself what part of you may need to commit suicide (be sacrificed) so that the rest of you can move forward with your life.

House

Universal Landscape: The Self; self-perception.

Dreaming Lens: Did you know the house in your dream? Was it your current home? Was it the home of someone else? What shape was the house in? Did the house represent a shift up or down in the quality of living from your waking life? What were your feelings about the house?

Personal Focus: Houses in dreams are the symbolic representation of the dreamer's sense of Self. No matter what other imagery or circumstances may present themselves in a dream, a house is always an unconscious expression of your identity. This applies to any home-like dwelling; such as an apartment, hotel room, trailer, grass hut, or any of the possibilities of "home" that exist in the imagination. The perspective or view of the house takes on specific meaning. The front of a house connects to the persona—the part of you that you show the world—while the back is what is private or hidden. What you discover on the inside reflects various, compartmental-ized aspects of yourself. Side views or alternate angles may connect to presenting yourself in the world in a limited, partial, or inaccu-rate fashion.

The size, style, condition, and reflection of abundance of the house will play a key role in interpreting this symbol in a dream. You will need to consider both the feelings evoked by the house in the dream itself, as well as what comes up for you when comparing it to your actual waking life home. Whatever shades of meaning you glean from your dream, they must be interpreted as reflecting an unconscious expression of Self.

A mansion on a grand scale may indicate a sense of your life getting bigger or opening yourself up to greater levels of abun-dance. Conversely, this could also be revealing a level of inappro-priate grandiosity, depending on your current level of self-esteem. A moment in life that feels constraining and steeped in lack might evoke a dream image of a house that is more hovel than home. Yet, this same image could be a symbolic representation of deeper levels of humility emerging within you.

A new house might mean a new sense of Self is on the horizon, or needs to be. Adding an extension indicates such an expansion may be occurring on a personal level. An older, dilapidated model could represent an outdated view of Self. A house on fire is expressing that powerful levels of transformation are afoot. Whatever the Dreaming

Lens is offering you about a house should be incorporated into an interpretation of your sense of self at the time of the dream.

If you dream of a specific home from an earlier time in your life, you are looking at the person you are today as a direct result of what was going on back then. This can refer to occurrences in the environment associated with the home and the people in it, as well as developmental issues based on your age at the time.

Ice

Universal Landscape: Absence of emotional warmth and fluidity.

Dreaming Lens: Where was the ice in your dream? Were you putting it to use? If so, how? Was the ice naturally occurring? Was it the result of weather conditions? Were you able to successfully maneuver over or through the ice?

Personal Focus: Water represents emotions and ice is frozen water. Symbolically, ice represents emotional content that has been dramatically altered. The resulting substance is cold and hard—adjectives that do not conjure pleasant sensations when applied to one's emotional nature. From the world of physics, we know that ice is not created by adding cold, but rather by the loss of heat. This tells us that when ice is present, warmth has been lost or given away.

Ice can also be dangerous, especially when one must maneuver over it. An icy road has the symbolic connotation that a lack of emotional fluidity can be treacherous on your path through life. This will be the case for most dream images where ice is being formed in nature. Glaciers, ice flows, ice storms—these are all symbolic representations of the negative impact to your forward movement that results from a freezing off of your emotions.

Ice has a positive side as well. It increases the enjoyment level of many of the foods and beverages we consume and is also responsible for the invaluable process of their preservation. On the symbolic level, you should consider these constructive uses of ice. But when examined at closer range, these useful attributes are more like consequences than intentions. Ice preserves perishable materials, because in its presence, very few organisms can live and thrive. This usefulness can also be said of a person who has shut off the emotional warmth of their heart: they may feel protected from life's occasional brutality, but only at the cost of losing life-sustaining warmth.

The Dreaming Lens will offer you insight by virtue of where the ice formed and how it impacted you in the dream. In your investigation, consider both sides of this equation. If there is danger present, then your interpretation is clear and should connect to where in your life you are withholding love, warmth, and expressiveness. If you are enjoying the value of ice in some way in your dream, you may have to probe a bit deeper for true understanding. Measure the value you are receiving against the impact and cost you may be suffering and you will be well on your way to receiving clarity about what this dream image has to offer you.

Infidelity/Affair

Universal Landscape: A circuitous route to meeting needs. Avoidance.

Dreaming Lens: Were you having an affair? Were you discovering an affair? Were you confronting or passive? Was there secretiveness involved? Was it a sexual encounter or more emotionally based?

Personal Focus: There is no intimacy need that cannot be met in a primary relationship. Going outside of a marriage or partnership for sex or affection is a way of meeting a primal need by a roundabout way. Simultaneously, there is an avoidance of some underlying problem that is not being addressed. Therefore, this image represents both a circuitous route to connection and avoidance of confrontation.

If you discover an infidelity in a dream, you may want to consider areas in your life where you are avoiding taking care of your self. If you are engaged in an affair, you might need to examine your life circumstances for signs of being manipulative or indirect in getting your needs met. As getting caught is always reflective of an unconscious desire to effect a change, being discovered as being unfaithful could indicate a desire to shift some area of your life.

Always be willing to look at issues of responsibility when this dream image appears: where in your life are you not allowing yourself to be accountable for your actions? If the dream involves details of constructing an affair, you may want to examine how genuine you are being in terms of expressing and manifesting your desires in life, both relationally and otherwise. Where in your life are you being authentic? How might you be betraying your own needs?

It is safe to assume that this image in a dream indicates a theme of intimacy issues in waking life, no matter what the marital state of the dreamer. This may have literal implications if you are actually involved in an affair or believe your partner to be.

Insects

Universal Landscape: Disturbing thoughts, hidden fears.

Dreaming Lens: What sort of insects were you seeing in your dream? Were there many, or just one? Were you frightened or curious? Was the insect recognizable from life, or a fantastic dream fabrication?

Personal Focus: Insects and bugs are generally found to be repulsive by most people. For some, they can evoke wildly irrational fears. As any animal is symbolic of some element of thought, any dream insect represents some small, but frightening unconscious thought. To arrive at an accurate interpretation, you may need to do a little research about the insect in question. Once you know a bit about it, you can come to an interpretation of what it might represent.

As an example, bees exhibit sophisticated forms of communication and a communal production of honey that represents enormous industriousness and the power of collective thoughts gathered for a common purpose. Cockroaches are famous for being hardy enough to survive a nuclear blast. They can, therefore, be said to represent the staying power of the creepy thoughts that live in the Shadow. Certain beetles manufacture a substance similar to paper or cardboard, embodying the powerful transformation that is available by attending to small details. The silk made by any number of different insects connects to the amazing power of creativity and strength that actually has its origin in the Shadow.

Flying insects connect to the vast mobility of our darker thoughts. Slimy, ground dwellers point to the ever-present underbelly of our psyche. If you have an insect show up in a dream, take a moment and look up some details about it. What you discover may trigger an important message that your unconscious is trying to give you.

Intercourse

Universal Landscape: Joining of personality Character Aspects; integration.

Dreaming Lens: Were you having sex? Were you watching sex? How many people were involved in the sex act? Were there multiple acts and/or partners? Were you having sex with someone you knew? Was it someone you have sex with in life? Was it someone you want to have sex with in life? Were you shocked at who you were having sex with? How did you feel about the sex?

Personal Focus: The essence of sexual intercourse is the joining of two individuals in a process that allows them to be as close to each other as the human body will allow. This translates into the concept of integration as the symbolic meaning of sex. Additionally, the potential for this act to result in the creation of a third entity reinforces this definition. If you remove all sense of eroticism, embarrassment, shame, or titillation, the purity of this symbol is profound. Any characters that appear in a dream engaged in sexual intercourse are expressing an unconscious desire to merge the Character Aspects of of the individuals involved.

If you are participating in sex in a dream, the focus of your investigation will be on your dream partner. The Character Aspects they represent are the qualities that your unconscious is expressing a need to be integrated into your present level of functioning. This will be easier to identify when you know the person from your waking life; however, this can also be the very element that makes examining such a dream uncomfortable. It is common to dream of having sex with people who you would never ordinarily do so, or even think of doing so, such as coworkers, family members, or acquaintances.

When using the Character Aspect technique in relation to sex dreams, you must add an element of transformation of the qualities that you identify. The process is not literal or concrete. For example, an authoritative boss might feel like an overbearing personality to deal with in life, but integrating such a person as a Character Aspect transforms that quality to an appropriate level of personal power. A harshly critical and negative personality may actually provide you with a much-needed sense of discernment or objectivity when incorporated into your life. A person who is so childish in their behavior as to be annoying in your waking world can be transformed into a new relationship with your inner sense of playfulness and joy. That arrogant and insufferable person you know may be providing you with new levels of confidence. Such is the power of the symbol of integration as represented by the act of sex.

If you witness others having sex in your dream, the same approach should be taken, but the process that is occurring is less about integrating new aspects as it is about exploring what existing skills you have that may be necessary for you to call upon to face some situation in your current life.

Internet

Universal Landscape: The collective unconscious and higher thought processes.

Dreaming Lens: Were you using the internet? Were you "inside" the internet? Were you trying to get connected and unable to do so? Were you surfing? What were you looking for? Were you successful in your online endeavor?

Personal Focus: The emergence of the Internet has radically changed the way we interact with the world in which we live. Through it, people can interact with others of like mind and connect with information and ideas that are shared by multitudes. In this way, it is an exact symbolic representation of the collective consciousness of human beings today. The speed with which it has evolved is alarming, and it has created a global culture faster than our ability to comprehend the rules that govern it.

A dream that features the Internet as a prominent image is inviting you to investigate your personal relationship with the overwhelming changes that have taken place in our world over the past two decades. If you are Internet-savvy in life and are logged on in your dream, you may not find this a particularly powerful image—therefore, consider this symbol as representing expanded and accelerated thinking. However, if you are someone who harbors resistance to the Internet, its appearance in a dream is inviting you to look into areas of your life that are overwhelming or moving too fast for your comfort.

In this way, the Internet would be a symbolic depiction of anxiety or chaotic thoughts. If the dream has you utilizing the Internet as a tool, you may want to look at areas in your life that are requiring a higher level of functioning or thought processes. Conducting research on the Internet might point to a search for meaning, agreement, or commonality with others through information that comes through the collective unconscious. If you are mindlessly surfing the Internet to kill time or eradicate boredom through escapism, your dream may be alerting you to the impact of compulsion or lower levels of thinking.

Itch

Universal Landscape: Unfulfilled desires and wishes.

Dreaming Lens: Did you have the itch, or did someone else? Was the itch related to a wound? Was the origin of the itch a mystery? Did you scratch it? Were you being asked to assist another's itch relief? Did the itch pass when scratched?

Personal Focus: In a dream, an itch represents the message that something needs to be cast aside. It indicates that the surface of some issue must be scratched to find the deeper layer of truth underneath. While on one hand this investigation can bring comfort and relief, it could also indicate a harmful, compulsive need to return to some troubling issue over and over again. The danger of scratching some itches can be quite intense.

Your investigation of such a dream must make an accurate interpretation of what type of itch you're being presented with: benign adjustment of comfort, or compulsive repetition that should be avoided at all costs? The first connects to the initial stirrings of an issue that are just being made known to you. The latter probably connects to habits or compulsions that you return to again and again that may not be serving you.

The source and cause of the itch is important to consider. An itch emanating from a wound usually indicates a healing process.

This might mean that resentments or unspoken thoughts about a recent emotional battle have left potential scars. An itch that spreads a toxin, such as poison ivy, would represent the addictive quality of what happens when you open the door to harmless satisfaction only to find the challenging compulsion to repeat harmful behavior. An itch in a socially sensitive area, such as the genitals, connects to thoughts and desires that are private, secret, and sexual in nature.

Jesus, Buddha

Universal Landscape: Archetypal Character Aspect: Ability to manifest thought into reality.

Dreaming Lens: Who appeared to you in your dream? How did they appear? In what form did they appear? Did they speak? Did you speak to them? Was there a specific message delivered with or without words? Was the experience blissful?

Personal Focus: Jesus and Buddha were remarkable teachers who were able to live the principles of pure love and manifestation in a fashion that can only be described as divine in nature. To limit this term to just these two is in no way meant to dismiss the many other prophets and teachers who have embodied this spirit. While both Jesus and Buddha once lived as men, they should be treated as Archetypes. Dreaming of one of them indicates that you are experiencing a high level of self-discovery and integration.

The male counterpart to the Goddess energy, Jesus and Buddha exemplify the masculine principle at its highest level of evolution. The masculine principle connects to the power of thought. Through very different teachings, both of these mystics taught the concept that what you think and believe becomes your reality. They exemplify that it is possible, through love, to experience states of bliss in this often-challenging life.

The appearance of one of these great teachers in a dream is to put you on notice that you are in a moment of elevating consciousness and integration of Self. It is not uncommon for an archetypal figure to be silent in a dream, as it is their mere presence that can be the dream's impact. If words and messages are present in the dream, take them to heart and do so literally. However, if this is not the case, your best use of such a dream is silent gratitude for the gift of a rare and powerful experience of elevated consciousness.

Jungle

Universal Landscape: Exotic, foreign territory; off the beaten path.

Dreaming Lens: Were you in a jungle habitat in your dream? Were you alone? Were you in danger? Were you excited and intrigued, or were you frightened? Were you able to maneuver or were you held captive by the landscape?

Personal Focus: By definition, a jungle is any land that is densely vegetative and essentially impenetrable by standard means. Only found in tropical climates, these vast, moisture-laden habitats are isolated, mysterious, and for most Westerners, completely foreign to our civilized mentality. This can make for a romantic view of such a setting in a dream.

If the jungle atmosphere in your dream evoked a sense of wonder and enchantment, you may be tapping into some new and interesting territory in some area of your life. The flip side of this coin would be this image expressing a desire for experiences that are new and different. Your dream could be a request for life to bring you a taste of the exotic.

Of course, your interpretation should match up with the Dreaming Lens. Jungle terrain can be quite inhospitable—from deadly animals to insects carrying disease, your life could be in peril in such a place. If this is the case, you will want to find an association with your waking life where a sense of isolation or foreign sensibility may be causing you fear or stress.

The rainforests are the lungs of Mother Earth, responsible for much of the oxygen that is released into our atmosphere. As we continue to decimate these precious resources, we put our very existence in jeopardy. Whether you consider yourself an advocate for saving the rainforests or not, you are connected to every inch of our planet through the collective unconscious. Your dream may be representing the callous destruction of resources, both globally and in your personal life. Consider both when forming your interpretation.

Kitchen

Universal Landscape: The heart-center of the Self.

Dreaming Lens: What kitchen were you in? Did you know it, or was it foreign to you? Was it from earlier in your life? Was it your childhood kitchen? What were you doing in the kitchen? Who else was there?

Personal Focus: As the nurturing center of a house, the kitchen represents the heart and hearth of the Self. It is where the family is fed and comes together in community. It is the room where people tend to congregate during parties. It is the symbolic realm of Mother and the feminine principle as it is expressed by the family structure. Food is stored and prepared in the kitchen, so the symbolic "food for your soul" is located in the kitchen of your dreams.

Consider how your dream may be informing you of how you are responding to your own spiritual cooking. If your life experience of family, mother, and kitchen were different from the ideal, your Personal Focus must include your individual paradigm. For example, much of a family's abusive interactions can occur in the kitchen, so such associations should be considered when interpreting a kitchen dream.

The activity in the dream will outline your current internal view around issues of nurturing, self-care, and healing. Any people who appear are key components in the process of exploration. If they are known to you, use the Character Aspect technique to integrate their qualities into your interpretation. If there were people in the dream not known to you, consider whatever you can remember about them in the Dreaming Lens. Any dream that takes place primarily in a kitchen has the capacity to offer you an overview of the status of your heart center. Use it to examine whether you are experiencing healthy levels of self-nurturance, or if you are in need of adjustments in this area.

Ladder

Universal Landscape: Transitions that seem risky or unsupported.

Dreaming Lens: Was the ladder in use? Was it in place for use or was it in storage? What was the integrity of the ladder's structure? Was it capable of bearing weight? What was the ladder made of? What was the ladder's height? Were you on the ladder? Were you comfortable or frightened?

Personal Focus: A ladder is an effective, but unstable, method of getting to a higher vantage point. Anything that helps a person move from one level to another is symbolically connected with transitioning from one realm of operating to another. However, a ladder is a tool used in the construction or fixing of things. So in this way, the symbolic meaning connects to the ability to achieve some sort of goal.

The presence of a ladder in a dream suggests that there is a transition afoot that may also connect to achieving some goal or fixing some area of your life that requires attention. If the dream merits the use of a ladder, but it is either ignored or inaccessible in some way, you may be missing the very thing needed for success with some goal in life. A broken ladder may be a warning that you are not taking the necessary step-by-step process to achieve your goals. This may also be expressing a feeling that some rudimentary items you need are not available to you. The instability of a ladder requires a slow and centered approach to your climb, signaling a need to take each step in your life with care, grace, and ease.

The size and shape of the ladder can offer subtle layers to your interpretation. A ladder that is too short is an indication that you have the right concept, but not quite enough of what is needed to achieve a goal in your life. Something on top of the ladder may signify a yearning for a higher state of consciousness or accomplishment. Looking down from the top of the ladder might represent acknowledging what it took to achieve what has recently occurred.

Languages

Universal Landscape: Unconscious messages not yet decipherable or understood.

Dreaming Lens: Were you speaking in a language that you don't know? Was the language real or made up? Was someone else speaking to you? Were you witnessing a conversation between others? Were you frustrated in not being able to understand, or were you able to glean some meaning?

Personal Focus: This interpretation applies only to a language that you do not know or was created out of the dream world. If you yourself know more than one language, then dreaming in different languages is a reflection of where you are in your life and what the language in question means for you from your past.

Words are the basis of all thought and all reality. When words that you do not understand show up in a dream, the unconscious is deliberately masking some information by changing the rules. Use the Dreaming Lens to assess the height of the stakes. This would

apply both to the information that is being expressed by the unconscious as well as the emotional meaning attached to your reaction
to being unable to decipher any literal meaning.

If you recognize the language being spoken by virtue of sounds
and cadences, then apply whatever associations you have with that
culture to the Dreaming Lens. If the language is made up and you
can remember any specific words, sounds, or phrases, use them in
your process to see if you can draw any parallels with words you
know. There may be a rhythmic or phonic connection to the non-
sense words of your dream. Do not be afraid of being overly literal.

If someone else is speaking to you in the dream, then the message is coming from the deep unconscious. If you are speaking the
foreign tongue yourself, it may indicate that the new information
is already integrated as part of you. More investigation will likely
need to be done before you will be able to understand and utilize
the information being presented.

Lesbian Sex

Universal Landscape: Integration of Character Aspects in the feminine principle.

Dreaming Lens: Were you participating in lesbian sex? Were you witnessing such a sex act? Were you aroused by this? Did it repulse or
confuse you? Was this in alignment with your sense of personal sexuality? Did it intrigue you? Did you know the sex partners involved?

Personal Focus: Any sexual act in a dream connects symbolically to the
process of integration and the joining together of different aspects of
the personality. In the case of lesbian sex, what is being highlighted
are elements of the feminine principle, such as nurturing, caretaking,
and creativity. This is included as a separate term as it is not uncommon for heterosexual women to have dreams of lesbian sex when life
events focus on this energy. Dreaming of sex with another woman is

often reported by women during pregnancy. If the dreamer identifies as a lesbian, then such dreams should be explored through the concepts outlined in the term Sexual Intercourse.

Watching lesbian sex is a waking-life fantasy for many heterosexual men. However, this image has more to do with integration of inner aspects of the feminine principle for a man when such a dream appears. It is a natural process of evolution for every man, as he matures through life, to become more in touch with his feminine nature. A truly integrated man has access to his own creativity, receptivity, nurturing qualities, and sensitivity.

Lighthouse

Universal Landscape: Indication of conscious awareness and emotional safety.

Dreaming Lens: Where was the lighthouse? Was it in operating condition? Was it daytime or nighttime? Was there a storm or fog present? Was there anyone inhabiting it?

Personal Focus: A lighthouse is located on a shoreline and provides perspective in an otherwise concealed landscape. During a fog, the lighthouse emits both a visual and audio clue to allow travelers to navigate through what would otherwise be dangerous territory.

To get to the core of this symbol, we begin with where a lighthouse is located. The ocean represents the deep emotional unconscious parts of the human psyche. Land is what is conscious and within our awareness. The shoreline is where these two vastly different landscapes meet. Because they are so very different in nature, the boundary that exists between land and sea can be a strange and sometimes treacherous place. This is true of the shoreline where the land meets the sea in the real world. In the world of symbolic meaning, these two dichotomous elements of the human condition interact with each other in a dramatic and sometimes violent way.

To be more specific, a person on land must be careful of the violence of crashing waves and the depths of the ocean so as not to be drowned. Someone traveling at sea must avoid destroying their vessel on the jagged edges of land that sometimes appear unexpectedly. Viewed through the prism of symbolic interpretation, when you are grounded in conscious awareness (on land), there is a danger that unconscious emotions can overtake you and drag you under. Conversely, when you are exploring the unconscious emotions (being at sea), you run the risk of being unexpectedly damaged by thoughts and ideas that may jut out and inadvertently trip you up.

The next layer of interpretation connects with what is happening when a lighthouse is put into operation. During a storm or heavy fog, the lighthouse provides a distinct indicator of where the land is located for the safety of boats and ships at sea. The important element for interpretation, however, is the conditions that cause a lighthouse to be necessary: storms, fog, or both.

Both of these weather-related phenomenon arise when water is drawn into the air. When emotional content (water) mixes violently with the thought process (air) it can produce a chaotic experience (fog or storm) that leaves you blind. If there is a lighthouse in your dream, you may want to consider what is happening in your life that may require a safe port in a storm or navigation through the invisibility of a fog.

A lighthouse in a still calm scenario points to the anticipation of difficulty to come. One that is inoperable may be expressing fears around being ready to face challenging interactions and still maintain your sense of safety. An abandoned lighthouse may hearken back to an earlier protective measure that no longer serves you. What you are doing at the lighthouse in the dream should contribute to your interpretation. (See also Beams of Light.)

Lightning

Universal Landscape: Sudden awareness or enlightenment born of divergent, confronting ideas.

Dreaming Lens: Where was the flash of lightning in your dream? Were you witnessing from a safe distance, or were you in danger? Were you indoors or outdoors? Were you actually struck by the lightning?

Personal Focus: Imagine you are in a dark field at night; you can't see where you are at all. Suddenly, there is a flash of lightning. For that brief moment, you can see everything around you. You see where it is safe to move and where it might be dangerous. Avoid the cliff off to your left. If you go too far to the right, you might be carried away by the rushing river. The lightning abates and you are plunged back into darkness once more. However, now you have the awareness of where you are and can navigate with much more confidence and surety. This is the essence of lightning.

Also consider how lightning is formed. Thick clouds contain both positive and negative charges. The positive charges gather on the top of the clouds and the negative charges drop to the bottom. When they are thrust together by the right weather conditions, the reaction of opposites explodes in an electrical charge of great violence. Therefore, lightning represents the flashes of brilliant awareness that come when polar opposite views come crashing together. These contradictory views should cancel each other out. However, what actually happens is that they reveal a brand new viewpoint that would otherwise have not been knowable.

At this point in time, there is no definitive theory as to why lightning forms. This scientific ambiguity must, therefore, be figured into the meaning of the image. In this way, the awareness and enlightenment that lighting symbolically brings is, ultimately, mysterious in origin.

Another nuance to the meaning of lightning comes from a little known fact. The most brilliant flash that we see when lightning strikes doesn't actually come from the sky. It is, in fact, a reactive charge that emanates from the ground and moves upward in response to the initial charge that starts in the clouds above. To use this distinction in your interpretation, remember that the initial spark of awareness may come from the heavens and, therefore, be associated with higher thinking or spiritual origins. But don't forget that the full charge of enlightenment comes from the ground, representing knowledge that was already present in human consciousness. It just needed a divine reminder to initiate it into full expression.

How you experience the lightning in your dream is key to your interpretation. If it is harmful or feels dangerous, then your dream is reflecting Shadow material. This could be anything that inspires the kind of fear that comes from gaining knowledge or information; as the saying goes, ignorance is bliss. Look to where you are being guided to choose a path that you are resisting, even though you may know it is your highest choice. If you are delighted by the beauty of the lightening, then your unconscious may be expressing gratitude for the sudden new awareness that is present or right over the horizon. (See also Thunder.)

Light Switch

Universal Landscape: Access to creative power. The assumption of success.

Dreaming Lens: Was the light switch turned on or off? Was it switched on and/or off repeatedly? Was it working properly? Were there exposed wires or was the mechanism safely covered? Was the switch on a wall or on a light fixture? Were you unable to find the light switch? What type of switch was it?

Personal Focus: Turning a switch reflects the need to make a change in some situation. Since most have only two positions, the desired effect is likely to connect to causing something to start or stop. We go through life with an inherent expectation that our light switches are always going to work, barring unforeseen circumstances. This implies a level of trust and faith in our ability to instigate the desired effect when this symbol appears in a dream.

Light connects to the power to create. Being able to access this energy and turn it on and off is the essence of this symbol. What occurs around a light switch in the Dreaming Lens will illuminate your current relationship with your ability to utilize this force at will.

Turning a switch on may point to a need to begin unleashing the creative force within you. Turning one off could mean a need to stop and take a break from some ongoing process. Be equally willing to consider that turning off a light can indicate an unwillingness to look at something as it really is. A working switch means your sense of control is intact, whereas one that is ineffectual means some area of your life is no longer responding to your demands. The safety of the switch is also important. Exposed wiring could mean that danger or uncertainty is present when you tap into your creativity.

The physical action required by a switch can add texture to your interpretation—an older style connects to older ways of getting things accomplished. A pull chord might mean there is more effort involved than with a modern fixture that works at the touch of your finger, connecting you to your source with ease. A dimmer might mean that subtlety is required in the area that is under transition. Additionally, if the switch cannot offer you the amount of light you require, you may be experiencing a dimming of your energy.

Lips

Universal Landscape: Control of communication, intimacy.

Dreaming Lens: Were the lips that were prominent in the dream your own or someone else's? Were they red, or another color? Were they painted with lipstick or other makeup? Were they attractive or grotesque? What were they doing? How do they fit in with the rest of the face? Were they disembodied?

Personal Focus: The lips are the sensuous guardians of the center of communication and intimate exchange. They are the *first mechanism of control* over what comes into the body with regard to nurturance. They are the *last mechanism of control* over what goes out from us in terms of communication.

The color of lips can range from blue to red, with the former associated with a lack of warmth, and the latter as filled with life-giving blood and, therefore, passion. When someone's lips turn blue, they are literally freezing to death, making this a potentially high stakes image. These details should be considered if the color of lips were prominent in the dream imagery. How much control are you exerting over your communication and your willingness to be intimate with others? The color of your dream lips may reveal this.

The essence of this symbol is intimate connection, whether that is to the world through words, or to another person via a kiss. Just as when lips meet in life, there is a mingling of fluids and all that that implies. Lips meeting in a dream can indicate a need or desire to mingle with and absorb another mode of communication. Lips that are too loose can allow communication to flow indiscriminately, whereas those that are pursed too tightly can indicate holding back with restraint. It is your job to decide whether this editing is necessary, or a function of fear and/or resistance.

Lost Objects

Universal Landscape: Preoccupation with lack and limitation.

Dreaming Lens: What were you looking for? Where were you searching? Did you know what you were looking for? How long were you looking? Were you alone in your search, or did you have help? How important was the item you were looking for?

Personal Focus: This is a fairly frequent universal dream that represents a primary human experience of discomfort. The feeling of searching for something important and being unable to find it is challenging enough when it happens in life. In the language of symbols, it also taps into a deep fear shared by all people; the elusive search for meaning that all of us have to face from time to time in our lives.

On the face of it, a dream of searching for a lost object has a primary purpose of helping us relieve stress so we can wake up the next day and face our day-to-day lives with more psychic balance. This is the purpose for all recurring dreams of this nature. If you have this dream on a regular basis, it may simply be a convenient way for your unconscious to process the pressures of everyday living. However, if your dream feels as if it requires a deeper investigation, use the Dreaming Lens to guide your interpretation.

What it is that you are searching for should be your first consideration. Your personal associations with the object will reveal what you sense is currently elusive. When in doubt, ask yourself, "What does this thing do, or what is it for?" Keys represent your access to the various compartments of your life. Your wallet connects you to abundance and the ability to meet your needs in the world. A more personal or specific item should be viewed through whatever meaning you assign to it. If there is no specific thing that you are searching for or you do not know what it is that you have lost, the dream may be pointing to a free-floating sense of being inadequately prepared for some situation in your life.

Where you are looking offers the next shade of meaning. Your own home connects to your personal sense of self. Any other environment should be used to guide you; where you feel that something has been lost may be telling you that a certain area of your life has left you feeling incomplete.

Magician

Universal Landscape: The power to manifest the unexplained or unexpected.

Dreaming Lens: Were you the magician or were you watching a magician? Did the magician have an assistant? Were you the assistant? Was the illusion well crafted? Was the magic presented typical, or dream-enhanced? Were your feelings about the magician comfortable or uncomfortable?

Personal Focus: The Magician is one of the primary archetypes that make up the human condition. They represent the part of us that can use magic, divine power, and the forces of will to create anything we desire. However, there is a large distinction between this as an archetypal figure and the popularized image of a stage magician engaged in the act of entertainment.

In the world of magic, the modern-day entertainer is an illusionist who presents us with the impossible. We know that there is a trick to what he or she is doing, yet we find ourselves awestruck. This type of magician relates to the concept of manipulation.

The personality, style of show, size of venue, and quality of the magician is what offers an accurate interpretation. A bad performance might lead you to consider ways in which you don't effectively wield your power to create. A mesmerizing performance in a majestic venue could be tapping you into the greater energy that is available to you through a belief in magical occurrences and synchronicity. The presence of an assistant invites you to consider that even a magician needs to call upon others for help in grounding them while they master an illusion.

Remember that an illusion that is self-serving is a betrayal of authenticity. A magician in your dream may be a call to investigate the amount of truth you stand in and the illusion you may still be hanging on to. An archetypal image of a Magician would appear in other scenarios than on the stage. He would not be dressed in costume, and his magic would be transformative in nature and not a function of hidden mechanisms. This distinction is important to make when such a character appears in a dream. There is a continuum being expressed here: on the one end is cheap showmanship while the other holds the true use of the mysteries of the invisible world. Where your dream falls on this continuum may give insight into your development in this area. Are you stepping into faith and your innate power to manifest your desires, or are you still trying to manipulate life into giving you what you want?

Mail

Universal Landscape: Anticipation of communication.

Dreaming Lens: Were you waiting for the mail to arrive? Were you sending mail? Was the mail in question delivered properly? Was the address known or unknown? Was the mail a surprise or something expected? Was the mail delivered to your home, or did you have to pick it up in a post office?

Personal Focus: Our relationship to postal mail has changed greatly since the advent of e-mail. It is now considered so slow that it is routinely referred to as "snail mail." While our current perceptions have changed, the essence of this symbol connects to the origins of mail and its impact on the world. Sending messages by way of traders who traveled between communities was the beginning of the spread of knowledge. The mark of a great civilization would have been a construct devoted solely to this purpose. In America, this was epitomized by the Pony Express and what we know today as the United States Postal Service.

Communication between two parties is symbolic of intellect and the inner process of deduction and decision-making. The slow speed and back and forth nature of mail adds the texture of anticipation. Putting a thought in writing connects to the permanence of a thought expressed.

Mail in a dream could connect to communication that is slower than desired. Junk mail is akin to anxiety and the background chatter in the mind, where information like an important letter can get lost in a pile of unwanted catalogs. A dream could connect to the need to ferret through the unimportant to find clarity. Since the majority of mail is comprised of bills to be paid, this might symbolize being put on notice for the price you will have to pay for some choice in life.

Mail Carrier

Universal Landscape: Connection to important communication.

Dreaming Lens: Was the mail carrier delivering mail in your dream? Was the mail delivered to your home? What was the gender of the mail carrier? Was the context of where you saw the mail carrier appropriate? Were you the mail carrier?

Personal Focus: This symbol may soon be going out of the collective consciousness. As computers and modern technology become the norm, the delivery of mail to our homes is becoming a less primary way of staying connected to the outside world. While this may be true, we still live in a time where on an almost daily basis, a human being comes to our front door and delivers items of interest and importance to one degree or another. As a Character Aspect in a dream, a mail carrier is the part of your own personality that remains connected to the larger circles of your life, but is detached from your core personality.

Because of the almost antique nature of this type of communication, this symbol should be thought of as a bit of a throwback to a slower time. The information sent through the mail has a different level of importance associated with it. Be mindful of this distinction; the message may be less important and, therefore, relegated to the slow transaction of snail mail. It is just as possible that possessing the original document is what the priority is, which can only be done through channels that involve human interaction.

The Dreaming Lens will offer key information for a satisfying interpretation. Also to be considered is your relationship (or lack thereof) to the mail carrier in your waking life. Whatever information you have about this individual should be factored into the Character Aspect you assign to this person from your dream. There is a fairly recent cultural meaning to a postal worker that has entered the collective. The term "going postal" has become synonymous with violent outbursts connected with overwhelming stress. If the dream has any dark or shadowy elements to it, you may want to explore the mailman as a Character Aspect of an undercurrent of violent feelings that are just waiting for an inciting incident to allow them to explode.

What a mail carrier is delivering in a dream offers an important second layer of meaning. What new information is your unconscious trying to send you? (See also Mail.)

Masturbation

Universal Landscape: Self-expressed sexuality.

Dreaming Lens: Were you masturbating in the dream? Was someone else masturbating you? Were you masturbating someone else? Were you watching the act of masturbation?

Personal Focus: Any image that involves sexuality is going to be complex and is best interpreted by at least starting with the symbolic meaning first, and breaking down the image to its basic parts. Masturbation has a specific purpose, which is to induce orgasm. There are two functions that might be assigned to orgasm. One is the pleasurable relief from stress that it provides and the other serves to remind the masturbator of their sexuality. The Dreaming Lens will offer some insight as to which direction to go with your interpretation. Also of importance is the current state of your sex life and your relationship to your sexuality in general.

If there is another person involved, consider him or her as a Character Aspect of your own personality. If you are watching someone masturbate (or you are masturbating someone else), then the qualities you assign this person may be the part of you that has access to elements of your sexuality at the time of this dream. The same is true if someone is masturbating you; however, this distinction connects more to an aspect of your personality that may be trying to stimulate a sexual response in you. The gender of this other person should be considered as well, no matter what your sexual preference. A man connects to the masculine principle of taking action whereas a woman embodies the feminine principle of being receptive.

The human sex drive contains the same power as the creative instinct. Masturbation in a dream may not necessarily be expressing the need to be sexual as much as the need to be creatively expressive. Look to where your life might be calling you to wake up your sense of passion. (See also Sex).

Massacre(s)

Universal Landscape: An enormous transformation in personal ideology.

Dreaming Lens: Who was massacred in your dream? How many people were killed? How were they killed? Did you come upon the end result of a massacre, or were you present for the killing? Were you responsible? If not, do you know who was?

Personal Focus: A massacre is an event of great magnitude by virtue of the number of deaths caused by a singular force. This extends to include the notion that the murders are indiscriminate and unnecessary. Any death is a powerful symbol of transformation and change, as it always portends a rebirth of some kind. A mass death is interpretable as any death would be—change so great that it can only be understood as the passing of something old to make way for the rebirth of something new.

The distinction of massacre adds several elements to this interpretation that should be considered. First, the large number of deaths that quantify a massacre implies an enormity to the transformation that is occurring. Look to your life for evidence of some change or shift that feels inordinately large in scale and you will probably find the stimulus for this dream. Since people in your dreams represent parts of your personality, the loss of large numbers could indicate that many old thoughts or patterns are being left behind.

Secondly, there is the indiscriminate and unnecessary quality of killing that goes along with the horror of a massacre. This implies callousness to the action, but such a perspective may only be from the victim's side. Since you are both killer and victim in your dream, this element of your investigation may prove more elusive. If you know who was responsible for the massacre, use that information to guide you to what part of your unconscious is acting out by expressing just how greatly things are being stirred up. If you are not aware of who the perpetrator is, you have that much more exploring to do before you find a satisfying interpretation.

Thirdly, there is often a political motivation to such events in the real world. In this way, you may be expressing change and shift of an ideological nature. Look to ways in which your beliefs and values may be undergoing transformation.

Mirror

Universal Landscape: Self-observation; cause and effect.

Dreaming Lens: What was the reality of the image in the mirror? Was there a disparity between the image and the object it reflected? Was the image clear? What was the integrity of the mirror (cracked, broken, or whole)? What was the style and age of the mirror?

Personal Focus: Mirrors can be confounding and confusing. Not only do they reverse everything that they reflect, but their images can give a sense of reality that they do not actually possess. They accurately reflect an image, but are not the image itself. A mirror is comparable to the basic principle of cause and effect. You can use it effectively as a tool to examine the current state of things. However, in order to change what you don't like in the reflection, you must work on the object being reflected rather than alter the mirror itself.

Who or what is seen in a mirror in a dream represents that which the *unconscious mind* is seeing. Consider whether the mirror image is accurate to how you see yourself in life. Looking straight into the mirror and being comfortable with what you see says that your self-appraisal is honest and real. If what you see seems off kilter in some way, it could be an invitation to look at where you are being inauthentic. This could indicate something you are deliberately hiding from others or something more mundane, such as being more concerned with how others see or how you *wish you were being* in the world, as opposed to how you really are being perceived.

The condition of a mirror should also be taken into account. For instance, a cracked mirror may be helping you process a feeling of ominous bad luck due to the Old Wives' tale common in Western culture that breaking a mirror brings dire consequences to the one who breaks it. A handheld mirror might be offering an intimate glimpse of self, one that is designed to privately monitor the image you project to the world. A full-length mirror could be pointing toward the need to see more of the whole picture of one's current life situations. Someone else's mirror might mean your individual sense of self is being determined at this time through someone else's values or perceptions. A mirror can contain the magical property of showing the truth about a situation when called upon, such as the queen's magic mirror in the story *Snow White*. Explore the theme of the dream for its profound truth.

Money

Universal Landscape: Abundance, power and freedom.

Dreaming Lens: Who had the money in the dream? Did you have more or less than you need or desire? Did you earn, find, borrow, or steal it? Was it clean conscience money, or money that had been laundered?

Personal Focus: Money is a complicated symbol to interpret because it stimulates intense emotional issues for most people. It is even more challenging to understand because of the illusive nature of money itself. Money is only as valuable as society agrees it to be. It wouldn't matter if we traded rocks or sticks instead of beautifully printed paper. What we call money is actually just symbolic of a commodity. Therefore, it is not wealth itself, but the representation of wealth. How much or how little you have is a measure of the power and freedom to attain what you desire by virtue of how much you possess.

In a dream, money often represents your inner resources. Your sense of personal value, power, or the ability to make something happen can be expressed by the symbol of money. As a symbol, large amounts of money can represent any sort of achievement or sense of fulfillment as an unconscious expression of desires met. No matter what the financial situation in your waking life, your dream state can find you available for limitless abundance or attached to absolute lack.

Since money in life is symbolic in nature, in the dream world it can represent *any form of abundance*. The appearance of money in a dream could connect to the acquisition of any desire, from a new sense of inner riches to outward expressions of expansion, such as a new relationship, job, or other appearance of a heart's desire. On the opposite side of the spectrum, money in a dream could be pointing out feelings of lack you are experiencing in life. As a wish fulfillment or compensatory dream, connecting to money could be balancing out feelings of limitation. Money that is counterfeit is revealing a relationship to abundance that is false or inauthentic. Though it may look real, it has been manufactured with dubious intentions. In a dream, this might point to ways in which you are trying to get away with presenting yourself as bigger than you really are.

Also be willing to look at the various elements in your current situation; are there circumstances in your life that are costing you more than you can afford? This can apply to both material and emotional conditions. Look at the amount of money or lack of money in the dream as connoting how much or how little of some needed commodity appears in your life. This can be spiritual, emotional, or physical. How abundant do you feel?

Monuments

Universal Landscape: Collective expressions of cultural greatness.

Dreaming Lens: What country were you in? What type of monument was in your dream? Was it something that you recognized from actual life? If it was from your imagination, was the location clear or was it also fictitious? Were you exploring the monument as a tourist or as a local?

Personal Focus: This term is designed to cover in a general way any number of dozens of images that might appear in a dream. Structures such as the Statue of Liberty, the Eiffel Tower, the Taj Mahal, and the Great Pyramids are all examples of a culture erecting monuments to their own importance. This has been happening since the beginning of civilization. These enormous expressions of power and technology are designed to celebrate the accomplishments of a society and provide a collective projection of greatness that help the masses feel safe and protected, as well as proud of their accomplishments, and feel a connection to their history.

There are several layers that must be explored if such a structure should appear in a dream. First, identify the culture being represented by the structure itself and consider your relationship to that culture. The presence of a monument in a dream may be revealing a sense of cultural pride. This can be so, even if you do not readily identify with the society that the monument represents. Dreams often emerge from the collective unconscious and when this occurs, it can be helpful and revealing to do some research exploring the civilization in question and how elements of that culture you may identify with at this time in your life.

If the monument in your dream is fictitious, it will be helpful to work with whatever you can remember about it when formulating your interpretation. Nothing should be considered unimportant and even the most insignificant detail can have meaning. Additionally, it is perfectly valid to use your creativity to work with this type of symbol; after all, the ideas that rise out of your imagination come from the same place in your unconscious as dream images. Ask yourself what parts of your deepest levels of expression want to see the light of day and just might lead you to a sense of greatness.

When this type of image appears in a dream, you are definitely exploring the realm of your life experience on a fairly large scale. Be willing to see if this is a dream about your connection to the world at large in a positive and powerful light, or if there is some area in your life where grandiosity is getting the best of you. The Dreaming Lens will offer you the clues you need to come to a satisfying interpretation.

Moon (Moonlight)

Universal Landscape: Feminine aspect of the life force energy.

Dreaming Lens: Was the moon full? Where in the sky did it appear? How bright was the moonlight? Was it Earth's moon, or a dreamscape night sky? Were you on the moon?

Personal Focus: The moon is a very powerful symbol, just as it is an enormous energetic force in our daily life on Earth. As the heavenly counterpart to the masculine energy of the Sun, the moon represents the feminine aspects of life. The primary essence of the moon is its constant changeability. In this regard, the moon symbolizes the ephemeral quality of life and all of the different cycles that human beings experience. If the moon plays a prominent role in your dream, your interpretation should begin with the notion that change is afoot.

A distinction should be made about how the moon appears in your dream. If the moon itself is visible to you in the skyscape of your dream, then you are looking at the source of emotional power. If your dream illuminates the light of the moon itself as it falls upon Earth then you are dreaming of the effect or impact of the moon's magic. If your dream actually takes place on the moon, then you are literally visiting the seat of your unconscious directly; such a dream should be considered a very deliberate snapshot of your current experience of how the invisible side of life is impacting the visible.

The emotional side of life is represented by the moon. This includes all that is changeable and all that responds to the ebb and flow of life. Because of its unquestionable universality to the human race, the moon in dreams should be considered with very broad strokes of interpretation. The Dreaming Lens is most important because it is the position, presence, or placement of the moon that is the key to its power. The moon also connects to cycles. It regulates the pulse of the Earth with its enormous gravitational influence. The presence of the moon in a dream may indicate the course of a cycle of an emotional process or transformation.

Mother Mary/Quan Yin

Universal Landscape: Archetypal Character Aspect: Healing through love.

Dreaming Lens: Who appeared to you in your dream? How did they appear? In what form did they appear? Did they speak? Did you speak to them? Was there a specific message delivered with or without words? Was the experience blissful?

Personal Focus: While there are many other archetypal representations of the power of love, this term will limit itself to these two as they are perhaps the most widely recognized symbols of divine forgiveness in the history of the human race. In dream work, they should be treated symbolically as Archetypes and their appearance in a dream indicates that you are experiencing a high level of self-discovery and integration.

Mary, the mother of Jesus, and Quan Yin, Buddhist goddess of mercy and compassion, embody the feminine principle in its highest evolution. The feminine principle connects to the power of love and receptivity. Both of these figures are revered by millions as the purveyors of forgiveness and unconditional love. Though the traditions that created each of them could not be more different, what they offer to those who turn to them in hours of need is exactly the same.

One of the most difficult challenges that all human beings face is the process of forgiveness. This applies to others, but even more elusive is the ability to forgive ourselves. The human mind is not built for unconditional love, even though it is a concept that many who travel the path of service continually strive for. No matter how she may appear to you, the Archetype of the Divine Mother can help you inch your way out of shame and resentment and move you toward the healing that can only come through love and mercy.

The appearance of one of these great figures in a dream is to put you on notice that you are in a moment of elevating consciousness and integration toward Self. It is not uncommon for any archetypal figure to be silent in a dream; it is their mere presence that embodies the impact of the dream. If words and messages are present in the dream, take them to heart and do so literally. However, if this is not the case, your best use of such a dream is silent gratitude for the gift of such a powerful experience of elevated consciousness.

Mountains

Universal Landscape: New ideas, constructs, or choices. Challenges or obstacles to surmount.

Dreaming Lens: What was your physical relationship to the mountains in your dream? Were you high in elevation or glancing up from the valley surface? What terrain did you see on the mountain-side, from barren rock formations to soft green slopes? Were you climbing a mountain?

Personal Focus: Mountains are formed when two opposing vectors of movement in the Earth's crust push against each other and rise upward to form a new land mass. Therefore, the mountain is symbolic of the newly formed, high vantage place that rises up out of conflict and confrontation. Remember that changes on our planet's surface first begin in the combustible core below. This relates mountains to the passion, aggression, and other friction-causing emotional states that occur in the lower depths of the unconscious that, in the long run, build new, higher terrain upon which you can see more of your life.

A person on or near a mountain may be filled with a need to conquer it, as in climbing Mount Everest just because "it is there." Given this, an obstacle or challenge that arises out of opposing forces and is generated by deeper conflicts is what your dream mountain describes. What you do with or on the mountain and how you feel about it is the next level of interpretation.

If you are resting in a peaceful mountain setting, consider that you are in a place of regeneration after a transformation that may have been created by a previously challenging time. Looking at the view from the peak indicates a higher vantage point from which to see the consequences of your inner conflict and where to go next. Climbing up is to be facing the challenges ahead of you, whereas climbing down, though easier, connects to the aftermath of conflicts that are already solved. The upward climber must remember that, once at the top, he or she has only completed half the journey.

Movies

Universal Landscape: Memories and desires; controlling reality.

Dreaming Lens: Were you watching a movie in your dream? Where were you and where was the movie being played? Was the dream itself unfolding as if it were a movie? Were you making a movie in the dream? What was the content or subject of the movie? How did it make you feel?

Personal Focus: Movies are so ingrained in Western culture it is difficult to separate them out from the human experience as something distinct from how we live life day to day. This is especially so with regard to the way in which a film can capture historical events and present altered versions of moments in time, which may be seen by future viewers as actual facts.

Research has shown that the areas of the brain that are stimulated by the images we see in movies are the same as those activated by real events. This blurs the line between fantasy and reality in an alarming way: Movies and dreams are not very different from each other. What is captured on film has a way of becoming real in the imagination of the human race. Even the most unbelievable storyline is made possible through the magic of film. In this way, the symbolic meaning of the movies is the incredible drive the human race has to make our most passionate desires come to life.

A common dream that many people report is to have the sense that the dream itself is a movie. The first distinction that should be made when considering the symbolic meaning of a movie in a dream is which side of desire the film is addressing. One connects to manifesting a fantasy into reality and the other embodies rewriting history as you perhaps wish it was. In either case, the presence of a movie in a dream is likely expressing a wish to have more control over how life is being perceived. Ask yourself what area of your life is feeling unreal, or that you wish were different. (See also Television.)

Music

Universal Landscape: Exalted expression and universal communication.

Dreaming Lens: Were you hearing music in your dream? Were you making music? Were you aware of the source of the music? Was the music familiar or strange to you? Was it pleasant or unpleasant? Was it in the background of your dream, or did it hold more primary focus?

Personal Focus: The structure of music is mathematical in nature. This is what makes it perfectly universal. Music might be considered the highest form of creative expression available to the human race. This is evidenced by the importance our society places on music, musicians and the powerful influence that music exerts over people. In all cultures throughout history, the presence of music has created the possibility of people being connected through joy. Not only does music have the capacity to bring human beings together in a shared sense of ecstasy, it has been shown to exert powerful influences over animals and plant life as well.

When music appears in a dream, your first consideration should be to examine areas in your waking life where you are allowing yourself (or not allowing yourself) to connect to spontaneous self-expression. If you are hearing music in your dream, you may be receiving messages from your unconscious to open yourself to a deeper, more joyful sense of life. The degree of pleasantness of the music in your dream may represent your current relationship to your intuitive and emotional nature that goes beyond intellectual understanding.

If you are making the music in the dream, you may want to examine areas of your life where creative endeavors are ready to thrive. If background music plays a pivotal role in your dream, you may want to consider this as an underscoring to subtle, emotional issues that may be getting ready to emerge into your conscious awareness.

In the same way that music deepens the emotional meaning in a film, music may serve to highlight the importance of a dream. If this seems to be the case, remember the manipulative nature of this use of music's power. You may want to examine ways in which your emotions may be influencing your view of some area of your life in ways that may not be organic or authentic. This could show up in the form of drama in a current situation where using a more pragmatic and less emotional approach might be more effective.

Naked

Universal Landscape: Vulnerability.

Dreaming Lens: Did you know you were naked? Was it a surprise to you that you were naked? What was your reaction? Was it horrifying, funny, scary, or perhaps not a big deal? Did you attempt to cover up? Was anyone else naked?

Personal Focus: This is one of the most common dream images experienced by almost everyone at some point or another. It expresses the fear we all have of being vulnerable or exposed in life in a way for which we aren't prepared. In Western culture, and especially in the United States, the public is generally not very comfortable with nudity. Given this predisposition to cover up our naked selves, it would be a natural representation in the dream state for nakedness to indicate feeling exposed in some area of your life. Where you are naked in a dream and who you are naked in front of will provide you with all the clues you will need for an accurate interpretation of such a dream.

Nightmares

Universal Landscape: Dreams that help us maintain emotional and psychological balance and equilibrium in the face of stress and fear.

Dreaming Lens: Was your dream a recurring nightmare, or something original? Did you wake up from the nightmare? Was there a specific theme to the nightmare (being chased, being in danger, known or unknown assailant)? Was the danger from something real or fantastical? Was the setting of the dream frightening, or was it innocuous with terrifying undertones? How did the dream leave you upon waking?

Personal Focus: Nightmares are those frightening and often very memorable dreams that can wake you up and leave you riddled with anxiety. While there may be underlying neurological causes for nightmares, for the most part they are simply a fact in the world of dreams: sooner or later, you are likely to have one.

There are many emerging theories about the neurological structure of nightmares and what some of the value of having them might be with regard to stress and psychic balance. However, these don't address the question that most people want answered, which is what causes them?

Of course, the answer to that question is that we still don't know what causes nightmares, or any dreams for that matter. We do know that there are some medications that can impact the quality and intensity of dreams, including the frequency of nightmares. There are plenty of old wives' tales associated with activities that can supposedly bring them on, such as eating red meat or other heavy meals before going to sleep. There are even those that believe the direction you lie in while you sleep can cause bad dreams. These are not, however, proven scientific facts, nor are they validated by my personal experience of interpreting thousands of dreams over many years.

There are a number of terms in the dictionary that connect to specific, universally experienced nightmares. If your dream contains any of the symbols that can be found within these pages, use the information you find to help you identify an effective interpretation. If the imagery of your nightmare is atypical and not to be found here, there are a number of ways to do further exploration.

The Internet can provide a means for research on anything that has some measure of reality associated with it. Anything more fantastical can be approached by using your creativity or the process of free association.

Nightmares are not easily forgotten and the residual emotional reaction they sometimes generate can linger in our conscious awareness far longer than the fond memories of our more pleasant dreams. However, this inherent capacity to remember them often makes them easy to work with. Additionally, people are sometimes highly motivated to understand them because of the upset they can create. If dreams are indeed messages from the unconscious, a nightmare is one way it has of telling us to pay attention as there may be Shadow material coming up. This always means there is something important to learn.

Numbers

Universal Landscape: The building blocks of all reality.

Dreaming Lens: Did a number itself feature in your dream? Was it the number of something that was significant? Was there more than one digit, or was your dream number from one to nine? Was there calculation involved? Did the number have a specific purpose, such as a phone number or address?

Personal Focus: Numbers are the building blocks for our understanding of how life is constructed. The movement of the Earth, moon, and other planets are geometrical in nature. Music is simply math expressed as tone. Digital technology reduces various data to numeric sequences and then back again to its original form. Our need to describe physical phenomena led us to create nine whole numbers that, in different sequences, can express anything from gravity to the speed of light, or the way visitors can identify which house on the block is yours.

The universally accepted meaning of numbers is what informs the discipline of numerology. From this tradition, we get the foundational and metaphysical interpretation of the nine whole numbers. Use this as a base to inform how you consider the image from your dream with which the number is associated. If there is more than one digit involved, add all the values together until you arrive at a final, single number. For example, if an address is 115 Main Street, you would add one plus one plus five and get seven.

The explanations below are meant to be read in order in one sitting, no matter what specific number you are interested in examining. There is a structure to the way the meaning of each digit expands on its predecessor, which will give you a powerful sense of the whole system and aid you in using numbers in the interpretation process.

One: One represents beginnings and is the starting point of existence. In human terms, it is the self alone. It is the idea before any action is taken. As such, it embodies the concept of potential and that which has yet to happen. In fact, the energy of one is limited by its inability to do anything by itself. However, it also connects to stillness and the cultivation of desire that precedes movement. One is the beginning of the journey, which can be a very exciting energy. However, the journey can bring with it the challenge of loneliness and isolation.

Two: When a second joins the one and two is formed, partnership is created. The concept of relativity evolves out of the energy of two, as the one has something to which it experiences itself as relative to. The one can now know itself as Self, because there is that which is *Other*. All of the elements of two are embodied in this idea—partnership, duality, opposites, yin/yang, balance, sharing, to name just a few. The Shadow side of two is the potential for collapsing into one another and losing the sense of Self.

Three: When two are gathered, eventually their energy will create a new element, and a third is born. Three is the number of creativity. A powerful energy, there are many examples of the concept of three.

Mother-father-child is perhaps the most universal. The holy trinity in Catholicism is another instance. The artist, the paint, and the finished work is just one case that can be applied to any creative endeavor. In music, a trine is the simplest and perhaps most pleasing harmony. In the world of geometry, it is only when you have three points to work with that you can create an actual shape and accurately define a location in space. The challenge of three is a lack of grounding and separation from reality. This is because three relates so strongly to the drive to create, that feeling unable to do so would be the fear-based side of this energy.

Four: When you add a fourth point to a triangle, you end up with a square. Four is the number of structure. Once the creative impulse has been satisfied, it is time for solidification, which can be accomplished by the power of four. A wonderful weight-bearing shape, a square is what allows for building the foundation on which the creative energies of three can be supported. Four connects to the establishment of institutions, order, rules, and regulations. While a number of great strength, it can engender a sense of limitation and the concept of restraint.

Five: What follows the foundational sense of four is the freedom of five. Once a structure has been established, there is now a sense of safety and security for exploration. The number five embodies this expressiveness. The human body expresses the number five as represented by the four limbs and the head. The ability for the body to move about through space is a vibrant and exhilarating experience. In this way, five symbolizes joy and bliss. With this, comes the shadow of freedom; indulgence. This expression of five can carry grave consequences such as compulsion and addiction.

Six: Six is the number of partnership, marriage, creative collaboration, and balance. After the freedom of five, there is a need for stability, which is provided by the even number six. This energy can also be seen as a pairing of two threes. If three is about primal creativity at an individual level, combining two systems of three allows for six to engender worldly partnerships and the concept of marriage and union. This number represents partnership on every level: business, social, educational, and spiritual. In personal realms, the number six represents the happy union of opposites within us and the integration of our own opposing forces, such as containing two powerful emotions that contradict each other. The challenge of the six energy connects to responsibility and a sense of burden.

Seven: After all the work in the external world that brought us to the concept of partnership, we are now prepared for a more elevated experience of human expression. Seven is the number of spirituality and higher thought, which is only possible after the basic human needs are met. We are now free to look up and contemplate our existence in a more esoteric manner. Meditation and any consideration of the interior landscape of our humanity is governed by the number seven. This includes thought, contemplation, mysticism, prayer, faith, psychology, and any endeavor that seeks to understand life from a higher perspective. This is a number we are all familiar with as significant: seven days of the week, seven deadly sins, seven notes in the diatonic scale. The challenge associated with this vibration is of getting lost in the ethers and losing contact with life on the ground.

Eight: After spiritual matters have been made manifest, great abundance is possible. Eight is the number of infinity and all that it implies. This includes wealth of every kind: love, money, bliss, joy, and every amazing experience life has to offer. The concept of infinity states that there is no limitation in the universe; that time and space continue forever and ever in a way that is beyond our ability to truly comprehend. When we combine an understanding of infinity and abundance, we begin to realize that there is an endless supply of anything we could possibly desire, even those things that you perceive as limited and unavailable to us. Eight is the magic of seven in action. The shadow side to this is greed, hoarding, and withholding love.

Nine: The final number in the system is nine, which represents completion and endings. All things must end in order for the inevitable new beginning to follow. Nine embodies that cycle of existence that demands that change occur and that the old give way to the new. We have started the journey alone in the infinite (one), discovered opposites and relativity (two), invented creativity (three), built a foundation (four), expressed freedom (five), partnered with another (six), went inward to find spirituality (seven), expressed and enjoyed the rewards of the outside world (eight), and now we come to a close (nine). The shadow side to the completion energy of nine is the fear associated with endings and death.

Nun

Universal Landscape: Extreme devotion to spiritual principles.

Dreaming Lens: Was there a nun or nuns present in your dream? Were they known to you? Was the setting connected to a church or parochial school? Was this from your past? Was the scenario humorous or religious?

Personal Focus: While the Catholic religion only represents about twenty-five percent of Americans that claim a religious affiliation, the proliferation of this image in the media makes it a universal symbol for spiritual devotion. Also because of the media, this symbol carries with it a great number of potential shades of meaning that range from intense levels of respect to humorous irreverence. Additionally, for those who grew up in parochial school, as well as through the media, there is a powerful connection between nuns and strict discipline that often connected to corporal punishment. Your personal associations with nuns will, therefore, play a prominent role in how you interpret a dream with nuns in it.

On the serious end of the spectrum, the nun is the symbolic bride of Christ and represents a level of dedication that is unparalleled in our modern culture. In this light, the Character Aspect of a nun in a dream connects to a deeply committed spiritual side of your nature that is willing to sacrifice much for the sake of your beliefs. For those individuals with experience in the Catholic school system, nuns can also connect to a level of strictness that represents obstacles to spiritual connection because of distaste for the authoritative severity they can be known for. Lastly, the figure of the nun in their habits have been incorporated into the world of comedy and, for many people, this image sparks feelings of amusement and parody.

With this image, perhaps more than with others, the Personal Lens of your waking life relationship to nuns both currently and from your past will figure greatly in how you interpret a dream in which one appears.

Obstacles

Universal Landscape: Blocks to moving forward in life.

Dreaming Lens: What was the nature of the obstacle in your dream? How did this obstacle keep you stuck? How dangerous was the obstacle? Were you able to free yourself? Was it you that was stuck or was it someone else? How did you feel about being blocked by the obstacle?

Personal Focus: This is one of the most frequent dream images and has a very literal meaning associated with it. Life is often experienced as a function of facing the obstacles that we must traverse to get from where we are to where we desire to be. This is a daily struggle. Dreams often help us balance out our sense of frustration and despair as we face this particular challenge that is an absolutely universal human experience.

There are two elements to consider when making an interpretation of a dream of this kind: the obstacle and the part of the body or type of movement that is being blocked. The more important of the two is how you are stuck. If the feet or legs are involved, it connects to how you are moving through your life. Feet guide us in the directions we choose, so if you cannot walk, your dream is reflecting an inability to make a new choice or find your footing firmly on the ground you desire. If the legs are more prominently blocked, then your direction might be clear, but your ability to move forward is being hindered.

If your arms are being impacted the most, such as with netting, webs, or ropes, than issues of capability are probably at play. If this is the case, there may be some area in your life where your effectiveness, strength, or creative power is what is being blocked. Some dreams of this nature involve obstacles to the face where something is blocking your ability to see, hear, or use your voice effectively. When this occurs, look to a situation in your life where you are not able to be as expressive as you need to be.

The other crucial element is what is causing the obstacle. Some obstacles that appear often in dreams include nets, quicksand, sticky floors, ground that opens up, and heavy legs or feet. If you can make an association to the stuff that is blocking you, add this to your interpretation.

Old Man/Old Woman

Universal Landscape: Archetypal Character Aspect: Wisdom and guidance.

Dreaming Lens: Was it an old man or old woman in your dream? Was the dream character the same gender as you, or the opposite? Did he or she speak to you? Were you drawn to the dream character, or frightened? Did he or she have anything for you, share any wisdom, or offer you an object?

Personal Focus: The Old Man and his female counterpart, the Crone, are staples in Jungian psychology, as they are the archetypes that represent human wisdom. This is a Character Aspect shared by every human being on the planet and connects us to our inner guidance and our highest thought. We can only connect to this powerful energy when we can learn from our mistakes, a trait often associated with the insight that comes with age and usually is unavailable to us in our youth.

An older person that you know from life may also represent wisdom, but an interpretation of any person must connect to their traits as you experience them in life. When the Old Man or the Crone appears in archetypal fashion, the dream character *will not be known to you* personally, and a gift, insight, or wisdom might be offered to you. This Archetypal Character Aspect is often the first one that most people encounter on their inner journey toward integration. This is because all human beings have access to the wisdom that comes with age, making this Archetype very accessible within each of us.

Use the Dreaming Lens to deepen your interpretation of this symbol. Examine the shift or change in the dream marked by the appearance of this character. If there was a "before" and "after" to the moment of meeting, how did the dream change as a result of their presence? A positive shift may indicate the new information that is now available for your integration. A negative shift may be a signpost that the next level of material you must face in your inner work is in the Shadow. As with many archetypal dreams, there may be very little chaotic content, and the dream may consist simply of a single scene in which you encounter the figure.

Oral Sex

Universal Landscape: Integration of verbal qualities and power.

Dreaming Lens: Was the sexual act fellatio or cunnilingus? Were you performing the act or was someone performing it on you? Were you watching others? Were you being watched? Was it pleasurable? Did the dream lack eroticism? Were there physical sensations and/or orgasm? Were the participants known to you?

Personal Focus: While some elements of sexual dreams are just that—sexual dreams expressing unrealized desire—there is symbolic meaning to each aspect of this symbol. Sex represents the desire for union; the joining together or integration of separate ways of being or other personality aspects. The oral aspect of this particular act indicates that communication is the area you are investigating.

If you are orally pleasuring a penis, you may be appreciating and experiencing a need to take more aggressive power into your speech. To be orally pleasuring a vagina means that the receptive, sensitive or creative elements of your personality want to be recognized and embraced. The active position indicates a higher level of urgency than if you are the recipient. If taking on new ways of communicating can be seen as an ongoing process, receiving oral pleasure connects more to the beginning of that process, while giving it might be associated with the end.

The object of your affection will give you a great deal of clarity on the matter at hand. This is where many people are disturbed by sexual content, for many dreams have us partnering with people from our life we would not ordinarily have sex with, sometimes to the point of being horrified by who they are. However, to the unconscious mind, sex is a symbolic expression of union and has none of the societal or personal stigma we may attach to it. If the person is known to you, use their Character Aspects to indicate what qualities you are integrating into your communication. If they are a stranger, use whatever information you can recall from the dream to inform your investigation.

Paint/Painting

Universal Landscape: Creative expression that refreshes and/or rejuvenates.

Dreaming Lens: What were you painting in your dream? Were you doing the painting or was someone else? Was it artistic or environmental?

Were there colors involved? Did the image evoke a positive or negative response?

Personal Focus: Painting a surface accomplishes several things. First and foremost, it covers whatever is on the receiving surface. It makes a blank canvas come alive with expression. A new image can also cover over an older one. A building or a room can reinvent itself with fresh color, or that which was old and dingy becomes clean with a fresh coat of paint. Seen in this fashion, painting will always connect on a symbolic level with the emergence of something new and expressive as a replacement of something either old or lacking vibrancy.

Paint itself is the stuff with which this form of alteration is executed. Symbolically, it should be considered as the raw material of change of an expressive nature. The control you are able to exert over this liquid, elusive medium, will illuminate for you how effectively you may be utilizing your current creative resources. The more control you are able to access, the more effective your expressiveness is likely to be and how well you are able to manifest your desired intention.

Environmental painting in a dream is likely to connect to your waking life surroundings, though beware of being too literal with your interpretation. Dreaming of painting a room in your home should be explored through the symbolic meaning of that room. The outside of your home connects to your persona, the part of yourself that you show to the world. Therefore, exterior painting, or the need for it, connects to your underlying relationship between your private and public sense of self.

Creative painting can be a little more complex to interpret and the Dreaming Lens will offer you the most information with which to consider the meaning of this symbol. A blank canvas can be synonymous with a moment in life that the artist wishes to capture and express. Covering up an original image with something new might be pointing to a need to reinvent some area of your life in a creative and expressive fashion. If you are the witness and not the painter in your dream, then it is a Character Aspect of yourself that will lead you to new territory. If unknown, your work will be to discover the hidden resources within yourself that can more powerfully express inner desires. Since color is intrinsically bound together with the act of painting, be sure to explore the symbolic meaning of the colors present in your dream (see Colors).

Paper

Universal Landscape: Commitment in communication.

Dreaming Lens: Were you using paper in the dream? Were you looking for paper? Were you making paper? Were you recycling used paper? What kind of paper was it, from newsprint to photographic? What was the paper being used for? What color was it?

Personal Focus: Paper has a rich legacy in the formation of civilization throughout history, and the spread of knowledge from the few to the many. The invention of paper allowed record keeping to become permanent. The mysteries of religion and science were eventually included in the cannon of knowledge that could be preserved for future generations through the use of paper. Eventually, the invention of wood-based paper became the standard for a mass-produced recording device. It holds the symbolic meaning of a communication that is made permanent by virtue of committing it to writing on paper. While the digital age and modern technology are fast making paper archaic, it still connects to communication that you are steadfast about or forced to adhere to.

How paper is being used in the dream will add dimension to your interpretation. Writing on paper connects to a need to gain clarity with your thoughts. Reading something written on paper is about attempting to absorb some new idea as an intrinsic part of your knowledge base. Folding a piece of paper might reveal a wish to keep something hidden from others, or possibly to break something down into more manageable pieces of information.

Doing something atypical with paper, such as origami or cutouts, could connect to being creative in a rebellious fashion. Blank paper might point to the requirement of definitive communication that you are not clear about or unwilling to commit to yet. Reams and reams of paper could align with an overwhelming sense of thoughts or feelings that need to be documented in some way.

In the business world, there is a phrase that something must "look good on paper," referring to the strategic planning that precedes taking action. This highlights the impermanence that exists prior to the permanence that a hard copy of a "paper trail" implies.

Parents

Universal Landscape: Inner sense of authority; who we are as a result of the parents we had.

Dreaming Lens: Which parent was in your dream? What were you doing at the time? Where were you? What age were you? What age were they? Were they the same as they are/were in life? Were they imparting information to you? Were they abusive? Were you?

Personal Focus: The voices of our parents become deeply imbedded as parts of our personality. This correlates with whatever information they repeatedly presented to us during our formative years. If their messages were ones of criticism and limitation, they live on within us as those inhibiting parts of our inner monologue. If they were supportive and loving, the same would apply. Chances are that they were a combination of all sorts of messages, some positive and others negative.

Depending on where you are in your life, you may be more aligned with the challenges they presented than the gifts they gave. It is usually most effective to deal with anger and resentment before authentically moving into forgiveness. The quality of the interaction in the dream will clue you in on where you are in that process. While dreaming of your parents may inform your actual relationship with them, it is important to consider what the dream is saying about how you parent yourself.

The Dreaming Lens will tell you if you are holding yourself back or encouraging yourself to move forward. If the context of the dream indicates being stuck, then you may be holding yourself back on account of messages you were given as a child. If there is positive activity or movement in the dream, the presence of your parent(s) may be giving you insight into ways in which you are empowering yourself.

A celebration or gathering where your parents are present can be considered a moment of inventory; of taking stock of who you are by virtue of who raised and guided you. If you lack a life connection with the dream parent, consider that their absence created just as powerful a Character Aspect of the inner parent as one who was present. Allow the Dreaming Lens to inform you of what area of your self-identity is being expressed. Allow the emotional sense of the dream to indicate how well (or poorly) you are functioning as an adult.

Pencil

Universal Landscape: Communication that is changeable or impermanent.

Dreaming Lens: Were you using a pencil or was someone else using it? Were you in need of one and motivated by that need? What was the proposed or actual use of the pencil? Was it used for artistic expression, writing, or accounting? Was it a No. 2 pencil? Was it oversized or small? Did it have an eraser?

Personal Focus: A pencil symbolically connects with communication issues. The fact that pencil is erasable adds an element of impermanence to the meaning and, therefore, a lack of commitment. By varying the pressure applied with a pencil, you can create different shades of gray, which implies a level of subtlety and textural meaning to the communication represented by this symbol in a dream. The Dreaming Lens should help inform what direction you should take with your interpretation.

If you are using a pencil so that errors can be fixed, you may be dreaming about a desire to undo something not aligned with your original intention. Look to areas in your life where you are struggling to be clear and accurate. Also consider your integrity with regard to recent communication. With a pencil, you can erase a statement you wish you hadn't made. A pencil without an eraser reflects reluctance to commit or be held accountable for what you need to express.

Pencils used for artistic expression connect to creativity in an organic and simple form. Such a tool is easy to obtain and likely to be within your reach. There may be creativity wanting to emerge from you and your access to it may be as simple as picking up a pencil. There is also a sense of freedom associated with using a pencil. Since it isn't permanent, you can be free to let yourself go with your expression as you can always correct something or re-do it.

Performing on Stage

Universal Landscape: Visibility in life; public exposure.

Dreaming Lens: Were you prepared for your role or not? How were you attired? At what level of success did you perform? Did you know the audience or were they strangers? What was their response? Was it familiar territory or a strange or odd setting? Is this a recurring dream or a single occurrence?

Personal Focus: Art imitates life and the theater has always been a metaphor for the unfolding drama of our everyday experience. In fact, dramatic structure replicates the process of conscious awareness on stage just as it happens on the personal level. First, there is an inciting incident that causes a crisis, which plays out in the story that is being told. After a climactic confrontation, the crisis resolves itself through an organic change in the psyche of the hero of the story. The catharsis that results alters both reality and the perception of reality for all involved.

Life can often feel like a performance. In this way, dreaming of this image indicates that your unconscious is expressing a sense of your current life as being under public scrutiny. This is a common recurring dream, signifying the dreamer's sense of feeling exposed or fear of performing up to standards. The subtlety here is in whether you are on stage because of heightened vulnerability or because you are hiding your true feelings by "acting" your way through an experience.

By considering the timing of the dream with regard to current situations in your life, you can discover your true sense of preparedness for what is being thrown at you at the time of this dream. By examining this thoroughly, you can assess whether this dream means you are feeling incompetent to face a challenge in life, or if you are feeling prepared to perform at peak capabilities. A highly stylized performance could indicate inauthenticity in some area. Conversely, it could connect to a powerful sense of creative originality. Forgetting your lines may represent your discomfort in some role or false persona you are putting on for the approval of others.

Life is often like a performance. How you feel about this dream reveals how you feel about how well you are performing at this moment in time.

Piano

Universal Landscape: Creative mastery and potential.

Dreaming Lens: What size and style piano was in your dream: upright, grand, concert grand, or spinet? Was it being played? Were you the player? Was it in tune? Were you part of an orchestra, group, or solo? What style of music resulted: classical, jazz, blues, etc.?

Personal Focus: The piano is a feminine image of creative receptivity and potential. It must receive the attentions of someone to play it in order to achieve this potential, aligning it with the concept of receptivity. As the music that emerges from it can vary from *Chopsticks* to Chopin, its symbolic meaning also connects to mastery. Anyone can cause a piano to sing by striking a key, but only a master can make it truly soar. The essence of music is the magic of joy, and a piano represents this potential lying dormant, waiting patiently to be unleashed.

To see a piano and want to play it reveals a desire to tap into your inner creative expression. Actually playing one in your dream may indicate a period of blossoming joy. If you actually play the piano in life, this may be more literal than symbolic. Playing above your skill level could point to issues around and desire to excel, and whether or not you are living up to your creative potential. Playing poorly could indicate feelings of inadequacy or a need for humility. If someone else is playing the piano, their Character Aspect represents the part of you that has access to creative mastery and expression, or its lack.

Where the music is being made and with whom also bears investigation. Playing alone could mean your creative expression requires some level of focus and concentration. Collaborating with others means that several qualities or skills within you need to work together for you to reach your potential. The magnitude of your connection to creative passion might be reflected in the size of your musical grouping, from trio to orchestra. The quality of the music produced reflects how in or out of harmony you are in some part of your life. A piano out of tune indicates that you may not be acting upon the relationship to your inner creativity often enough.

Picture Frame

Universal Landscape: Compartmentalized feelings. Memories.

Dreaming Lens: What was the style of the frame in your dream: was it opulent, shiny or austere? Was the frame intact and complete? Was it broken or cracked? If so, did you know how it happened? Was there an image in the frame? Did you recognize it? Was it mounted to a wall or resting on a stand?

Personal Focus: The frame around a picture completes it. We display imagery that reflects parts of who we are through pictures of loved ones and moments in time from our past. A picture is not the thing it represents, but a reflection of it, often imbued with our fantasies and projections. What we place around such captured moments has great significance to explain our feelings about them. This can represent how we have *framed them in our minds* to make sense of them.

If a picture frame is a prominent image from a dream, you may be processing issues represented by the picture in the frame. The frame connects to some explanation, justification, or limitation in thinking about the person or circumstance being displayed. If the frame was empty, the rest of the Dreaming Lens may point to something that needs to be placed inside the boundaries of understanding or acceptance.

A broken frame relates to old boundaries and constraints that need to be repaired or let go of. Fixing a broken frame could indicate the process of healing and moving toward forgiveness. A very opulent frame might indicate the elevation of something or someone to higher status than it currently holds. Something complex in design could reveal defensiveness or obsession. A heavy frame with straight edges and simple lines might point to more definitive boundaries around some person or challenge. A collection of different frames might indicate variety in your perceptions. Uniformity in the way you frame things might point out a perception that may be limited, or lacking in flexibility.

Pills/Medication

Universal Landscape: Instantaneous alteration of mind or mood.

Dreaming Lens: Did you take medication or did someone else take something? Did you administer it? Were you aware of what the medication was or its effects? Were you considering whether to take the pills in your dream? Was there an overdose situation?

Personal Focus: A pharmaceutical medication is a compound that causes the brain to either create or inhibit the creation of certain chemicals that alters an experience in the body. This chain reaction occurs relatively fast after swallowing a pill. In this way, the symbolic association with any kind of medication is to create an instant shift in some state of affairs.

Whether it's aspirin for a headache or a narcotic for pain, the notion that you can take a pill for anything that ails you is firmly imbedded in the collective psyche. The popularization of anti-depressants and the introduction of Viagra have increased the power of this concept.

If you are taking a pill in a dream, there may be some area in your life that you wish would transform or go away with relative ease. An overdose might indicate a more extreme search for an easy way out of a challenge or issues of indulgence. If you have health issues in your life, there may be a more literal relationship between the medication in a dream and the desire to get well.

Not knowing what kind of pill you're taking or what it might do to you is a possible indication of some ignorance or naiveté in the way you are approaching a situation that needs attention. The specific action of a medication also needs to be taken into account. For example, a pain medication might relate to a desire to escape something difficult. An antibiotic might indicate a reaction to dark, unwanted thoughts. An anti-depressant might reveal an avoidance of unpleasant emotions. An anti-psychotic medication could connect to feeling a loss of control of your emotions or chaotic thought patterns.

All drugs have side effects, which must be considered when making a decision to take one. Often, the resulting symptoms are worse than the condition they treat. Some carry with them very dangerous risks. This perspective must be considered in a dream where a medication is a prominent symbol. You must be clear about whether the cure is worth the curse.

Possession (Demonic)

Universal Landscape: Release of pent-up rage without regard to responsibility.

Dreaming Lens: Are you possessed in the dream or is someone else? Do you know the person who is possessed? Do you know what force is responsible for the possession? Is the image from the film *The Exorcist*, or is it some other image of possession?

Personal Focus: Many of the associations in this term connect to the film *The Exorcist*. This enormously popular and infamous movie in which a twelve-year-old girl suffers demonic possession created several permanent images in the collective about this phenomenon. It is a fairly common dream image and represents a sudden outburst of any number of pent-up, dark emotions, such as guilt or rage. At the heart of this symbol, however, is the concept of not feeling responsible for the behavior in question or the intensity of the feelings being expressed. As the saying goes, "The devil made me do it."

In Aboriginal cultures before written history, demonic possession was a community illness that was treated by the local shaman. It was frequently a way for hidden grievances to be expressed in a public way. A person possessed by a demon was free to say things and express that which normally would be kept private. This could be as simple as marital dissatisfaction or resentment between family members. The appearance of the symptoms of possession and the public exorcism that followed, allowed for such conflicts to be aired, addressed, and resolved.

This illuminates how to interpret such an image in a dream. When someone is possessed by a demonic force, deeply hidden frustrations, resentments, and pain are at the root. The only way to free yourself from such a challenge is to express that which has been held back. This is often true of anger and other hostile expressions over which we either have no control, or about which we fear we may lose control. When these pent-up feelings gather enough force, the image of demonic possession may be the dream expression of daytime frustrations.

A person who has trouble controlling outbursts of rage may dream of being possessed. Examining this can help them identify the small feelings that spark the fear of being overtaken by bigger feelings. If possession shows up in your dream, it is a call to action to investigate the authenticity of any of your expressions and your willingness to take responsibility for all of them—both the pleasant and not so pleasant.

Pregnancy

Universal Landscape: The formulation of a new idea or way of being.

Dreaming Lens: Were you pregnant? Was someone else pregnant? Was it the beginning, middle, or end of pregnancy? Was the pregnancy showing? Was there fear of the labor or birthing process? Was there shame or joy around the pregnancy?

Personal Focus: A pregnancy represents the appearance of something new on the horizon. The distinction with this versus Baby or Birth is that pregnancy represents the inner process that precedes any outward expression of whatever is being created. All ideas, changes in direction, and physical shifts must first be created in the vat of ideas within the mind. Everything that we create in life is first felt as the spark of a new thought. To dream of pregnancy is to be connecting powerfully to this part of the creative process.

Consider that something in you or your life is about to change dramatically. Dreaming of pregnancy is not relegated to women alone—men will often dream of being pregnant. Many men report such dreams when their significant other is literally preparing to give birth and in the dream world, this represents the dramatic change of life that is about to take place as fatherhood descends upon them.

Shame or fear of being exposed as pregnant because it is unwanted connects to uncertainty of how the shift in you may be perceived by others in your life. The closer the pregnancy is to birth, the more imminent the change that is germinating. If the pregnancy is experienced by a character within your dream then consider that it is an element of your personality as represented by that Character Aspect that is undergoing the change that is afoot.

If the term of the pregnancy is clear in the dream, you might want to consider what was going on in your life at the time conception would have been likely. For example, if you were pregnant seven months in your dream, look back seven months in your life for some new element that could be making itself known at this time.

Of course, it is very common for women who are actually with child to dream of their pregnancy. This is a literal and direct expression of the symbolic representation of a new chapter in life, that just so happens to be a new life itself.

Priest

Universal Landscape: Extreme devotion to spiritual principles.

Dreaming Lens: Was there a priest or priests present in your dream? Were they known to you? Was the setting connected to a church or parochial school? Was this from your past? Was the scenario specifically religious? Was there an aura of authority involved in the dream? Were there any sexual overtones to the imagery of the dream?

Personal Focus: While the Catholic religion only represents about twenty-five percent of Americans that claim a religious affiliation, the proliferation of this image in the media makes it a universal symbol for spiritual devotion. Also because of the media, this symbol carries with it a great number of potential shades of meaning: from intense levels of respect, to humorous irreverence, or even intense antipathy. Your personal associations with priests will, therefore, play a prominent role in how you interpret a dream with priests in it.

On the serious end of the spectrum, the priest is the symbolic representation of Christ on Earth and signifies a level of dedication that is unparalleled in our modern culture. In this light, the Character Aspect of a priest in a dream connects to a deeply committed spiritual side of your nature that is willing to sacrifice much for the sake of your beliefs. Priests also connect directly to the power of ritual, as the Mass is the most stylized practices still in existence today that harkens back to forms of devotion that are all but lost in our modern world.

Because a priest is the authority within a church, they can represent an archetypal aspect of the self that is deeply committed to the role of spiritual leader, either for yourself or for your community. If the dream has a reverent quality to it, consider this meaning to be part of your interpretation.

There is no getting around the current perception that the institution of the priesthood is also embroiled in deep controversy over sexual improprieties. The enforced role of celibacy also plays an important role in interpreting this symbol. If a priest should play a prominent role in a dream, issues of sexuality and sexual expression/ freedom may be present. If you know the priest, then use them as a specific Character Aspect. If not, a more generalized sense of sacrifice or denial of sexual impulses may be what is being expressed.

Prison/Jail

Universal Landscape: Restrictions and consequences of choices made.

Dreaming Lens: Were you in jail? Was someone else? Were you visiting a jail? Were you in a cell? Why were you imprisoned?

Personal Focus: When you break the law, you go to prison. And while you have to engage in criminal activity to find yourself in jail in real life, the idea of being imprisoned by something can easily apply to any number of circumstances where you feel bound to some person, place, or thing in a way that feels severely constricting. In fact, the phrase "like a jail sentence" is often used in casual conversation to refer to anything that obligates a person beyond their comfort level.

There is a difference between jail and prison, which may be significant, especially if the dream was clearly taking place in one or the other. While they have very similar sensibilities, a jail is where someone is taken when they are suspected of committing a crime or when the crime is of low severity. Prison is where convicted criminals of more serious crimes are sent to pay their debt to society. If this distinction is made clear in your dream, recognize that jail is a more temporary form of bondage. Prison indicates that a more serious matter is being expressed.

At the core of the symbolic meaning of prison is what you did to get there. The inciting incident that ends in jail time is always a choice that may have seemed like a good idea at the time, but has consequences resulting in the removal of freedom and comfort in some area of your life. When this environment plays prominently in a dream, examine your life for where you may be feeling that a decision you made in the past is feeling like something you can't escape in the present.

Prostitute

Universal Landscape: Trading on that which is intimate or personal for material gain.

Dreaming Lens: Were you a prostitute or were you soliciting a prostitute? Was the prostitute female or male or somewhere between female and male? What were your judgments in the dream around prostitution? Was it a street hooker or high-class call girl?

Personal Focus: The essence of prostitution is making public that which is ordinarily considered private. They say "money can't buy you love," but it can indeed buy you sex, which can be a substitute for love and intimacy. The challenge with prostitution lies in the judgments we place on selling something as intensely personal as one's body, and the act of performing sex for money. This makes it something intensely *im*personal.

If you dream of being a prostitute you may be experiencing something in your waking life that is pointing toward a sense of selling out or taking the easier, softer way through some challenge. If you are hiring a prostitute you may want to look at that part of you that is willing to sell yourself short. If there is prostitution around you in the dream, notice your sense of connection to the concept: if you are in judgment or fear, maybe consider the idea that there is a lack of integrity in the way that you are handling some person or situation. A more open attitude toward prostitution might point to a need for a more careful appraisal of your self-judgment, whether it be too severe or whether you might benefit from utilizing more discretion with your choices.

No matter what your belief system, on some level, prostitution leaves a legacy of shame, which is really the essence of this symbol in the dream. Is the price you are paying for your freedom worth it?

Public Speaking

Universal Landscape: Communication on a grand scale; pressure

Dreaming Lens: Were you speaking in public? Were you watching someone else speak? Where were you speaking? What was the topic you were speaking about? Were you comfortable or nervous?

Personal Focus: Speaking in public is challenging for most people. For some, that challenge is so intense that even the idea of it can bring on a terrorizing attack of anxiety. Since there is a literal connotation with this symbol to the act of speaking, a dream that involves this activity will naturally point to an area in your life where your communication is being put on the spot.

A person speaking in public is usually a figure of authority on some level. In this way, a dream that includes this as an image is probably expressing some area of your life where you are either in your authority or where your authority is being put to the test. This is especially so if you were the one doing the speaking. If you were in the audience and someone else was talking, use them as a Character Aspect of yourself to figure out what part of your personality has something to say. It could be that the power and authority you desire in life is speaking to you through your unconscious in your dream. (See also Performing on Stage.)

Purse/Briefcase

Universal Landscape: Access to tools for daily living.

Dreaming Lens: Were you carrying a purse or a briefcase? Had you lost one? Was the dream focused on the carrying case or was it secondary? What was inside the purse or briefcase? Were you aware of its contents? Did the contents play a prime role in the dream?

Personal Focus: The key to this symbol is in what is carried inside of it. Whether it's a pocketbook, briefcase or shoulder bag, the personal carrying case has become a fixture of necessity in our fast-paced world. They provide mobile access to important items, which may be needed for when you are out in the world, such as your wallet, driver's license, credit cards, and all the things that represent your identity. Hence, there is a strong association for this image with what might be referred to as tools for life on a day-to-day basis.

A pocketbook, handbag, or purse is generally carried by women and often contains grooming products. This connects it symbolically to the feminine principle. The items found in a purse will likely be associated with self-care and nurturing. Whether being carried by a male or female, a briefcase is connected to the masculine principle by virtue of its association with work and career.

The interpretation of this as a symbol will depend largely on the Dreaming Lens relationship between the dreamer and the object as it appears in the dream. A solid connection to a purse or briefcase in a dream indicates effective access to the tools carried within. Losing, searching for, or being robbed of such an item points to difficulties in this area. One that is too heavy may indicate burdens with being overly cautious, just as one that is empty reveals issues of lack or being ill-prepared.

The function of the bag in question will also offer clues to the appropriate interpretation. This is most true in the world of women's purses, as they come in a variety of styles that connect directly with the use intended for it. A dress clutch is not the same thing as a leather handbag. The first indicates having the bare essentials associated with looking good, while the later implies a more grounded ability to contain what might be necessary in any situation. The specific type of carrying case will indicate what area of your life is being highlighted by the dream.

Your waking life associations to a purse or briefcase are important. If you routinely carry some sort of bag, then your ongoing relationship with this object will feature highly in your interpretation. The more attached you are to your purse or briefcase, the higher the stakes of the symbolic meaning in a dream, especially in dreams that feature loss or separation. The items you generally carry with you each day should also be considered.

Quicksand

Universal Landscape: Obstacles to movement; emotional overwhelm.

Dreaming Lens: Were you stuck in quicksand? Was someone else in the quicksand? Were you attempting to save someone or yourself from sliding deeper into quicksand? Was someone trying to save you? Did you successfully avoid falling into quicksand? What environment was the quicksand in?

Personal Focus: Quicksand is Earth and water in a treacherous combination whereby the water is abundant and the makeup of the Earth is such that the water is not readily absorbed. The result is land that appears solid but is anything but, and stepping into it can be dangerous—even deadly. If you or someone else is stuck in quicksand in a dream, it may be reflecting something in your life that is causing you to be stuck and this stuckness may be putting you in some sort of danger.

Any time water is present with regard to a symbol, issues of emotionality are in play. Since quicksand's water content is essentially imperceptible until you find yourself engulfed in it, your interpretation should reflect this sense of being initially unaware of the danger and the astonishment of discovering that you are suddenly in peril. In this way, the emotionality of the situation inspiring the dream may not be readily apparent. However, once you are immersed in it, there is enough feeling and confusion to drag you down into immobility and overwhelm. This symbol in a dream may be an indication that there are emotional issues that you have not been aware of up until this point. Having been stopped in your tracks by these issues, you are being forced to go deeper (hence sinking into the quicksand) in order to deal with the matter(s) at hand.

If you are the one that is stuck in the quicksand, look to where you may be being brought down by situations in your life, especially where emotional issues need more attention. If someone else is challenged by quicksand, use them as a Character Aspect to identify what elements of your personality are causing you to be stuck. Remember that this image can pertain to any number of dream images that involve obstacles to moving on foot, from cement, to unknown substances or invisible forces. (See also Obstacles.)

Rain

Universal Landscape: Emotional expression; tears.

Dreaming Lens: How severe or gentle was the rain? Were you prepared for the results of the rain? Did you enjoy it or was it unnerving to get wet? Did the rain feel romantic, sinister, welcome, limiting, or frustrating?

Personal Focus: Water is always a symbolic expression of emotion. Since falling rain is very similar to tears, rain is the closest representation to the act of crying. As such, it symbolizes the process of allowing our feelings to flow freely. Rain is considered cleansing for it washes away dirt particles and leaves the air clearer. Tears can also be said to wash debris from the soul. Rain indicates that an emotional experience is taking place that is ultimately healing. The Dreaming Lens will offer clues to what area of your life is evoking such a deep, emotional response. Your reactions to the rain as well as the quality of the rain itself will provide even more information for your exploration.

A light, gentle rain could indicate a small disruption in your life that is causing some emotional reactivity. Torrential downpours, such as hurricanes, point to more intense undercurrents of feelings being expressed. The relative intensity of the rain in your dream will mirror the intensity of what your unconscious is trying to express. How you respond to the rain in your dream will illuminate for you the level of resistance you are in. The mightier your attempts to escape the onslaught of the downpour, the more likely you are avoiding the free flow of emotional expression.

Rainbow

Universal Landscape: Hope; abundance; the promise of good to come.

Dreaming Lens: Where do you see the rainbow? How vibrant or dim was it? Was it lasting or fleeting? How did you react to the sight of the rainbow? Were there others with you when you saw it? Did you see the end of the rainbow?

Personal Focus: A rainbow is formed when waves of sunlight interact with droplets of water in the Earth's atmosphere. The reflective droplets of water break the white light down into the seven colors that make up the visible spectrum. The result is one of the most magical phenomena that can be found on Earth. Part of the meaning of this symbol can be taken from the emotional reaction a person can have when looking at one. They are breathtaking and can inspire deep feelings of elation. In this way, a rainbow is almost always going to be thought of as a positive image.

There are several major cultural associations to a rainbow. In the Old Testament, God sent the rainbow as a promise to never destroy humanity again, which is the origin of the theme of the promise for the future. The Celtic tradition tells us that at the end of a rainbow is a pot of gold, associating this symbol with the search for abundance. However, both of these time-honored interpretations bring with them darker meanings that bear consideration. The former implies past destruction and the later is a paradox in that it is impossible to ever actually find the end of a rainbow as it constantly shifts as you move toward it. However, each of these counterparts is what infuses the rainbow with its most powerful symbolic element: hope.

The physical construct of a rainbow is filled with beautiful symbolism. They contain all the colors of the spectrum and, therefore, represent a sense of wholeness in a majestic and highly spiritual expression. Rainbows appear when the Sun and rain are present at the same time. To be able to experience sadness (rain) and joy (sunlight) at the same time is a true sign of consciousness and wisdom.

Rape

Universal Landscape: Integration of the aspects of personality through violent, forceful means.

Dreaming Lens: Were you being raped in a dream? Were you witnessing a rape? Were you aware of who the rapist was? Were you the rapist? Was the rape a violent act, or was it an erotic pseudo-rape?

Personal Focus: Although it is conceivable that in the waking world, a woman could rape a man, the notion of rape as a symbol connects to the masculine principle. Women will sometimes dream of being the aggressor in sexual situations and may even have a penis in their dream, or perceive themselves as having one. Because the act of rape is sexual in structure, the symbolic meaning must reflect the same theme as sex that is consensual, which is the coming together or integration of different Character Aspects of the personality. However, rape is an act of violence and when this is combined with the absence of consent, it puts a very different spin on how to interpret it if it should appear in a dream.

When a dream includes something as heinous as rape, it is important to remind yourself—whether you are male or female—that dreams are symbolic, not literal. Rape in a dream is not like rape in life. It simply means that the integration that is occurring within your psyche is being experienced as so abrupt and potentially frightening that the symbolic expression of it appears dramatically. The unconscious will often use nightmares and frightening dreams to get our attention.

If you were raped in the dream, consider the rapist. If he was known to you, then use that person as a Character Aspect to see what part of your own personality is demanding to be dealt with. If he was not known to you, then consider the dream a precursor to a powerful shift that is going on under the surface and is not yet clear. If you cannot glean more helpful insight from this dream, trust that future dreams will inform you of whatever shift is taking place.

If you witnessed a rape, you must look inward to see what aspects of your personality are at odds with one another, for they ultimately need to be integrated and made whole. The rapist would be the part of you that is demanding to be recognized and the victim is the part of you that needs to accept the merging, but may be in resistance to the process. If you were the rapist in your dream, consider the victim as a Character Aspect that represents the part of you that you wish to subdue.

Rape fantasies are common for many people and can be quite erotic and satisfying when handled in an appropriate manner. If the dream of rape was erotic in nature, the meaning is the same, but the integration that is taking place has much lower stakes and may, in fact, be a source of pleasurable anticipation.

Rats

Universal Landscape: Pervasive underbelly of Shadow.

Dreaming Lens: Where were the rats in your dream? Was there just one or was there an infestation? Were you frightened of them? Were they being destructive? Were they harmless? Were they pets?

Personal Focus: Rats are considered pests as they can overpopulate and bring with them destruction and disease. They are inexorably bound up in our history to the bubonic plague, because rats carried the fleas that transmitted the disease. The consequences for not attending to them properly are recorded in our mythology as a loss of innocence, as in the story of *The Pied Piper of Hamlin* who, when not paid for his services of ridding the town of their rats, took away the children of the town and led them to their deaths. This adds the element of a loss of innocence as a possible interpretation if your dream reflects this theme.

Rats can be found in sewers, basements, and dark corners. This expands their association with Shadow material, which is all the things about ourselves we wish were not true or that we would rather not look at. If rats appear in your dreams in any fashion, there is something to investigate under the surface. The consequences of not exploring these dark places are that it can lead to some sort of destruction.

An interesting juxtaposition to all this darkness is that laboratory rats, which live in sanitary conditions and are usually white in color, are responsible for enormous benefits to mankind by giving up their lives for scientific experimentation. More has been done with rats to advance science and medicine than with any other animal. The meaning here is that if you diligently and systematically investigate your Shadow, enormous benefits can come to you and your path of transformation.

What the rats are doing in your dream will inform you of where you are in your process of lifting your shadow. If they are very frightening to you, then you are just beginning your search of the underlying troubles in your path. The more open you are to their presence, the more open you are about your own psychic shadow. Needing to exterminate them may parallel a need to uncover, discover, and discard some element of your thinking or behavior. It is important to investigate your personal pestilence. And don't forget to pay the piper!

Rebirth/Resurrection

Universal Landscape: Rebirth, resurrection.

Dreaming Lens: Were you reborn in the dream? Was someone else? Was it a literal birth, or more figurative? Did your dream include images of resurrection? Was it religious in nature, or more fantasy-based?

Personal Focus: The repetition of this term and its Universal Landscape is not a typographical error. By its nature, this term is identical to its meaning. This concept is such a vibrant part of human thought; it can appear in dreams in its pure form—the notion of rebirth or resurrection itself. This can be an image of literal birth/rebirth in biological detail or in a more subjective form as in resurrection as mythological or metaphorical. Often the dream image of being reborn is experienced intuitively as an inner knowing rather than as an action or occurrence.

Rebirth implies that a death must first take place. It is crucial to investigate this side of the equation, whether your dream includes something being sacrificed or not. If that which is dying is clear in the dream, you can ruminate on what it brings up for you. If it is not clear in your dream who or what is dying, you may want to make exploring this a large part of your investigation. Rebirth implies that some previous way of being in the world has died away. This gives way to a new way of being that benefits from the new without discarding wisdom from the past.

When an image and its symbolic meaning are so similar, the Dreaming Lens becomes an even more important guide to a satisfactory interpretation. Consider the feelings and sensations in the dream and apply them to the concept of new beginnings.

Restaurant

Universal Landscape: Self-care and the celebration of abundance.

Dreaming Lens: What type of restaurant were you in? What meal were you eating or intending to eat? Were you well-served? Was the food palatable? Who were you dining with?

Personal Focus: Any establishment that concerns itself with food connects to nurturance. This especially applies to a restaurant, as the ritual of being waited on and served is also a form of self-care. The expense of eating out is always going to be higher than the expense of preparing something at home. The cost factor adds the color of celebrating abundance to the meaning of this symbol. If the Dreaming Lens focus was more negative, it could be indicating feelings of lack in this area of your life.

Waiters are responsible for the tempo and structure of your dining experience. Ideally they are informative, pleasant, and efficient. In this way, they are a Character Aspect of the organization and control that surrounds your issues of nurturance and self-care. The service you receive in your dream restaurant will inform you of how effectively you are managing the constant flow of meeting your needs in life. Ask yourself if you are happy with the service you provide yourself with each day.

The quality of your meal connects with both abundance and the ability to discern excellence. Responsible for this element is the chef, the unseen heart and soul of a restaurant. The chef also represents the creative power within your psyche. A fine meal could reveal that you are indeed being careful to ensure that your life provides for your needs in a way that reflects a consciousness of deserving abundance. However, a dream in which you are served unacceptable food indicates that there is something out of balance in this area. If the dream includes something as severe as food poisoning, you may want to examine your attitudes more closely.

The atmosphere and ambiance, or lack thereof, can be thought of as reflecting your sense of values and what you are attached to in life. There is nothing wrong with demanding and expecting luxury, especially if it is readily available to you. However, any visceral reactions to the setting of your dream restaurant may offer you insight into how your current value system is impacting you on an unconscious level. If the dream centered on issues connecting with the mood, setting, or attitude of the restaurant staff, you can use this information to inform you of any imbalance you may be expressing from your waking life.

The company you were keeping in such a dream can offer a wealth of additional items for consideration. Treat each person as a Character Aspect. Their qualities will inform your choices around receiving abundance, and also your commitment, or lack of commitment, to taking care of yourself.

River

Universal Landscape: Emotional flow.

Dreaming Lens: Were you in, near or on the river? Did it feel safe? Were the rapids swift or gentle? Did you want to cross it? Were you able to cross it? Were you traveling downstream? Were you fighting to move upstream? Was the river running dry? Did you know where it lead to, or originated from? Were there any boats or other people present?

Personal Focus: Any dream that involves water connects to emotions. In the case of a river, the essential meaning relates to the expression of feelings and emotional flow. All rivers eventually deposit their contents into the ocean, the symbol of all that is unconscious. This adds the perspective of emotions that move freely across our conscious awareness as they travel back to their ultimate mysterious source. The intensity of the river's flow in a dream is a direct barometer of the level of emotionality of your life that is being expressed by this image.

The force of a river can run the gamut from a babbling brook to a torrential powerhouse. The volume of water involved can also vary greatly. A dry or barren riverbed indicates a lack of expression and a desperate need for emotional content. One that is overwhelmed by flooding might point to a situation that may feel dangerous and threatening to the stability in your life. An obstacle that blocks a river, such as a dam, reveals some level of emotional blockage. All of these distinctions will figure prominently into an accurate interpretation.

The underlying message to be considered when a river appears in a dream is that of surrender. Over time, the path of a river has enormous impact on the land surrounding it. With a mind of its own, it carves its way with force and determination. Symbolically, a river would be the emotional experiences in life that rush upon you. While sometimes frightening, if you surrender to them, you will be carried to the next destination on your journey, possibly even your heart's desire.

Rivers often appear in dreams when you need to let go of things in your life as they are and go with the flow. A river is in charge of the journey it takes you on, often pushing you up against obstacles or inviting you to maneuver around them. The call to action here may indicate a need to trust your feelings, no matter how frightening they may be. Human beings, by nature, resist change and are often overwhelmed by the sense of vulnerability that comes with it. Your unconscious mind may be calling you to relinquish control and move gracefully from where you are to where you are going.

Road

Universal Landscape: Your path or direction in life.

Dreaming Lens: Were you on a road or trying to get to a road? What type of road was it? Was it urban or rural? What was the quality of the road? Was it a side road or a main thoroughfare? Was it rocky and steep, or winding through a forest? Was it a never-ending straightaway? Did you know where you were heading? Was the road busy, dangerous, empty, or treacherous? Were you on foot or in a vehicle?

Personal Focus: Each of us is on our own path in life. It is a combination of past choices we have made and current circumstances and decisions we are about to make that determine the road we're on in any given moment. Such an image in a dream is representative of your current life path. It can be a snapshot of where you are and how you feel about the present moment of your journey.

The Dreaming Lens will offer you the foundation for your interpretation; however, the type of road and its environment will give you deeper shades of meaning. The more isolated the road, the more the dream relates to your private life and personal issues. A public or widely traveled road will likely connect to aspects of your life that are more social in nature.

If the vehicles in your dream are traveling fast enough to inspire anxiety, you may be expressing fears of being able to match the speed of life around you. Heavy traffic that slows you down may indicate feelings of frustration with the pace of your life and the presence of obligations and responsibility. If the road is straight and smooth, you are probably moving along comfortably toward your goals; whereas if it is bumpy or treacherous, you may be complicating your journey in some way. The sophistication of your vehicle may mirror the skills you have at your disposal; from feet to sports cars (see Driving).

If you know where you are heading, the interpretation you attach to the road will inform you of your feelings about your destination and the process you are in to get there. Not knowing where you are going is not the same as having no destination. The former implies ignorance while the latter could indicate a moment of surrender. Being on the wrong side of the road going against traffic could be mirroring resistance you are meeting in your life.

Robots

Universal Landscape: Productivity; emotionless activity.

Dreaming Lens: Was there a robot in your dream? What was it capable of doing? How human-like was it? Was it effective at what it did? Did you make the robot? Did you purchase it? Did it belong to another individual or institution? Was it benevolent or potentially destructive?

Personal Focus: A robot is a non-human entity that is designed to replicate some level of human functioning. While the field of robotics is advancing in the scientific community, most dream robots are more of the fantastical variety.

From a consumer mentality, robots are machines that have been created to replace human labor. In theory, they ought to be more effective than we are and should be free of physical limitations and devoid of self-judgment, doubt, or low self-esteem. In this way, a robot in a dream may represent a wish to be highly effective, but without the scary feelings associated with taking risks. Dreaming of one may reveal your own personal relationship to emotional responses with regard to accomplishment. It is important to also ask yourself if there are areas in your life where you might be operating in such an automatic fashion that it might be draining you of vibrancy and joy.

If you have created the robot of your dreams, you may have another angle to explore. While you should still examine the possibility of a robot as emotional defense, the power of the creative impulse should not be ignored. From the beginning of civilization, the human race has sought to use its expanding knowledge to improve the quality of life.

If you are attracted to the notion of the robot in your dream, you will find clues for yourself in what tasks the robot frees you of having to complete. However, once you have identified the area of your life that you are fantasizing about delegating to an outside source, your next task will be to attempt to uncover the vulnerable, frightened part of you that drew you to this notion in the first place.

Science fiction is fascinated with tales of robots and other forms of artificial intelligence rebelling against the human race and creating our ultimate demise. Since this notion exists in the creative mind of the collective unconscious, it must be considered in your interpretation whether you relate to this futuristic possibility or not.

Roller Coaster

Universal Landscape: The up-and-down nature of life.

Dreaming Lens: Were you riding the roller coaster or watching it from a distance? Who was on the roller coaster? Was there a feeling of danger or a presence of excitement? If riding it, how did it feel to be on the coaster? Did the ride come to an end?

Personal Focus: When the ups and down of life are dramatic, we often express this by using the analogy of a roller coaster ride. Just as in life, these extremes can be simultaneously thrilling and terrifying. As a ride in an amusement park, it is something that one chooses to experience, knowing that it will contain surprising twists and turns. If one resists the sensations of the journey, it can be terrifying. If one welcomes them, there can be great exhilaration. Which end of that continuum you find yourself on in the dream illuminates your relationship to the ups and downs your life is currently throwing at you.

A roller coaster symbolizes one of life's biggest challenges: sudden changes in intensity and direction. These rapid shifts constitute the rhythm of life that we have all come to expect, especially when transition is afoot. Dreaming of such a symbol indicates that life is currently (or about to) hurl itself up to the heights, plummet into the depths, or both. Remember that if you find yourself riding the roller coaster of life, you have chosen to benefit from all of the possibilities life has to offer. It is through the challenging ups and downs that we are able to create brilliant manifestations of our heart's desires.

Santa Claus

Universal Landscape: Innocent belief in the magic power of love.

Dreaming Lens: What was Santa Claus doing in your dream? Were you dressed as Santa? Was the Santa Claus the real thing or a man in a costume? Was the dream pleasant or punitive? Were there presents involved? Was it Christmas?

Personal Focus: Christmas comes with the Winter Solstice, the time when the days are shortest in the Northern Hemisphere. During this darkest time of the year, we reminisce about the bounty of sunshine with a tree that is decorated with the symbolic fruits of spring. Santa Claus is the icon at the foundation of this mythology. He represents the magical power of love to transcend all darkness. This power is associated with the innocence of childhood, for once the belief in it is abandoned, it can be very difficult for people to fully believe in magic again.

There are two developments around the idea of Santa Claus in modern times that are worth mentioning. Somewhere along the line, parents began to use the promise of what Santa might bring to a child in order to manipulate them toward good behavior. If a child is good, they receive presents. If bad, they get a lump of coal. To solidify this notion, he was bestowed with the power to see what was occurring during the year as a sort of moral compass. This was popularized by the famous lyric, "he sees you when you're sleeping, he knows when you're awake, he knows if you've been bad or good, so be good for goodness sake." While on the surface this is a charming notion, Santa's voyeurism is a falsehood, so the spirit behind instilling this sort of fear into children is manipulative and judgmental. Look to see where in your life you may be overly concerned with whether you've been bad or good and what the consequences might be. Conversely, the appearance of Santa in a dream could indicate a desire to exert control over someone else's behavior (or to be feeling controlled by another) in a way that is indirect or passive aggressive.

If your Santa Claus is in any way dark or menacing, look to where your consciousness may be reflecting the misuse of love or magic. When an archetypal Character Aspect is reflecting Shadow material, they might be engaged in behavior that is contrary to what is expected of them. Are you manipulating some situation to get what you want by being over-generous or giving too much? Sometimes the impulse to be generous comes with a hidden hook of trying to snare what you secretly want in return.

The concept of the "secret Santa" is a prominent modern day way in which this Archetype is fully present. While an adult knows that there is no Santa Claus, we refresh our workplace spirit by agreeing that not only does Santa exist in our own hearts, but the best way to keep that energy alive and equally experienced by all, the identity of the giver must be kept secret. In this way, the essence of this energy is that yes, with apologies to Virginia, there really is a Santa Claus; but he exists within the heart of all human beings just waiting for an organic moment to express love through the generosity of giving.

Scars

Universal Landscape: Evidence of previous transformation or change.

Dreaming Lens: Did you have a scar or was it on someone else? Were you aware of what caused the original wound? Was it surgical or violent? Did it form in the dream or was it already present? Was it visible to others or hidden? Did you find it repulsive or interesting?

Personal Focus: Scar tissue is the body's way of healing invasive wounds. When a scar is present it always relates to some previous event that was damaging or otherwise altering. Sometimes the original wound is purposeful and connected to healing, such as with surgery. Other times it can be the result of an attack of some kind. We use the term *emotional scars* to represent memories of things in our past that stand out as particularly painful and worth avoiding in the present. No matter what the backstory is, the presence of a scar *today* means something powerful and invasive happened *yesterday*.

This image in a dream has the same connotation of evidence of challenges from our past. If the wound was surgical in nature, then the experience is something that you either chose or was necessary for your evolvement. If the wound was inflicted in violence, the same holds true, though the attack may point to resistance on your part.

Seeing a scar on someone in a dream is inviting you to consider that some previous wounding and subsequent healing is connected to a Character Aspect of yourself. Consider the meaning you assign the person who bears the scar very carefully. If the scar is on yourself, or if the person is not known to you, the answer may be found by considering where on the body the scar is found. A scar on a face points to one's persona and how you show up in the world. The torso relates to matters of pride, courage, and matters of the heart. The belly connects to feelings and secrets. Scars on the arms and hands are likely to be about things you do, while the legs symbolize where you've been or may be headed. What is most important to remember is that a scar indicates a healing has taken place, though you may still fear the circumstances around its origin.

Seeds

Universal Landscape: Potential and possibility.

Dreaming Lens: Where were the seeds in your dream? Were they in an environment suited for growth, or were they dormant and in need of planting? What type of seeds were they? Who had access to them? What was your intention for them in your dream?

Personal Focus: Seeds are pure potential. From something very small and unremarkable, spectacular expressions of life force can emerge. In and of themselves, they are unimpressive. Place them in the right environment and a miracle occurs.

One of the most significant things about seeds is their specificity. Each type of seed will transform into one expression only. If you plant a radish seed, you cannot expect a carrot to grow. Every seed has a consciousness about this—as long as it finds itself in the proper conditions, it knows what it is and knows what to do.

The essence of the universal meaning of seeds is in its potential, but the less obvious meaning connects to the independence of development. You could hardly expect your garden to grow if every day you dug up the seeds you had planted to see how they were coming along. They must be left alone to do what is innately inside of them to do. In this way, patience for the possibilities to come is also indicated by this symbol.

When you dream of seeds, look to areas of your life that are somehow expressing a desire to manifest or multiply. If the seeds are planted, then you know that you have already begun this process in some situation. If they are not, then explore your consciousness for some area where your desires are lying dormant.

A seed can also indicate an unmet need or the readiness to meet it, depending on whether or not the dream involves getting them into the proper space for growth. The type of seed will inform you of what is trying to get your attention. Something edible will connect to basics, such as self-care and nurturance. Flowers could indicate a desire

for more beauty in your surroundings. A tree might represent a longing for something of permanence and strength to be added to your
life. If the seeds are unknown to you, your assignment is to recognize
that there is some potential within you that wants to be expressed and
the call to action is to plant all the seeds in your life in a spirit of faith
that whatever grows will be the right and perfect result.

Seizure

Universal Landscape: Intense, debilitating confusion.

Dreaming Lens: Did you have a seizure? Did someone else have a seizure in your dream? What was the end result of the seizure? Was it
painful? Where did the seizure take place?

Personal Focus: A seizure is a neurological phenomenon where cells
in the brain and the nervous system begin to fire rapidly and out of
control. While there are a number of different causes of a seizure,
the net result is often dangerous. On a symbolic level, anything that
involves the brain connects with how we think. The chaotic nature
of a seizure represents a kind of thinking that is confounded and
confused to an extreme degree.

Where in your life are you suffering from confusion, chaos, or
anxiety? If you are the one having a seizure in your dream, then
look to where in your life confusion may be hurting you on a deep
level. If someone else in your dream is the victim, then use them as
a Character Aspect of the part of your personality that is suffering
due to confusion.

Sex

Universal Landscape: Primal instincts around connection.

Dreaming Lens: Who was having sex in the dream? Was the dream about
the sex act itself, or was it just a part of the narrative of the dream?

Were you engaging in sex, or witnessing it? Were you comfortable or uncomfortable with what you were seeing or experiencing?

Personal Focus: Sex is perhaps the most misunderstood of dream images. This is certainly due to the complicated nature of sex itself, both individually and culturally. When sex appears in a dream, it is imperative that you put your personal reactions to sex and sexuality aside in order to arrive at an accurate interpretation of a dream which contains a sexual element. Detaching from the thoughts and feelings triggered by the characters involved in the act of sex in your dream is even more crucial to this process. This can be difficult for many people to accomplish.

Sex in dreams can be an area of great concern for many people. While some sex dreams are experienced as pleasurable and erotic, more often than not people report dreaming of sexual encounters as troubling because of the nature of the sexual act they dreamed of or the partner with whom they were engaged. However, once examined through the language of symbols, sex loses its potency and charge, while revealing so much more.

When two people have sex, on at least some level, they are trying to get as close to each other as they possibly can. The act of sex can be defined symbolically as two separate energies attempting to merge into one. Therefore, sex is symbolic for the process of integration. If you remove any personal projections that come up around sex and how it was played out in your dream, the interpretive meaning rises above any potential embarrassment or shame. Though sometimes more difficult to accept, this also applies to sexual encounters that have societal taboos associated with them, such as those involving incestuous relationships or illegal activities.

Whoever you are having sex with in your dream represents a Character Aspect that your unconscious is telling you needs to be integrated into your personality. If you are witnessing a sexual act, then you will need to consider what Character Aspects of yourself are being expressed by the people having sex. The message of integration still applies, but it will connect more to parts of your personality that need to join forces. Perhaps a life situation is demanding different areas of your skill sets that, if combined, will empower you to be effective in a way that is currently eluding you.

This symbol can be so challenging, it merits an example to help clarify the best approach to interpreting sexual dreams. One of the most frequently reported sex dreams that people generally find disturbing centers around coworkers. Here is an example of a dream to help illustrate how to find the value of an interpretation by removing that which is distressing:

> *I dreamed that I had sex with a coworker while my boss watched. It was creepy in a way because I think he's gross. But worse was that, in the dream I was enjoying it. We were in a private booth at a baseball game, the kind where they serve food and it's all very fancy. Just as it was about to finish, the batter in the game hit a home run. My boss got up and went to the glass window to watch the game, at this point, and was cheering for the home run hitter.*

This young woman was feeling very stifled at her job, as if no one really valued her. In fact, she reported that most of her colleagues didn't even know what she did at the company. She often talked about wanting to be promoted but didn't think that would ever happen. While the coworker in the dream was definitely not a potential sex partner, he was a self-assured, outgoing person who had no trouble verbally expressing confidence in his skills to others.

The dream is not about actually having sex with this man; it's a symbolic depiction of the woman's need to discover her own inner resources as represented by the Character Aspect of this self-assured colleague. If she can access this part of herself and integrate it into her personality more effectively, she has a much greater chance of hitting a home run at work. Had she not moved past the embarrassing and upsetting images of sex with this undesirable coworker, she may have missed the real message of the dream. (See also Intercourse, Oral Sex, Lesbian Sex).

Shoes

Universal Landscape: How grounded you are.

Dreaming Lens: Were you wearing shoes? Were you looking for shoes? Were you shopping for shoes? Were you putting them on or taking them off? Were they yours or someone else's? Were you aware of whose shoes you were wearing? Was someone else wearing your shoes?

Personal Focus: Shoes simultaneously protect our feet as well as express our sense of style. Our feet symbolize how grounded we are and our ability to maneuver effectively on our chosen path. The shoes that we wear or see in a dream reflect two things: how we protect the stand we take in life and how we express ourselves with regard to the steps we take as we walk through life.

Looking at a particular pair of shoes to wear in a dream connects to a direction you have not yet embarked upon but may be considering. Noticing someone else's shoes might point to a number of thoughts about others, including envy, judgment, or compassion—the latter of which can only occur when you have walked a mile in another person's shoes.

A single shoe means a path that is only half-considered, or a switch that occurs midway through a process. Losing or looking for shoes might point out insecurity that keeps you from moving through life in a more grounded fashion. Sneakers or athletic shoes connect to speed and increased performance. High-heeled shoes make a statement about a deliberate presentation that has impact, but can debilitate movement. Wearing a very expensive shoe might illuminate issues around the desire for abundance.

Siblings

Universal Landscape: Character Aspects related to waking-life siblings.

Dreaming Lens: Were you dreaming of your own brother(s) or sister(s)? Do you have siblings in waking life or were these dream characters? Were the siblings in your dream related to each other but not to you?

Personal Focus: All people in dreams relate to some aspect of your own personality. If you dream of your actual brothers or sisters from your life, the Character Aspects that they represent as part of your psyche should be investigated in the same manner as any person known to you who appears in a dream. However, because of the powerful dynamic of family systems, the relationships between siblings will connect to various roles each member of the group often find themselves locked into. When a sibling appears in a dream, there is a great deal of complexity to explore—from your current relationship to your childhood history, and even how parenting styles impacted each family member. With careful and unbiased investigation, a sibling dream can offer a penetrating snapshot of where you are in your development as an individual, separate from the limitations of your personal history.

If there is little or no complication associated with the sibling you dream of, treat the interpretation process the same as with any cast member in a dream using the Character Aspect technique. If you have no brothers or sisters in waking life, the Character Aspect of one appearing in your dream will be based primarily on the context in the Dreaming Lens.

Silverware

Universal Landscape: Tools for nurturing. Social grace with meeting needs.

Dreaming Lens: Were you using the silverware to eat or preparing to do so? Was the silverware clean or dirty? Did the set match? Was the use of the silverware connected to food or something unrelated to usual use? Was someone being taught to use it properly?

Personal Focus: Silverware and its use is a symbol of civilization and sophistication. Food is what sustains us and represents nurturing and self-care. By using an implement to connect to our food, we add yet one more separation between ourselves and animals. The meaning attached to silverware must combine the primal instinct to eat for survival with the restraint of social acceptance and grace. Parents struggle to get their children to use silverware for both these reasons; so that they will be able to feed themselves and simultaneously fit in with society. The more sophisticated the circle one travels in, the more silverware there is to contend with. This illuminates the symbolic association of silverware to civilization and cultural hierarchy.

Using silverware in a dream connects to your sense of propriety and conformity. Needing utensils to eat might reflect an unwillingness to get down and dirty when meeting your own needs. Being told you must use silverware when your hands will do just fine might indicate an area of your life that your more primitive approach is not suitable for the arena in which you are operating. Not knowing what piece of silverware to use may symbolize a fear of not being prepared in a social setting. How you feel about your lack of knowledge is important to consider. Hiding your ignorance may indicate a need to conform, whereas feeling intimidated might show areas where you are shut down from lack of information. Aversion toward what is considered proper might symbolize an area where rebellion may need to be explored.

Singing

Universal Landscape: Passionate expression that is so great that it demands more energy than just speaking.

Dreaming Lens: Are you singing or is someone else? Is there a group of people singing or just one voice? Are you witnessing the singing? Is it recorded or live? Is anyone else listening?

Personal Focus: Singing is an ancient, primal expression of passion. When words are not enough, singing becomes the next heightened form of communication. The ability to sing is so revered that we elevate superior voices to high status in our media and culture.

Technically, singing is merely a sustained extension of speaking—the basic principle here is the power and passion of the expression. If someone is singing in your dream, the message that is being communicated is very important. So important, that the spoken word was not enough to carry the force of the weight of that message. Therefore, it is important to consider what is being sung and incorporate the message into your interpretation.

Losing one's voice in a dream might correspond to a feeling of lack of passion in your waking life or a loss of expression due to some challenging circumstance. If you can sing in your waking life, your personal relationship to your singing is crucial to consider. If you are critical, you may be connecting to being judgmental of your passion, or lack of it. If you cannot sing as well as you wish you could, you might be longing for more passionate encounters by dreaming of being able to sing in your sleep state. Singing before an audience may connect to a need to rally inner resources behind some common desired aim or goal. If someone else is singing in your dream, use the Character Aspect technique to determine what part of you is expressing a passionate need to get your attention.

Skeleton

Universal Landscape: Hidden structure, old or outdated foundations.

Dreaming Lens: Is the skeleton complete or fractured? Is it a medical skeleton that is clean and pristine, or is it buried and partially decayed? Is the skeleton recognizable as having once supported someone known to you? Does it frighten you, or intrigue you?

Personal Focus: Skeletons support the physical body and are not readily visible to the outside world. They are the foundation on which everything else is built. In the dream world, they represent this same underlying structure of our bodies, ourselves, and our lives. A skeleton is the invisible underpinning of any physical, conceptual, emotional, or spiritual construct in your waking life.

The skeleton of our lives is the structure of ideas, beliefs, and myths around which we superimpose our sense of self. When you can see the skeleton of something, you have a better idea of what is supporting it or holding it upright. If you dream of this image, you might be getting a message that something in the structure needs to be examined.

Discovering a skeleton in a closet may suggest that some of your thought structures may be outdated and need to be taken out and contemplated. If a skeleton is being studied in a laboratory, it may be time to explore the underlying structure of something—ask what's underneath so you may better discover ways of managing an area of your life.

Consider in what context the skeleton appears in the dream and how you respond to it emotionally. A sense of fear, of feeling "shaken to the bones," means you may fear confronting some underlying structure that you have perhaps taken for granted. Do you need to reconsider your beliefs about something or someone? If so, you may dream of a skeleton appearing as a result of such an investigation. Your familiarity or comfort level with seeing the skeleton will match the insight you are having as the essence of that area of your life is exposed to your inner view.

Skyscraper

Universal Landscape: Expansion to higher levels of conscious awareness.

Dreaming Lens: How tall was the skyscraper in your dream? What was the building made of? Were you inside or outside of the skyscraper? What floor were you on? Were you on the roof? How far could you see?

Personal Focus: Any building is a reflection of the consciousness of human beings. If a house in a dream symbolizes your sense of personal self, each successively larger building can be thought of as expansions of this consciousness. In this way, a skyscraper is the ultimate expression of human consciousness reaching from the ground to the heavens.

The skyscraper is also a very American icon and is directly connected to the explosion of urbanization that marked the movement into the current modern era. When steel began to be mass-produced, it paved the way for the bustling city environment to push upwards. This ascension, then, is symbolic for the consciousness of mankind erupting toward higher levels of awareness and intellectual functioning.

There is an interesting linguistic nuance in the meaning of the skyscraper as a symbol. A tall building is understood in terms of just how tall it is. And every floor is also commonly known as a "story." The taller a building is, the more "stories" it has: the higher into consciousness one gets, the more life-stories are required to unfold in order to gain the wisdom reflected in the high vantage point that a skyscraper has to offer.

Consider your relationship to the skyscraper in your dream. If you are inside the building, then your dream is reflecting a deeper rumination of thoughts. Being outside and looking up at the building is to be contemplating thoughts you have yet to grapple with. If you are enjoying the view from someplace high in the building, then the dream is connected to the awareness that results from higher levels of thought. If the height is frightening or menacing, then the dream may be expressing fears and overwhelm around too much thinking.

Smoke/Smoking

Universal Landscape: An indicator of transformation or change.

Dreaming Lens: Where was the smoke in your dream? Were you aware of the source? If the dream included a person smoking a substance, what was being smoked and by whom? Was there any color to the smoke? Were you in danger of asphyxiation? Were you creating the smoke? Was it increasing or decreasing in your dream?

Personal Focus: The saying goes, *where there's smoke, there's fire.* Since fire represents drastic change, smoke is an indication of the occurrence of transformation without necessarily having the ability to see the actual source of the shift. Smoke can cause asphyxiation by blocking the lungs from receiving oxygen, so dream smoke may indicate a suffocating life situation about which your unconscious is sending you an alarm.

A smoke screen is a mechanism for keeping something hidden. It is a battle technique that was used during the Civil War and thereafter, associating it with danger and violence. It has entered our language as something that indicates a deliberate desire to obscure a person's true intention or create a diversion in order to perpetrate some act of betrayal. If your dream smoke obstructs your sight in any way, you may want to consider what current difficulty in your life may be blocking your view of things as they really are. Ask yourself if you are focusing on what's really important and not being distracted in some way.

Cigarette smoking is a hotbed of controversy in today's society, such that the symbolic meaning attached to it can be complicated. The media has always connoted smoking as glamorous and sexy, though that is changing. Those who smoke may have a relationship with their smoking that runs the gamut from frustratingly addicted to apathetically indifferent to the consequences. Health conscious, nonsmoking individuals can be quite virulent in their objections and many states and cities have banned smoking in public places altogether.

Given these radically different perspectives, if a cigarette features prominently in your dream, you must use your own associations with smoking to arrive at an accurate interpretation. No matter what your Personal Focus is, the health risks associated with smoking make the symbolic meaning connect to making choices that are not impacted by your knowledge of the consequences. The factor of addiction is an important element to consider. Smoking can represent any choice in life that is not healthy, but difficult to avoid.

Snake

Universal Landscape: Change or transition; healing; death and rebirth.

Dreaming Lens: What kind of snake is appearing in your dream? Is it poisonous, dangerous, or innocuous? What was your fear level or lack thereof? Did the snake have human qualities or abilities? Does it have a message?

Personal Focus: Snakes can inspire great and varied personal emotions and, therefore, can ultimately connect to very different shades of meaning based on your Personal Focus. Because of this continuum of response from fear and loathing to fascination and sensual stirrings, they need to be considered carefully when they appear in a dream.

First and foremost, snakes represent change and transformation. This connects to the fact that they shed their skins in their growth process and that many of them are capable of causing fatality to their predators, implying the symbolic rebirth that follows any death experience. There is a healing element of this, as many snake venoms can also be used as curatives. This may connect to the two snakes that appear on the physician's caduceus, representing the challenge to life and the response of the healer to match it.

In the Judeo-Christian tradition, the snake bears the responsibility for tempting Adam and Eve. As such, a snake can represent a confrontation with a change in your value system. It is important to remember that their yielding introduced the human race to the knowledge of mortality and the birth of consciousness. A serpent in your dream may actually represent a major shift in your awareness that may bring about the death of an old paradigm that brings you into a whole new world.

In Eastern cultures, the awakening of spiritual power is often referred to as a snake. Known as the Kundalini, it is experienced as an incredible energy which undulates up the spine. Stimulating this can induce a tremendous healing force, which contains the ability to purify the nervous and glandular systems. The practice of yoga is designed to awaken the snake that lives dormant at the base of the spine. As a dream symbol, a snake could represent the potential for power and energy if properly channeled.

If a snake appears on a particular part of your body (such as choking you) you might want to make an association between that body part/energy and what in your life needs to be transformed. How you feel about the presence of actions of the snake reveal your deeper emotional responses to the change that is occurring.

Snow

Universal Landscape: Emotional disconnect, ignorance of underlying issues.

Dreaming Lens: Was it snowing in your dream? Had it already snowed? Was the snow melting? What did you do with the snow? Were you outside in it or indoors and warm? How heavy was the snowfall? Did it hamper visibility or mobility?

Personal Focus: There are few sights as beautiful as a landscape covered by a blanket of fresh, undisturbed snow. While this may conjure idyllic thoughts of serene landscapes, the symbolic meaning of snow connects more with what it is covering up than with the beauty it embodies while doing so.

Snow is frozen water. Water represents emotions. Emotions that are frozen imply a disconnection from authentically experiencing them in their raw, wet form. When snowfall is particularly heavy, it can impede visibility and render you immobile or housebound. When seen through the perspective of emotional avoidance, it is easy to see that a large dose of emotional expression that is not being dealt with can seriously limit any forward movement in your life.

The joy that snow can impart is not to be discounted completely, but should be added to your interpretation only after exploring the more universal meaning described above. Consider your own experience of snow, both now and from childhood years. As an example, if you loved playing in the snow and the dream image evoked joyful feelings, your interpretation might combine the avoidant qualities of a cold-shouldered approach to an emotional stimulus with the joyful abandon that can sometimes result from putting off dealing with a sensitive issue until a later time. Since snow melts, facing the underlying issue is inevitable. The snow just postpones the confrontation and does so with beauty and the promise of temporary peace.

Soul Mate

Universal Landscape: An inevitable expansion of your total Self.

Dreaming Lens: Did you meet your soul mate in your dream? Were you pursuing your soul mate? Did you know your soul mate? Did your soul mate know you? Was he or she elusive, or responsive? Was there anything in the way of you connecting with your soul mate?

Personal Focus: The idea of soul mating is a complicated one due to the attachment of expectation to the concept. Most of us want our soul mates to be in the form of lovers with whom we live happily ever after; however, a soul mate is simply another individual with whom we share an energetic synchronicity and a powerful recognition. A soul mating can occur across any matrix of relationship: lovers, partners, friends, siblings, and so on. The kernel of the meaning to soul mating is in its feeling that it was destined that you meet.

If the soul mate in your dream is someone you know, the interpretation should connect to the Character Aspects you associate with them. If they are not known to you, use the Dreaming Lens to round out your investigation. Whoever they are, the qualities being presented are to be integrated into your Self as part of your journey toward integration.

Searching for your soul mate indicates that wholeness and/or the blocks to wholeness have not yet been identified. A successful connection with your soul mate may mean that integration is at hand. If there are challenges to connecting with them in your dream, those challenges represent the obstacles to wholeness in your current life. The dream may be telling you it's time to face them and that no matter how frightening the challenge, you may as well surrender to the task at hand. After all, just like meeting your soul mate out in the world, it is meant to be.

Special Powers

Universal Landscape: Increase in confidence and ability.

Dreaming Lens: Did you have a special power in the dream? Did someone else? What was your special power? Did you know about your special power? Were you able to use it effectively? Did you gain or lose power in the dream? Were you the only one with special powers or did you share them with others?

Personal Focus: We associate special powers with the fantastic world of comics and video games. This notion of accelerated abilities is particularly appealing to adolescent males, who form the largest fan pool of these types of media. As a symbol, special powers should be considered primarily as a fantastical reaction to feelings of inadequacy. Through them, an average person can be suddenly endowed with abilities that enable them to transcend the challenges of a mundane life.

Most special powers can be related to one of the four elements of fire, air, water, or earth. A power associated with heat or flames should be considered as a function of combustion and the transformation that fire can generate. Any power associated with water connects to emotions: use and manipulation of water relates to channeling the power of emotion whereas transmuting water to either steam or ice has the impact of altering emotional energy for one's use. The grounded element of earth is represented by anything rock-like or strength-oriented power. Air is the element in question when powers such as invisibility or flight are concerned.

If your special power does not conform to one of the elements, the key to your interpretation will lie in discovering the underlying use and essence of the power you possessed in the dream. Ask yourself what area of your life needs amplification based on the area of your skills and abilities that were amplified by the increased power.

Spider/Spider Web

Universal Landscape: Powerful feminine energy. Patience.

Dreaming Lens: Were you encountering a spider or spider webbing? Was it frightening? Were you in danger? Did you kill the spider? Did you want to? Did the spider want to harm you? Was the overall scene macabre or more magical?

Personal Focus: Spiders are a powerful image of the feminine principle, which relates to creativity and receptivity. Spiders embody this by virtue of the creative act of making a web and the patience involved in awaiting their prey. Many, if not most people, have an aversion to spiders, which makes them a creature of the Shadow.

Spiders can be found everywhere, which is one of the reasons why they feature prominently as a common dream image. While not all are venomous, the most widely known spider is the Black Widow, famous for mating with and then killing her male counterpart. This is the feminine principle in its most ferocious expression.

A spider's webbing is a miraculous feat of engineering and unparalleled beauty. Its purpose is twofold. On the side of nurturing, it is a home. However, it is also a weapon of prey—a trap set to capture, kill, and eat. Spiders also connect to the numerological expression of abundance because of their eight legs. (See Numbers.) Any or all of these themes may be being expressed in a dream that features this image.

A spider web may point to creative ideas that are currently being spun. This also indicates that a period of waiting must follow in order for success to be achieved. A spider bite may indicate that an infusion of the feminine principle may be in order for your current dealings to succeed. The irritation, illness, or death that is possible with a spider bite indicates the level of sacrifice that will be required of you on an emotional level at this time.

Stabbing

Universal Landscape: Penetration; deep impact.

Dreaming Lens: Were you stabbed or did you do the stabbing? Were you or someone else hurt badly? Was the stabbing fatal? If you did the stabbing, who was your victim? Who was the assailant? Did you know them or were they a stranger? What sort of weapon was involved? Where did you get it?

Personal Focus: The act of stabbing creates a very narrow, deep penetrating wound that can do a surprising amount of damage, while compromising a fairly small amount of flesh. In other words, a little goes a long way. Harsh or sharp words can have the same effect. The right phrase delivered with the proper tone can cut very deeply and wound a person at a surprisingly deep level. In fact, any penetrating action that occurs suddenly and contains a touch of violent intention could be represented by stabbing in a dream: Sudden changes in loyalty are often referred to as a stab in the back. Unexpected news can feel like a stab in the heart. The nature of a small wound that produces a great deal of blood symbolizes the devastation that can follow even the smallest of hurts.

Examine the structure of the dream for an accurate interpretation. If you hold the knife and stab another, use the Character Aspects of your victim to explore the part of you that you are attacking. If it is the other way around, your assailant is a part of yourself that is demanding to be heard. They may represent a way of being that is harmful to you in some way. They could also indicate a Character Aspect of your self that, if ignored, will get your attention in a destructive way.

If you are witnessing a stabbing, the unconscious process may be more internal. Looking at the people involved will guide you to a deeper understanding of the conflict. A stabbing dream could also be triggered by a waking life experience where you are feeling hurt by another's behavior. This is equally true if you are the one doing the wounding. Such a dream could be your unconscious letting you know how important it is to remain vulnerable, even when to do so might feel dangerous.

Stairs

Universal Landscape: Transitions in life, often directly connected to personal growth or assessment.

Dreaming Lens: Were you climbing the stairs? Were you ascending or descending? Where were the stairs leading to and from? How many steps were there? What step were you on? What shape were they in? Were they steep? Were they dangerous? Did you slip or fall?

Personal Focus: Stairs represent transition, change, and personal growth. When we use them, we make direct contact with our feet. This makes them symbolic of change on a very specific, personal level. Climbing up stairs should be interpreted as ascending to higher levels of consciousness. Going down stairs connects to revisiting places you have already been or moving into lower levels of thought, such as anger and envy, or facing your own emotional development by revisiting old issues.

Where the stairs are is important to consider. A stairway in a home is about personal transitions, whereas stairs in public environments reveal issues around how we operate out in the world, in full view of others. There may be literal elements of this image in a dream, as a dream that takes place on a stairway at your workplace will likely connect to issues that are work related. A stairway in a public park may reveal shifts that involve issues of relaxation and leisure. Use the Dreaming Lens to focus your interpretation.

Your actual experience of climbing the stairs is the key to working with this symbol. A treacherous experience may reveal fears attached to issues you are currently facing. Running up and down stairs with ease may point to an ability to operate at different levels with grace if your life is calling you to do so. Fear of where the stairs may lead correlate to investigations that lay ahead of you where the outcome is not clear. The number of stairs, if known, can be considered using numerology (see Numbers). Escalators indicate more ease in the transition, but must also be looked at in terms of the potential to gloss over the change that is occurring. Remember that going down is as important as going up in life. We must often revisit where we have been below before we can move upward effectively. Eventually, we must be able to easily exist on many levels at once.

Stealing

Universal Landscape: Acquisition of resources without consideration.

Dreaming Lens: Were you stealing, or were you being stolen from? Were you a witness as opposed to a participant? Did you know the perpetrators? What was being taken? Were you present for the act, or was it something you discovered? Were you hiding facts or attempting to uncover truths?

Personal Focus: To steal is to take something that belongs to another. The objects of theft are often things of value. Therefore, the symbolic meaning implies resources or levels of abundance that are coveted and then taken without permission or regard for consequences. The opposite of stealing is being stolen from. This uses the same themes, and adds the elements of violation and loss.

Begin considering your interpretation of this symbol from the appropriate perspective, based on which side of the act or consequence of stealing appeared in your dream. Often inherent in the act of stealing is the presence of betrayal, so look for areas of your life in which this may be present. For deeper clarity, take note of the category in which the stolen property might fall. The more valuable the item or items that are stolen, the higher the emotional stakes are being expressed by the dream. Personal items might spark you to consider more intimate issues in your life, including circumstances of an emotional, private, or hidden nature. Theft in a corporate or institutional environment may be revealing underlying issues surrounding your more worldly considerations, such as politics, your workplace, or your larger community.

If you were a witness to thievery in your dream as opposed to the victim or perpetrator, a more complicated process will be called for to reach an accurate interpretation. If this is the case, use the Character Aspects of both sides of the theft to examine what elements of your personality might be compromising other areas of your thinking. When faced with unknown elements associated with this symbol appearing in a dream, incorporate your ignorance or lack of awareness into your interpretation. Stealing in a dream may be the inciting incident of an investigation that needs to commence.

Strangling

Universal Landscape: Deliberate constriction of communication and/or life force.

Dreaming Lens: Were you being strangled in your dream? Were you strangling someone else? Who else was involved? Were you witnessing something that was occurring between two other people? Was the strangling fatal?

Personal Focus: Since strangling involves cutting off the air supply at the neck, communication is the focus of the interpretation of any dream with this image in it. It is important to recognize that there is a specific intention associated with strangling that is to cause death. Any death in a dream should be considered a transformation of such magnitude, that an inevitable rebirth must surely follow.

Strangling necessitates that two people are involved, which means you should consider the other person as a Character Aspect of yourself. If you are the aggressor, then the person you are choking is a part of your personality that you are attempting to or needing to stifle. You will have to decide if this is because you actually need to silence an inner voice that doesn't serve you, or if your unconscious is expressing fear around an idea that wants to be expressed that you are not quite ready to listen to.

If you are being choked, look at who is attacking you. This represents some element of your psyche that is rising up and attempting to silence you or rob you of the breath of life. If you are witnessing two other people engaged in this act, use the Character Aspect technique to identify what parts of yourself are involved in some sort of inner turmoil. This conflict is likely going to be about one way of being (the strangler) attempting to control, stifle, or eliminate another way of being (the victim). (See also Choking.)

Stroke

Universal Landscape: The dangerous impact of destructive thoughts.

Dreaming Lens: Did you have a stroke? Did someone else have a stroke in your dream? What was the end result of the stroke? Was it painful? Where did the stroke take place?

Personal Focus: A stroke is caused by some sort of disturbance in the integrity of the brain. Caused by a blood clot or the eruption of a blood vessel, the damage that results can leave the victim of a stroke with a range of symptoms from innocuous discomfort to death. The brain is the symbolic center of the intellect and thoughts. When thoughts are compromised by some sudden challenge, a symbolic dream stroke may occur if the cause is severe enough.

There are two basic types of strokes. One form of stroke results from the buildup of pressure within the brain; as a result, a blood vessel breaks and a stroke occurs. The other type starts with a blood clot from somewhere else in the body traveling into the brain, causing damage or death. Even if your dream doesn't clearly indicate which cause created the stroke, it may be a helpful piece of dream work to consider the distinctions of each.

The first type, where the damage is a result of pressure within the brain connects symbolically to some specific, repeating thought or pattern of thinking that causes enough stress or tension to eventually explode, shutting down all thought and functioning. This may indicate that the thoughts or ideas in question have been present and building up for a long time, though probably below the level of consciousness. Ignored for too long, they burst into consciousness in a way that is damaging and stops anything else from taking place till they are dealt with. What nagging thoughts have you been ignoring?

When the culprit is a clot that starts elsewhere in the body, the initial cause of the shutdown is more likely in the realm of action than thought. Look to where in your life something is causing repeated stress that you have been overlooking or ignoring altogether.

If you are the one having a stroke in your dream, then look to where your thoughts might be hurting you on a deep level. If someone else in your dream is the victim, then use that person as a Character Aspect of the part of your personality that is suffering due to misaligned thoughts.

Sun

Universal Landscape: Life force; life itself. Consciousness.

Dreaming Lens: Was the Sun rising, setting, or mid-sky? Was it the Sun as we know it in our solar system? Was it closer than normal? Further away? Was the heat of the Sun oppressive or dangerous, or was it warm and comforting? Did you experience it from the vantage point of Earth or space? Were you traveling toward it or perhaps even into it? Was the Sun being eclipsed in your dream? Was solar energy the focus of the dream?

Personal Focus: The Sun is the source of almost all life on Earth. There was probably no prehistoric civilization that didn't worship the Sun as a god or supreme being. Though modern science has demystified the Sun somewhat by expanding our understanding of what it is made of, its awe-inspiring nature is just as magnificent today as it must have been for early humankind.

As the focal point of the system that we call home, it is the symbolic center of life itself. Not only do we literally revolve around it in space, we also have created our lives to revolve around our relationship with it. The power contained within the Sun is so enormous, it is almost unfathomable. From the impact of the seasons to the rhythm of day and night, the Sun truly embodies human consciousness. The condition and position of the Sun in your dreams, as well as your proximity to it, are crucial to an accurate interpretation. If you dream of comfortably basking in its embracing warmth, it could indicate a sense of contentment with life. If you experience the harmful and dangerous effects of too much Sun in your dream, you might want to consider paying more attention to some of the more powerful forces in your life. In the same way that a sunburn can sneak up and surprise the unwitting sunbather, forces of power left unchecked can do damage that go unnoticed until the damage is done.

A sunrise may point to new beginnings just as a sunset may indicate an ending of some sort. If your dream Sun is blocked by clouds, you may want to consider where in your life your personal power is being limited or held back. To dream of tapping into the technology of solar power may allow you to recognize that every human being has a birthright to an endless supply of abundance and limitless life force. If your dream finds you in fantastical close proximity to the Sun, such as flying through space toward it or even through the Sun itself, you could be dreaming of connecting with a new surge of personal power. However, be warned: To whom much is given, much will be required.

Surgery

Universal Landscape: Violent alteration toward healing.

Dreaming Lens: Were you having surgery in the dream? Had you, or someone else, already had a surgery? What type of surgery was it? Were you performing the surgery? If so, on whom? Was it excessively violent or scary? How was your recovery?

Personal Focus: Surgery is usually thought of as a painful and invasive procedure undertaken when some form of healing needs to take place. In its essence, it is a process that fundamentally alters the structure of some part of the body. Whether it is to remove something harmful, assist in recovery from trauma or enhance one's appearance, the surgeon never leaves things as they were found. This makes the symbolic meaning connect to the alteration as the primary result of the surgery, and healing as secondary.

All surgeries can be categorized as either removing or adding something to the body. If something is being removed, begin your investigation in areas of your life where you are facing loss or release. If you are being surgically enhanced with new material such as replaced joints or a pacemaker, look to ways in which you are taking on new paths or ways of being that are currently foreign to you.

The area of the body involved will be prominent in your interpretation. If your organs and intestinal area are the site of a surgery, you are likely dreaming about issues around emotional expression. If bones and/or joints are involved, then what is being altered connects to the foundational structures that underlie your sense of self or belief systems. Brain surgery points to intellectual or thought-based changes, whereas heart surgery would imply shifting around the expression of love or passion. Plastic surgery deals with the more superficial elements of change.

No matter what the surgery is, there is an implication that some area in your consciousness requires dramatic healing. The healing that is taking place is big enough to warrant this image to express itself, which is a further indication that an alteration will be required if the healing is to be successful. As with all change, there may be pain and suffering. Most importantly, there will be a recovery period before the new way of being will be fully accessible to you.

Sweat/Sweating

Universal Landscape: Restoring balance from stress, fear, or guilt.

Dreaming Lens: Were you sweating in your dream? Was someone else? Was it subtle or profuse? Was the sweat visible, or was it evident by other means, such as stained clothes? Was the sweating connected with a specific physical activity and did you know what that was? Was it healthy sweating or indicative of fear or anxiety? Did you wake up sweating?

Personal Focus: There are both emotional and activity-orientated correlations to sweating and the appearance of sweat. However, the essential meaning assigned to sweat must connect with its most basic and primal function: to regulate the temperature of the physical body. We would die if this process did not operate effectively.

If you are sweating in your dream, your interpretation may uncover an unconscious message that some life experience is posing a threat to your equilibrium and balance. Heat represents a visceral reaction to perceived danger in the form of anger or aggression. Sweating represents your desire to restore balance from whatever might be the cause of these feelings of threat. If someone else in your dream is sweating, consider what their Character Aspect might represent for you. It may be that a particular way you have of being in the world is heating things up and a restoration of balance is necessary. Sweating also serves to rid the body of toxins, so dream sweat may point to the presence of underlying thoughts, ideas, or behaviors that are ultimately poisoning your sense of well being.

On a social level, sweat is sometimes evidence of inner stress. This can reveal the presence of guilt or panic that betrays the person beyond their ability to control their sweating. If you feel this may be the case in your dream, your interpretation should involve investigating secrets or issues in your waking life that you might rather keep hidden. Sweating may indicate that these thoughts have the power to reveal themselves through inadvertent means. Sweat appearing on the face or brow likely point to issues related to your persona and how others may perceive you. Underarm sweat connects directly to stress and anxiety. If this includes the presence of body odor, then your interpretation should look at situations that may be causing feelings of shame.

Swimming

Universal Landscape: Moving with effort through an emotional transition.

Dreaming Lens: Were you swimming or were you watching someone else swim? Was there a specific purpose or destination involved, or were you swimming for pleasure? How difficult was it to stay on your course? What sort of body of water were you in? Were you swimming above the water or down deep fully immersed?

Personal Focus: Water represents the emotional realm of our feelings, both conscious and unconscious. Swimming is specifically about progress and making your way through the emotional territory in your life. The intimate connection suggested by being immersed in water makes this an image that reflects your personal emotional journey as an individual. The effort of propelling yourself forward is completely self-motivated and generated exclusively by your own body. This reveals how effectively, or ineffectively, you are pushing yourself through an emotional challenge in your life.

The ease, pace, and depth of your swim offers a great deal of texture for you to investigate. The harder you have to work, the more effort is required to arrive at your destination of emotional growth. How fast you are moving will inform you of the speed of the process you are undergoing. The level of immersion communicates the emotional territory through which you are traveling—being on the surface reflects the emotions you are aware of, whereas swimming underwater implies deeper areas of feelings that reside in your unconscious mind.

The body of water you are in plays a strong role in arriving at an accurate interpretation. Small amounts of contained emotion connected to single issues in your life will be reflected by images of man-made constructions, such as pools or spas. A natural body of water expands the symbolic meaning to processes that are shared with others. The ocean represents the collective unconscious and an emotional connection to the human race. A lake might be more personal, but is reflective of your life as a whole. Water that flows, such as a river or a stream, connotes issues of emotional flow and the expression of your feelings.

Swimming upstream might mean that the current challenge is significant and requires effort. Moving with the current or tides could indicate that surrender to the emotional shifts is taking place. The fear of drowning can represent being overwhelmed by the transition you are in. Swimming laps might point to facing a recurring emotional issue that you are confronting over and over again. Competitive swimming could indicate that your struggle is both visible to others and may be producing elements of performance anxiety.

Taking a Test

Universal Landscape: Anxiety over knowledge; accountability.

Dreaming Lens: Were you prepared or unprepared for the test in your dream? What was your level of anxiety? Were you alone, or were there others with you sharing the experience? Was it present time, or did you return to an earlier time in life?

Personal Focus: Taking a test is to allow yourself to be held accountable for what you have learned in some area of life. Quizzes, tests, and exams are part of the structure of education that most people in the West first experienced in childhood. This is imprinted in the brain as a permanent memory associating the sensation of performance anxiety with images of being tested in school. In dreams, these become a metaphor for the ways in which we are tested by challenges in life. We only pass such tests if we have gained a sufficient level of knowledge from past lessons learned. When you dream of taking a test, your unconscious is letting you know that there is underlying anxiety around how prepared you feel to face your life.

Examine your life for areas where you feel you are being held accountable, even if the only person holding yourself accountable is you. This is often a recurring dream for people who experience high levels of performance anxiety, fear of failure, or frequent feelings of judgment from others. It can also indicate a hidden need to be acknowledged by those in authority in your life and to feel validated for your accomplishments. In this way, a test dream can be a compensation for feeling undervalued.

The emotional timbre of the Dreaming Lens will help you clarify the meaning you give your interpretation. Failing a test can leave you open for new choices and directions. Cheating on a test can indicate an issue of fairness, entitlement, or heightened inadequacy. Obsessing over a test and its results could indicate that you are driven by your perception of how you are measured by others rather than your own self-evaluation. If you don't get to take the test in your dream, consider areas of your life where fear of failure has obstructed your path to success.

Teachers

Universal Landscape: The steps toward mastery.

Dreaming Lens: Who was the teacher in your dream? Was this a real teacher from your life, or an unknown character? How did you feel about this teacher? What class were you taking? Was the teacher out of the context of a classroom? Were you the teacher?

Personal Focus: Learning occurs by accumulating small increments of data that build upon each other. This results in the eventual ability to understand a theory or concept. A teacher in a dream is a Character Aspect of the dreamer. It represents the part of your personality that is aware of your current level of knowledge in some area of life. Teachers know what piece of information needs to be added next in order for learning to take place.

A figure of authority, the teacher is the one person at school who knows what the lesson plan is. They have both the questions *and the answers*. They not only control what happens in the classroom, but they also know why things are ordered in a particular way. Each of our teachers presented us with the specific information needed to master a particular level of our functioning. As we mastered one grade level, we moved on to new lessons and new teachers. While this ideal may not have been the actual schoolroom experience for most people, the principle is the same. Any teacher in a dream represents the part of you that understands this concept of step-by-step mastery and provides the mental environment in which learning and advancement occurs, or when it is blocked.

There is great patience built into this process, even though many of your teachers in life may have lacked this quality. When a teacher appears in your dream, examine him or her as a Character Aspect of yourself. Their behavior toward you in the dream and your resulting feelings will offer you insight as to how well your inner guidance system is operating and to what degree you are showing yourself patience with the pace of your growth. A kindly teacher will result in a very different interpretation from one who is abusive.

If the teacher in your dream was one from your waking life, how you feel about him or her is the interpretation itself. A positive role model will have very different meaning than your hated nemesis. If the teacher is unknown to you, then you must look to other elements in the dream to inform your investigation. Are you receptive to the lessons that life is serving up at the time of your dream, or are you resisting? Will you pass your examinations and move up to the next grade level, or be left back to repeat what you have not yet learned?

Teeth Falling Out

Universal Landscape: Insecurity.

Dreaming Lens: Were your teeth loose, or falling out of your mouth? What was the amount of pain or bleeding experienced? Did you swallow any of your teeth as they fell from your gums? Did you have trouble removing a loose tooth? Were they crumbling, disintegrating, or coming out whole?

Personal Focus: Teeth serve three primary functions. They allow us to process our food so we can nurture ourselves. They express joy when revealed in a smile and they can indicate aggression when exposed in a snarl. All of these things—nurturance, joy, and protection—connect directly to security and well-being. If a person is not able to be self-nurturing, attract loving connections, and maintain a sense of being safe from danger, the basic constructs of a secure life are not likely to be available. Without these three important parts of life, fear would prevail. Therefore, when this dream image appears, issues of personal security are at the forefront of your unconscious expression.

There are various levels of intensity associated with this symbol. It can fluctuate from a slightly loose tooth to having them all crumble out of your mouth in a bloody mess. The scale of intensity of the dream will indicate the amount of fear being expressed. Whether it is a general fear of being out of control, looking bad, aging, or other issues of unmet needs, the appearance of this dream indicates underlying insecurity in some area of your waking life.

The teeth are used for chewing and this association can indicate a need to "chew on something for a while" as in mulling over a choice or course of action. Sinking your teeth into something refers to taking on life wholeheartedly. Losing your teeth in a dream could indicate an inability or unwillingness to do so. Losing our teeth as children is such a powerful rite of passage. On some level, losing your teeth in a dream will connect to the process of growing up, even in adulthood.

Telephone

Universal Landscape: Direct communication with a buffer of safety.

Dreaming Lens: Did the phone ring or did you initiate the call? Were you using the telephone or did you need to and could not? Was someone else using it? If so, was that an obstacle for you? Were you waiting for the phone to ring? Was the phone ringing off the hook or silently hung up? Was it a pay phone, cell phone, new, antique, large or small phone?

Personal Focus: Most people in the Western world are accustomed to the instant gratification of picking up the telephone to contact people with whom we want to speak. In a dream, this points to the need or desire to communicate, with the added texture of ease and immediacy.

The most powerful element of a telephone is the ring. We are conditioned to respond to that sound with a visceral and instantaneous reaction. The feelings elicited by this run the gamut from relief and excitement to dread, depending on who we think may be calling. Hearing a phone ring can be a sign that some part of your psyche is attempting to get in touch with your conscious awareness. Wanting or wishing it to ring may connect an area of your life where you need some information. Whether it is reassurance you crave, validation of some kind, or the solution to a problem that requires insight that has yet to occur to you, your hope with regard to who is calling will let you know what it is that you need.

Being involved in a conversation on the phone implies that various aspects of your personality are collaborating in some fashion. Whom you are speaking with will offer insight into what qualities within you need to be consulted at this time in your life. The nature of the conversation will, of course, reveal a great deal of data for an accurate interpretation. Hanging up connects to the desire for control. If this is the case, notice how politely or abruptly this is done, as this can reveal the level of defensiveness you may be expressing.

An important perspective to consider when a phone is being utilized for communication is the absence of a face-to-face connection. The physical distance that a telephone allows may imply the presence of vulnerability and fear around an issue in your life. Using a phone rather than connecting in person could indicate a number of darker motivations, such as a lack of authenticity, the need to avoid, or a deception in the works. On the lighter side, a telephone can unite loved ones separated by distance. If this is the case in a dream, it could represent that integration is taking place between aspects of your personality.

If you remember a telephone number from a dream, there may be some meaning to explore through using the meaning of numbers. Add up all the digits you can remember until you get to a final, single digit between one and nine. See Numbers for an interpretation of the numerology being revealed.

Television

Universal Landscape: The collective consciousness. Manufactured truth.

Dreaming Lens: Was the TV on or off? Was it broken? Were you watching TV? Was someone else? Who else was present in the dream? Did you know what show you were watching? Was it on, but in the background? Were you part of the television programming itself?

Personal Focus: The television media has completely shaped modern life. Through it, the entire Western world is united in a common thread of corporately controlled information that we as a culture accept as truth. In the same way that the collective *unconscious* contains the shared, but hidden, elements of the human mind, the collective *consciousness* contains the shared knowledge of which people are actually aware.

Television represents this collective thought in action. Through programming, especially the news, there is an almost hypnotic experience that makes the general population accept what is seen on

TV as the truth about life, whether or not that is actually so. The line between what is truth and what is fiction is continually blurred and this has increased with the advent of so-called "reality television."

Whatever the proximity between yourself and the television in your dream should be considered to represent your current relationship to the impact that television and its content is having on your life. Some people never watch TV while others are addicted. Where you fit on this continuum will affect how you view this symbol in a dream. First examine the Dreaming Lens for an accurate, contextual theme of what messages the dream may be offering you. Then filter this perspective through the Universal Landscape of manufactured truth and race mind thoughts. Ask yourself how you might be being manipulated by what other people think as opposed to your own authentic notions about life. It may be time to turn the television off and start living life in real time.

Thunder

Universal Landscape: Evidence of dramatic moments of enlightenment.

Dreaming Lens: Was there a storm in your dream? Was there also lightning present? How much time was there between the lightning flash and the thunder? How loud was the thunder? Were you frightened?

Personal Focus: Thunder is the auditory evidence of the presence of lightning. If lightning is to be understood as sudden bursts of enlightenment and awareness that appear in an instant and change things forever, thunder is the booming announcement that comes along with the moment.

There is the old adage that the amount of time between the lightning strike and the clap of thunder determines the distance of the storm. If thunder and lightning are both present in the dream, it raises the stakes of the interpretation. It can also point to the distinction between a moment of awareness and the secondary impact of the change it initiates. (See also Lightning).

Timepieces/Clocks/Watches

Universal Landscape: Your relationship to the flow and pace of life.

Dreaming Lens: What type of time piece were you dreaming of? Was it working? Was the time accurate and, if not, was it fast or slow? If it was a clock, how public was it? What were your feelings around what the time was? What were your feelings around the accuracy or inaccuracy of the time?

Personal Focus: Time is a creation of the human mind as a way to systematically measure the passing of moments. Its primary purpose connects to the ability to create agreement in a diverse society. Early humans relied on the repetitive cycles of the Sun, Moon, and seasons to invent the agrarian societies that led to the birth of civilization. As civilization expanded, it became necessary to expand this concept in order to accommodate the complexity required for larger communities to function effectively.

From sundials to watches and clocks, timepieces are the tools by which the measurement of moments becomes accessible to all. They are symbolic of the effectiveness with which someone monitors the pace of their movement through their day-to-day lives. Additionally, timepieces are the screens onto which people project their emotional relationship to time, whether that is anxiety connected to feeling it is moving too fast or depression stimulated by a sense that it is moving too slowly.

Your personal relationship to time must be factored into your interpretation. Consider whether you are operating on one of the extremes: always late, always early, or compulsively prompt. Another important factor is the feelings that come up for you around time, from complacency to anxiety. The more prominent issues of time integrity factor into your waking life, the more rigorous you should be when creating your interpretation.

The type of timepiece will offer different shades of perspective in the meaning and correlates with size and proximity. A watch connects to the very personal and is reflective of you, the dreamer. A house clock expands this view to a more complex sense of self that reflects your role within the dynamic of your family and/or your most intimate associates. An institutional clock would point you toward considering time issues that relate to the specific location: A school clock connects to feelings around knowledge and learning. A workplace clock could be expressing issues about productivity, effectiveness, or remuneration. A public clock in a town or city expands this view to a more collective and social level.

A timepiece that has stopped may be expressing a wish for more available time to relieve pressures around productivity. Inaccuracy in a timepiece, fast or slow, may be pointing to a lack of awareness of time and its impact on your life. The more ominous the feelings around the timepiece in your dream, the more likely your unconscious is expressing that something is out of balance in your relationship to time, its passing, and all that comes with it.

Tongue

Universal Landscape: The ability to articulate. The sense of taste.

Dreaming Lens: How was the tongue featured in the dream? Was it your tongue or the tongue of another person? Was the tongue human or animal? Was kissing part of the dream? Was the tongue attached to a person or detached from a mouth? Was the tissue living or dead? What was your visceral reaction to the tongue in the dream?

Personal Focus: The tongue's ability to form different shapes inside the mouth endows human beings with an enormous catalog of sounds. This has allowed us to create one of our greatest assets—language.

The tongue is symbolic of our innate human desire to be understood and relates to issues around communication. This can reflect everything from being soft spoken to possessing a sharp tongue. If communication is too passive, the speaker may be rendered ineffective. If it's too pointed or overly direct, wounding can occur, often in opposition to the communicator's intention.

A damaged tongue could indicate a need for you to examine how effective you are in this area. If your tongue is paralyzed, you may not be speaking powerfully enough to achieve your intentions in your waking life. In the world of crime, whether fictional or real, to have a tongue removed is a punishment for speaking out of turn, or revealing secret information. Dreaming of losing your tongue can relate to consequences of things you have said or wish to say in some situation.

The other primary meaning associated with the tongue relates to the physical sensations of taste and sensual pleasure. Consider that tasting food is erotic in nature and falls into the same category as do sexual acts. If eating is involved in your dream, the tongue relates to pleasure associated with self-care and abundant living. The ability to taste delicious food is a luxury, and if this interpretation feels right, the Dreaming Lens will inform you of your current relationship to this in your waking life.

The act of kissing with the tongue is extremely personal. If this is the focus of the dream, your interpretation must examine where in your life you are allowing or avoiding intimacy. Joining through the mouth is symbolic of two people exchanging and integrating communication skills. If you are kissing someone in a dream, use their Character Aspects to inform you of what traits you need to incorporate into your communication.

Tornado

Universal Landscape: Destructive force of opposing energies.

Dreaming Lens: Where was the tornado in your dream? What happened before and after its appearance? Was it fearful or exciting? Were you at risk or at a safe distance? Did you witness the formation or the aftermath of a tornado, or both?

Personal Focus: These weather phenomena are incredibly destructive and completely unpredictable in their movement. The devastation that they leave in their wake is almost unfathomable. There is also an element, however, of creation in their symbolic meanings, which lies in their formation. A tornado is the result of two air masses of very different temperatures colliding with each other. Under the right conditions, these two systems meet up with each other and each tries to force the other to submit to their direction of movement. As a result of this conflict, the two form a third energetic system, which combines the force of both, creating a tornado.

Resistance is at the essence of the interpretation of this image, so look for areas in your life where you may be in resistance when a tornado appears in a dream. In addition, the chaotic nature of a tornado's path makes this a perfect expression of waking-life chaos. This dream may be indicating an unconscious reaction to the unpredictable nature of how things are unfolding around you, especially in areas where you are facing direct opposition to your desires.

The film *The Wizard of Oz* has added a magical perspective to the power of a tornado. In this classic hero's journey, the cyclone is a force strong enough to transport a person to another place without harm, while destroying other things in its wake. In this way, tornadoes can be both creative and destructive and your interpretation should consider both possibilities.

Traveling

Universal Landscape: The path through life.

Dreaming Lens: Were you planning your trip, beginning it, in the middle, or at its conclusion? Did the dream span the entire trip? Where were you going? Were you moving toward something or away from something? Were you excited? Were you anxious? Were you spontaneous or hesitant?

Personal Focus: This is a very broad image and the meaning described here can be applied to any dream imagery that resembles traveling in any fashion. It is best to break this symbol down into very basic segments. The location you are leaving is likely tied in with your past and elements of your life that you are letting go of and moving away from. Your destination, if there is one, may offer clues to where you are heading or desire to be. An unknown destination can point to a need to move your life into new territory, even though you may not currently be aware of what that might look like. The emotional qualities of the traveling can be a good snapshot of how your unconscious is responding to your current life path and the movement inherent on your journey.

The mode of travel will reveal issues around the way your life is supporting the desires you have. The effectiveness of your vehicle and the control you are able to exert over your direction may be a reflection of how these themes are playing out in your waking-life. The obstacles that present themselves are to be considered as a barometer for challenges you are facing that may be impeding your progress. Being stuck or unable to control where you are going might connect to some element of your life that is stagnant.

The speed of travel is important to decipher your perspective on how fast an area of life is moving. A train might indicate things speeding out of control whereas a cruise ship could feel impossibly slow. Very often only a small bit of a journey is what appears in a dream. In this case, the context and location will help identify what path in your life needs to be examined specifically by stopping and paying closer attention to where you have been and where you are going.

Tree

Universal Landscape: One's growth through life.

Dreaming Lens: Was it a single tree or a forest? How old did the tree appear to be? What type of tree was it? What was its size and strength? Did you recognize it from your life? Was it from a scene in your past? Did you climb it, swing from it, cut it down, or prune it? Was it healthy? Did it bear fruit?

Personal Focus: Venerated by many cultures throughout history, the tree is a standard symbol of life and growth. Its roots are symbolic of our need to feel connected to something foundational, such as our homes and families. The trunk of a tree represents the physical body and how we grow in wisdom as we age. The branches mirror the need to reach toward our goals and desires. The fruit and foliage of a tree is much like the fruits of our own lives through what we create and express to the world.

At the heart of this symbol is the measurement of growth and wisdom, as the rings of a tree can be decoded to reveal its age and history. A tree in your dream is offering you an indication of where you are on your journey through life. If you return to a childhood tree, you may be considering how far you've come since that time. Cutting one down is to stop growth in a particular area suddenly and permanently. Climbing a tree could indicate a need to more closely examine the path your life is traversing or possibly a need to be less serious about issues of maturity. A barren tree could indicate a lack of creative expression. A plush green tree can mean a new level of spiritual awakening or self-discovery is unfolding.

The type of tree could reflect your level of strength and flexibility. A weeping willow has a large, immovable trunk that sprouts much thinner branches that easily sway with the wind. This implies a strong center that supports free emotional expression. An oak has more limitations in its movement, but with a sense of fortitude that reaches out to its very edges. A palm tree is almost invincible through its ability to bend, but not break. Many life circumstances require us to do just that. Examine the qualities of the tree in your dream and apply them to your interpretation for added meaning.

Your dream may contain many trees. A forest is a magical place where change can occur hidden from the view of the outside world. If you dream of being surrounded by many trees, you may be exploring the mysterious side of life through your unconscious. This image might be a call to rely more on your intuitive, feminine side for guidance. Trusting in this aspect of your self will help you find your way out of the woods and back home again.

Tribal

Universal Landscape: Ritualistic connection to primal urges.

Dreaming Lens: What was the setting of the dream? Were you participating in a tribal activity? Were you watching something from a distance? Were you in danger? Were you part of the tribal society? Who else was present in the dream?

Personal Focus: Before the onset of Western civilization, all humans were gathered in aboriginal groups of hunter-gatherers. In this way, we all connect back through the history in our DNA to a primal sensibility that lives on today in images of tribal culture. The media has conjured images of this and movies have been filled with scenes of dancing hoards that are simultaneously engaging and dangerous. We are both drawn toward and repelled by our more primitive nature. In the dream world, a tribal scenario may be expressing a need to connect to this passionate element of our humanity.

Your first order of business with this symbol is to determine which direction the dream is pulling you in: toward this energy or away from it. The Dreaming Lens will provide this information. The more compelled or comfortable you feel, the more likely you are being called to tap into this part of your nature. If on the other hand you are frightened or in actual danger, you may be resisting the very qualities this scenario is pointing out.

What is actually taking place in the dream should also be examined. A celebratory dance has connotations that are different from a cannibalistic ritual. Use this dream to assess your unconscious relationship to waking up deeply routed passions that may be becoming more activated in your psyche. (See also Jungle)

Truck

Universal Landscape: Resource management on life's path.

Dreaming Lens: Were you driving a truck in your dream? Were you watching it from a distance? Was it moving or still? Was it functioning in a particular way? What type of truck was it? Was it carrying any type of cargo? If so, were you aware of what it was?

Personal Focus: As with any mode of transportation, a truck connects symbolically with the movement on your chosen path through life. A vehicle that is not your usual mode of transportation points to an underlying shift in perspective of where your life is heading. A truck is a utility vehicle that is used when there is a need to move heavy cargo with ease. When one appears in a dream, the need being expressed connects to traveling into new territory that may require a considerable inventory of resources.

The size, structure, and purpose of the truck in your dream will give you the most informative clues for your interpretation. In identifying its specific use, you will have a better sense of the shift that is underlying this symbol's meaning. A moving van has implications that are far greater than a pick up truck might have, as one indicates the need for a complete reorganization of some aspect of your unconscious while the other implies only a minor alteration. A truck with towing capacity points to the need to carry something old and broken into the new landscape that is emerging. A more specialized vehicle such as a cement truck or a construction vehicle might lead you to consider what structural or foundational changes in your life may have sparked this image. Body type, age, and color of the vehicle can also be considered for shades of meaning. An older truck could mean that you've made this change before, whereas something new could be commenting on the newness of what you are going through.

Tunnel

Universal Landscape: Transition through lower levels of consciousness.

Dreaming Lens: Were you in a tunnel? Were you about to go through a tunnel? Had you just come out of a tunnel? Were you afraid to go into a tunnel? Was there a light at the end of the tunnel?

Personal Focus: A tunnel allows for movement underground and safe passage underneath a body of water or other above-ground landscape. The creation of a tunnel is dangerous work that can sometimes even be fatal. But the results are well worth the risk as the increase in productivity and convenience are enormous.

There are a number of things to consider when interpreting the symbolic meaning of a tunnel. First and foremost is what two landscapes are being connected by the tunnel itself. The above ground elements are parts of your conscious environment that you are aware of; one as origination and one as destination. If this information is available in the dream, assign some interpretive meaning to each and consider the tunnel as a journey that seeks to connect these two elements. The tunnel symbolically represents the deep, hidden place you must often go in order to be outwardly successful in some endeavor that is visible in the outside world.

Be sure to expand your interpretation to include what obstacle the tunnel is bypassing. If a tunnel goes under a river, look to where emotional issues are being avoided. If the tunnel runs beneath a city environment, the area being subjugated may connect with the way in which you structure your life and how you navigate your movement through daily tasks.

Being inside of a tunnel can also connect to a transition into new territory in your life. The part of this transition represented by the tunnel itself is the most difficult part, often characterized by a sense of loss and lack of direction. Very often when you find yourself inside a tunnel that is symbolic of a transition, you may not know where you are coming from and, more frightening than that, you may not know where you are going to wind up. The thing most often looked for while in a tunnel is the light at the end. And, of course, you must make sure the light is not an oncoming train!

UFO

Universal Landscape: Exploration of very high levels of consciousness.

Dreaming Lens: Were you watching a UFO in the sky? Did it land? Were you abducted? Did you go willingly? Was there a sense of threat and danger? Did the presence of the UFO portend good or evil?

Personal Focus: Much time has passed since the UFO craze swept across our consciousness. Since then, the term Unidentified Flying Object has permanently entered our cosmopolitan vocabulary. For the sake of defining this term, UFO is referring to any extraterrestrial mechanism of travel as it may appear in a dream, no matter how fantastic or out of the realm of possibility it may appear to be.

As with any mode of transportation, the essential meaning must connect to your path in life. Clearly, if you are traveling through outer space or being visited by beings from outer space, you are dreaming of some deviation from your more grounded life on

---

Earth and your interpretation should incorporate some sense of this atypical, expansive exploration.

Typically, this image in a dream will spark either fear or fascination or some combination of both. Your reactions to your UFO dream experience will inform you of your emotional relationship with esoteric elements of spirituality that the dream is trying to express. Being abducted adds a shade of meaning that connects to expanding processes of thought that may be occurring in your unconscious whether you want them to or not. If this is the case, look to your present circumstances where you may be feeling forced to think way outside of your usual thought paradigms. If you were not abducted but were actually proactive and perhaps even motivated to go with the aliens, this may indicate a readiness to explore new intellectual territory in some area of your waking-life.

Seeing a UFO from the ground could be a precursor to new, higher levels of consciousness that are making themselves known to you before they fully arrive. Your emotional reaction to what you see in your dream will illuminate for you how open or resistant you are at this time to the inevitable expansion of consciousness that comes when you step onto any path of self-investigation.

Uphill/Downhill

Universal Landscape: Exertion or ease in your current life's journey.

Dreaming Lens: Were you going uphill or down? Was the uphill challenging? Was the downhill easy or frightening? How much further was there to go? What was waiting for you up top or down below? Was the hill an obstacle in your flow or an expected part of your movement?

Personal Focus: Any path in a dream such as a road, trail, or walkway connects to your journey through life. The degree of inclination or declination is key to understanding how your unconscious is experiencing the current level of stress involved. This should be applied literally to the interpretation of how you are understanding some life experience. Consider the direction: uphill points to difficulty and challenge while downhill brings you ease and speed. Both perspectives have positive and negative associations to them.

While going uphill can be exhausting and debilitating, a modicum of exertion can also be very stimulating and the accomplishment of the climb can be very satisfying. Going downhill may be easy and exhilarating, but the sense of free fall can also breed terror and create danger or misfortune. These dichotomies must be examined when coming to an accurate interpretation. Your Dreaming Lens will guide you, but you will also want to factor in your own physical abilities and/or limitations. If you are debilitated in life in some way, challenged movement in your dream could be an expression of frustration with your limitations. Similarly, ease of movement could be compensatory in some way.

If the uphill journey in your dream stops your ability to move at all, you may be working out feelings of inadequacy and may be shut down in the face of a life challenge. Similarly, a downhill plunge that leads to calamity and injury could indicate the fears that are stopping your movement in life. If there is a view at the top of the hill, you may be looking at the motivating forces that underlie your current choices. If you are sailing easily and safely downhill, your unconscious may be signaling the end of a previous dilemma or signaling a need to proceed with blind faith—that no matter what the consequences, you will survive and proceed successfully. Pay attention to the road ahead and you cannot falter.

Urination

Universal Landscape: Release of toxicity.

Dreaming Lens: Were you urinating? Was someone else? Were you in a bathroom setting? Did you have an accident? Were you in bed? Did you wake up from the dream and have to urinate? Was the dream erotic? Was it repulsive? Were you urinating on someone? Was someone urinating on you?

Personal Focus: We mostly think of urination in terms of the elimination of waste and urine as the fluid that bears toxic material out of the body. Our blood picks up chemicals and other harmful materials, which are then transferred by the kidneys into a solution held by the bladder. If this doesn't occur, the body would poison itself. Urination in a dream may be pointing to a buildup of negative thoughts or unexpressed anger, hence the phrase, "pissed off."

There are other perceptions of urine that come through the collective from other cultures. One such distinction comes from the many societies where the drinking of one's own urine is considered vital and healthy. Dreaming of this may indicate that there is a mechanism you are unaware of or that might seem unpalatable, but that could be quite good for you. Issues relating to anger might need some reconsideration, like a "taste of your own medicine" as the saying goes.

There is a sexual subculture in which urinating on someone or being urinated on by another is considered highly erotic. It is also a symbol of the hierarchy of power between two individuals. In sexual role-play, while it may appear that the dominant party holds more power by virtue of the act itself, in actuality the receiver, or "bottom," is the one with the control in any interaction. Therefore, in any dream involving this sort of activity, consider that if you are the giver you may be experiencing toxic backlash from some area in life where you are being insensitive or lacking compassion. If you are on the receiving end of urination, then you may want to consider where in your life you may be compromising yourself through manipulation or some other hidden motivation.

There can be a physiological function involved in this dream image and the body may assist in the unconscious process: if you have to pee, you just might dream about it first. This does not alter the interpretive meaning, and such a dream deserves investigation of its imagery as much as any other.

Vampire

Universal Landscape: Drain of life force.

Dreaming Lens: Were you the vampire or was someone else the vampire? Was the vampire a stranger and a figure of mystery? Was the vampire someone you know from life? Were you the intended victim? Were you trying to save someone from a vampire? Were you bitten? What was the level of danger, intrigue, or sexual stimulation?

Personal Focus: Vampires are creatures of death that survive by drinking the blood of the living. Blood represents passion and life force. A vampire in your dreams represents some aspect of your personality or way of being that has the potential to drain you of your vibrancy and energy.

Because vampires can only move about freely at night, they are in the symbolic realm of the Shadow. This indicates that whatever issues are robbing you of your vitality, they are hidden from your conscious awareness and must be examined with this in mind. We keep in the shadow those parts of ourselves that we can't accept and have difficulty integrating into our personal identity. Not integrating the Shadow can suck the life force out of us until we face what we resist.

Often portrayed as sexy or seductive, consider that the vampire may represent a situation or person in your life that seemed alluring at first, but is now exhausting or depleting. As a Character Aspect of your personality, there may be some habit, behavior, or emotional trait that is literally sucking you dry. Since vampires cast no reflection in a mirror, this may be a part of you that you may be unable or unwilling to see directly.

Feeling responsible for things can have a very draining effect on you. You may want to become more aware of those things you are attached to in a negative way. Holding on to old attitudes and beliefs can be draining. Consider that it can be just as draining to avoid responsibilities that are legitimately yours. It is the ignorant victim who foolishly leaves the window open and unwittingly invites the vampire to visit. Other internal vampires include neediness, self-doubt, lack of forgiveness, and judgments. All of these feelings kill passion for life. Commit to emotional healing and your vampires will return to the grave where they belong.

Victory/Winning

Universal Landscape: Mastery over challenge.

Dreaming Lens: What was the victory in the dream? Was there an adversary? If so, who were they? Did you win at a cost and, if so, what did you have to sacrifice to win? Was there a lack of integrity involved in winning? How did it feel to be the victor?

Personal Focus: A game or contest divides the participants into two categories: winners and losers. From many perspectives, winning is the entire point of engaging in competition because of the wonderful sensation that accompanies victory. Losing can be both humiliating and frustrating, often bringing out the worst in people. There is an old adage, "it is not important whether you win or lose, but how you play the game that counts." This wisdom is not always honored in our aggressive society, and an individual's response to winning or losing can reveal a great deal about his or her moral and ethical makeup.

Life is very much like a game. Any competitive event in a dream may be symbolic of the game of life. Games of strategy, like chess, represent areas of life that require a tactical approach. Cards and other games of chance rely on luck and highlight how you are handling what life may be currently dealing you. Anything involving mental activity is symbolic of your intellect, while physical contact implies a connection with your emotions and your bodily functions.

Something violent, such as a wartime battle, might indicate a more intense inner conflict, where winning represents a high stakes victory for you.

Winning in a dream is either compensating for feeling beaten down by some area of life or celebrating an accomplishment. If choosing one interpretation over the other is not obvious by your current situation, examine the emotional content of the dream for clues. Anxiety is an indication that your unconscious is expressing conflict and a desire to have it resolved.

Video Games

Universal Landscape: Total and utter escapism; mindless thought.

Dreaming Lens: Were you playing a video game in your dream? Was someone else? Did you want to play and weren't able to? Was someone else trying to play? What was the game being played? Was it a satisfying experience to play? Were you inside a video game environment?

Personal Focus: Video games are a modern phenomenon that will have very different symbolic meaning based on your personal relationship to them. While the Universal Landscape connects to escapism, the diehard gamer will have a joyous experience of that escapism, while a critic might hold a more judgmental perspective. Where you stand on this continuum will furnish the full picture for your interpretation. There is a perspective of video games that connects to a type of skill building; however, those skills have very little practical value outside of the realm of playing the game repeatedly. This is where the element of "mindless thought" enters into the symbolic meaning of video games.

Most video games are environments unto themselves, where a whole world is recreated in the digital realm. The player merges with that world through the act of playing it. This informs the part of this symbol's meaning as "total and utter." It is not uncommon for people to play video games for hours at a time, getting completely lost in this alternate reality. This provides the element of "escapism" in the Universal Landscape. A dream is also an alternate reality in which we seek to find meaning and self-discovery. The presence of a video game in a dream is an ironic appearance of detachment and should be considered as a possible defense against what the unconscious mind may be attempting to express. If someone in your dream is playing a video game, understanding the Character Aspect of that person will identify for you what area of your self is avoiding reality.

Volcano

Universal Landscape: Feeling rage; destructive expression after prolonged constraint or restraint.

Dreaming Lens: Were you near the volcano? Were you under its reach? Were you witnessing it from above or at a distance? Was it erupting? Was it dormant? Were there people in harm's way? Were you experiencing fear? Were you exhilarated?

Personal Focus: The outer image of the volcano reveals the aftermath of the essence of this symbol: constraint or restraint. The Earth's crust can only hold back the brewing force of heat and combustion for so long before the build up of pressure generates an explosive eruption that permanently changes the landscape.

The intense heat and molten lava connect to feelings of rage, anger, and any other suppressed emotions of great power. The eruption would be the breaking point that is either imminent or close at hand. A dormant volcano connects to past issues of pent-up stressors no longer threatening your comfort and safety. An active volcano indicates an ongoing, volatile situation that may just currently be emitting steam, but can re-erupt at any moment. The lava flow itself is the dangerous aftermath of expressing feelings of rage. The ash that rains down after the explosion aligns with the way an outburst tends to leave the entire environment coated with some evidence of the conflict.

Whatever is at risk of being destroyed by a volcano will reveal the parts of life that feel vulnerable to the experience of withheld anger. A city or town might indicate that your social associations and circles of friends play an important role. A lush valley might point to the dissolution of serenity. An urban center might mean that institutions or your greater community is at the cause of your building frustration. Whatever lies in the path of a volcano's destruction can be explored for clues to what your unconscious is harboring resentment toward. Evacuate, if you can.

Vomiting

Universal Landscape: Rejection and expulsion of harmful emotions or ideas.

Dreaming Lens: Were you vomiting or was someone else? Did you make yourself vomit or was it involuntary? Were you aware of what was coming out of you? Was it food or something other than food? Was it painful and uncomfortable? How did you feel afterward?

Personal Focus: The body possesses a natural reflex for getting rid of something harmful that has entered the digestive system. This regulatory impulse senses the presence of toxins or poisons and triggers a muscular contraction to expel the unwanted material. While this can be caused by different stimulus from tainted food, viral infection, to self-inducement, the symbolic meaning is the same—getting rid of something that is perceived to be bad.

Because of the connection between vomit and food, this image will always have something to do with nurturance and self-care. If it shows up in a dream, there is something amiss in how you are being nurtured. This may signal a period in life where you are pushing away the nurturing you need. The other side of this could be a need to reject the nurturing habits or relationships in your life that might be unhealthy. Vomiting could also signal the purging of previously unexpressed feelings that have been stuffed down for too long. Since vomiting is a primal reflex, this could hearken back to patterns established early in life. On a positive note, this reflex is associated with the body caring for itself, so vomiting in a dream could point to instincts that protect you and keep you safe.

If the vomiting has been purposefully induced, as in bulimia, you are dealing with an attempt to control the expression of feelings. Not wanting to take in food could connect to a desire to reject some thought or idea in your waking life. Examine how well you are caring for yourself, including accepting the behavior and words of others. If you have to "swallow something" that doesn't agree with you, you may find yourself vomiting those ideas right back up in your dreams.

War/Battle

Universal Landscape: Shifting boundaries.

Dreaming Lens: Were you in a battle? How much danger were you in? Were you connected with others on your side or were you close to the enemy? Were you advancing the front line or attempting to damage the resources of your enemy? Did you know the cause for which you were fighting?

Personal Focus: The object of war is for one entity to obtain the land and/or resources of another. Therefore, war in a dream indicates change on such a large scale that it can only be accomplished by the use of major force. Our world is a set of organized boundaries we know as countries. Our psyches are divided in a similar way. These boundaries are, ultimately, fluid. Things change—sometimes dramatically—which leaves us feeling vulnerable. When the change is sudden and violent, the unconscious may use a dream of war to express the enormity of the internal shift that's occurring.

There is a distinction between war and battle. War implies an ongoing state of flux whereas battle is the actual shift taking place in a small increment of upheaval and change. If you dream of being in wartime, then your life may reflect a grand cycle of transformation that is currently taking place. Most people living in America have never experienced wartime, but to live under the threat of war is to be in constant, hyper-awareness of danger lurking just about everywhere. If this is the case in your dream, look to where in life your defenses might be running on high. If you dream of an actual battle, then the immediacy of the symbolism implies something much more current in your waking-life. Look to where changes in boundaries are eminent, both in your outside world as well as within, as many battles are with ourselves.

Generally speaking, there are two points of focus for modern war: one is to advance the front line in either direction, essentially shifting the land borders between countries. This connects symbolically to the establishment of boundaries that we must carve out each and every day of our lives. The greater intensity of the war in your dreams, the more intense the daytime conflict being expressed is likely to be. The other focus of war is to destroy the resources of the enemy. This has a more complex symbolism as it involves invasion and aggression; qualities which imply assumption and risk. When this is the focus of your dream, know that you are in some dark and dangerous territory. If you knew the cause you were fighting for, you must add this information to your interpretation.

Warehouse

Universal Landscape: Unfinished business. Unattended issues. Postponement.

Dreaming Lens: Were you inside the warehouse or outside? Was the place abandoned or filled with activity? Were you aware of what was stored in the space? Was there danger afoot or was the atmosphere mild?

Personal Focus: Warehouses are places where we gather and store items which will later be distributed for their intended use. What is key to this symbol is that the storage is temporary—what is kept in a warehouse is eventually going to be moved somewhere else. In a dream, they are symbols of change. In the arc of any transformation, a warehouse points to the middle of a greater shift; a point at which resources are gathered, but have not quite yet arrived at their final destination.

In films, warehouses often appear as empty and dilapidated, adding a futility and uselessness to the image. Additionally, they are frequently the place where criminal elements hide harmful things with bad intentions. This colors how the collective may be using this image to express Shadow material of the danger that can result from not attending to certain life challenges in a timely and above- board manner.

There is an underlying theme of abundance that is implied with a warehouse. The products stored inside are in the middle of being transported. When they get to their final destination, they have the potential of generating profit for the person who owns them. If the warehouse feels like a place of good, then you are in a transition that may be of long duration, but is clearly in your best interests. If the dream takes place at night or feels scary and dangerous, there may be layers of Shadow material to examine.

Washing/Bathing

Universal Landscape: A process of creating socially acceptable states of being.

Dreaming Lens: Were you bathing or was someone else? What types of structures were involved? Were you in a private or public place?

Who else was present if you were not alone? What parts of your body were you washing? What was the state of the water?

Personal Focus: Regular bathing is a relatively new phenomenon in modern Western culture. Many older civilizations had bathing as a regular part of day-to-day living, however, early Christianity discouraged the practice as a way to deal with the perceived sinfulness of the naked body.

The impulse to bathe connects with a desire to be socially acceptable. Human beings are the only animals on the planet that actively remove their natural scent. As civilization began to modernize, we found it desirable to smell more pleasant and the practice has stuck. In this way, the primary symbolic meaning for any kind of bathing connects to this desire to be clean and available for social interaction with others. This can connect to unconscious feelings of dirtiness that are both literal and metaphorical. In what ways and in which areas of your life are you feeling unclean and in need of purification?

The health-related advantage to being cleaner was an almost accidental result of the practice of regular bathing. As such, this offers a secondary shade of meaning for this symbol connected to safety and the precautions needed to stay clean in all of your affairs.

Finally, remember that anything that involves water in a dream is going to connect somehow to issues of emotions. Using water to bathe might point to a need or desire to immerse yourself into the realm of your feelings in order to cleanse yourself of the pain that life sometimes brings.

Water

Universal Landscape: Emotion. The unconscious.

Dreaming Lens: What was the body of water? How large, small, manageable, or fearsome was it? Were you in the water, or did you consider jumping into it? Were you wet or in danger/fear of becoming so? Were you drinking it? Was the water natural or contained in man-made constructions, from cups to pipes or even aqueducts? Was the water related to the weather?

Personal Focus: Water is symbolic of the emotions. On a biological level, this is so because of the connection between emotional expression and tears. The human body is primarily made up of water held together by protein-based structures. When we cry, we lose some of that water in a stream emanating from the eyes. While we do not really understand why we cry, we do so when we are deeply moved. This mysterious leakage of precious water is akin to the feelings of loss that accompany it.

If all water is viewed as a symbolic representation of emotions, both conscious and unconscious, it is the structure that the water takes in your dreams that will inform you of the size and scope of the expression being illuminated by your dream.

As a general rule, weather-related water connects to conscious emotional expression and flow, whereas bodies of water contain some element of that which is unconscious. Rain and storms occur in the atmosphere and often over land, which represents the emotional content of the conscious mind. When large portions of water are only partially visible, that which is below the surface and unseen is symbolic of the powerful, hidden emotions of the unconscious mind. When water is contained in any way, the dreamer's impulse to control some element of their emotional nature is being expressed.

Violent movement of water, such as rapids, waves, riptides, and storms represent the overwhelming power of emotional material. Your response to such images in a dream is indicative of your level of fear and resistance or lack of it. Lying near water may reflect being close to a willingness to explore the emotional territory outlined by the dream.

Being thirsty and/or drinking water could indicate a strong need to take more emotional sustenance into your life. Drowning might indicate an overwhelming amount of unmanageable emotions or the fear that any emotional outpouring might result in suffocation. A waterfall represents the way feelings can cascade down upon us suddenly and with great force: both sensual and exhilarating or painful and overwhelming. Using water to clean (from laundry to grooming) could mean the need for an emotional healing through working directly with your emotional issues.

Wedding

Universal Landscape: The beginning of the process of integration.

Dreaming Lens: Were you the bride, the groom, or a witness? Did you know the couple? Were you happy or opposed to the union? Were you late, early, intoxicated, or surprised at the altar? Did you arrive on the wrong date? Were you marrying someone you know or don't know? Was someone else marrying the person you desire?

Personal Focus: A wedding is a ritualistic joining of two life paths that choose to merge. The theme being explored with this image is integration on a major scale. The Dreaming Lens will inform you of what areas of life are coming together and whether the process is going well or not. The first area of exploration should be with the individuals who are getting married. If one of them is yourself, then the wedding represents incorporating a Character Aspect into your personality with a sense of commitment and permanence. If you are watching two other people, the process is more about finding a resource within yourself by joining together two distinct ways of being.

A wedding dream represents integration of those desired qualities within ourselves that could lead to a level of wholeness that might allow us to attract the partner of our heart's desire. The first step to this is to create a loving union with all aspects of our selves, inside and out. This development is not always smooth sailing. The level of chaos in the dream may be reflecting unconscious responses to changes that are occurring in your waking life.

There may be some literal meaning to be explored if you are approaching a wedding in your waking life at the time of your dream. If this is the case, use the Dreaming Lens to inform you of your deeper emotional responses being stimulated by this huge event.

Well

Universal Landscape: Availability of emotional sustenance.

Dreaming Lens: What type of well was in your dream? How deep did it go? Was it filled with water or empty? Was there anything surrounding the top of the well? Was it usable? Was it private or for public use?

Personal Focus: Any time water is featured in a dream, what is being expressed is the state of your emotional life. Water is the necessary ingredient to sustaining life. A well is dug to provide consistent access to this life-giving elixir. In the symbolic world, there is a correlation between water as emotion and water as life-sustaining substance. We need water to live and our souls need emotional balance to thrive. A well is often a community resource, so the state of the well in your dream may be revealing your current life's relationship to your own feelings and how much you may have to give to others. If your well is running dry, you may need to consider your own needs first. If it is overflowing, take a look at how your emotional life may be more than you can contain. (See also Water, Fountain.)

Welts

Universal Landscape: Evidence of wrongs done; the aftermath of attack.

Dreaming Lens: Where on the body were the welts? How severe were they? How recently were they formed? Were they visible to others or covered? Were they painful? On whose body did they appear? How did you feel about their appearance?

Personal Focus: Welts are the visible remnants of an injury and appear after some sort of violent blow to the body. They form as a rise in the skin as a result of the body sending fluid to an injured area to begin the process of healing. In this way, they indicate that there is a raised awareness of some kind relating to a rapid shift or change in consciousness where the newfound awareness is painful. Welts appear right after an injury is inflicted, adding a sense of immediacy to what is occurring.

Your interpretation will vary depending on the part of the body that is affected. The arms relate to strength and action, the legs connect to movement and motivation. The hands represent creativity and the face connects to the persona one shows to the world. See "Body Parts" for more thoughts to augment the meaning you assign this symbol. Additionally, consider that a welt on an exposed part of the body means your wound is visible to others. An area that is generally covered by clothing may connect to the ability or desire to hide your wounds.

Whispering

Universal Landscape: Revealing of previously unconscious or private thoughts.

Dreaming Lens: Were you whispering in the dream? Was someone else? Were they whispering to you or was it two others whispering to each other? Were you aware of what the content of the message was? Was it for privacy or emphasis that the whispering was happening?

Personal Focus: People whisper for two reasons: to keep something private or for dramatic emphasis. In both instances, there is a secret nature to the information being expressed. Words are thoughts and thoughts are expressions of consciousness. Since the unconscious mind is a realm steeped in the unknown, it is fair to assume that it will at times reveal something previously hidden. Such expressions would likely be the thoughts that hover close to the edge of the barrier between these two realms. This is the case with a dream whisper.

A disembodied whispering voice that you can discern is a powerful message from your higher self. If you choose to whisper to someone else in your dream, consider what you are saying and notice if it connects to something about which you are not quite ready to take ownership. If you are witnessing others whispering, know that you are being shown information that is likely on its way to being conscious, but is not yet quite clear. Use the Dreaming Lens to clue you in on what area of your life is being uncovered and revealed. If the whispering is for dramatic emphasis, you may want to examine areas in your life where you need to express yourself clearly but are currently in hesitation or resistance.

Wind

Universal Landscape: The movement of collective thought; ideas.

Dreaming Lens: Was there wind blowing in your dream or an absence of wind? How hard was it blowing? Were there strong gusts or was it a steady force? Did it have an affect on your balance or ability to move? Was it blowing in the direction you wanted to go or was it going against you? Did anything blow away?

Personal Focus: The wind is like the constant flow of thoughts and ideas in our minds. If you think of the Earth as the collective consciousness of all the beings that live on it, the wind would be akin to the ceaseless stream of information that passes through our heads. We may not always be aware of it, but it is a constant force to which we are forever adjusting. It is only when it changes suddenly that we tend to notice it. It can vary in intensity from a pleasant breeze to a howling gust. However, like all forms of weather, it never stops and it blows where it wants without any concern for how we feel about which way it is moving.

Air represents the intellect, so its movement is symbolic for the direction of our thinking. Like the wind, thoughts often flow through our minds in a ceaseless fashion that seems unstoppable. These thoughts can push us in certain directions in life. Sometimes we go with the flow, whereas other times we resist and push ourselves against the direction the winds of thought are blowing. Since we all experience the same wind at any given moment, what becomes important to notice is your individual response to it. A gentle breeze could be either pleasant or uncomfortable depending on the temperature. Dramatic gusts can be exciting for some people, while others may find them maddening.

The behavior of the wind in your dream and your response to it will provide you with an accurate interpretation. The strength of the wind is indicative of the amount of power some life circumstance is exerting over you. Your movement with regard to its direction will illuminate whether you are being supported by your choices or meeting resistance. A constant wind could mean there is an obsessive thought pattern running through your mind. This can be very creative when they are affirmative thoughts of creative manifestation. However, compulsive obsession is one of the most destructive activities the mind can engage in. It can take your life in directions that don't serve you. The more fear present in the dream, the more likely you are facing something that needs your attention. Identify what life situation is in the process of shifting. The winds of change are powerful and unpredictable. Your dream may be an assessment of how you are responding to the things you cannot control.

Window/Window Treatment

Universal Landscape: An opening in perspective.

Dreaming Lens: Were you inside or outside? Were you looking through the window? Was the window covered or decorated? Was it open, shut, or boarded up? Did you or someone fall through the window? Did you break it? Was there a view?

Personal Focus: Houses and buildings represent the Self and windows are the portals between the interior and exterior of any structure. They are the symbolic opening where the outside world gets a view of what's going on under the surface of our behavior. Simultaneously, we privately peek out through the windows of our selves, penetrating our public personas with snippets of who we really are. There is a flow of information between your inner and outer experiences in life and it is through windows that this exchange occurs. The more exposed you feel by a window, the more vulnerable you are feeling around your current challenges. As such, window treatments reflect your desire to both obscure and control the information presented by you to the outside world.

The more covered the windows, such as with heavy drapes, shades, and so forth, the more you are trying to block the flow. The presence of window treatments that are open indicates a willingness to see, but with a sense of control that signals the view is temporary—take advantage of it while you can. A broken window reflects an even less blocked flow, but one that might feel dangerous, depending on the level of violence associated with the breakage. If you broke the window, then it is your need to be more authentic that may have sparked the breakthrough. If any outside force is responsible, you may be feeling pushed into confrontation by something in your life and, therefore, an expansion of authentic persona may be in process. Since the eyes are the windows to the soul, pay close attention to how open your dream windows are, for it is your soul's light that wants to shine through them.

Witch

Universal Landscape: Archetypal Character Aspect: Purveyor of magic.

Dreaming Lens: What was the witch doing in your dream? Was she frightening or fascinating? How dangerous did she seem? Was she able to do magic? Were you the witch? How did the witch relate to you in the dream?

Personal Focus: The witch is a creature of relatively modern invention with little, if any, origins in the older mythologies that have shaped Western culture. They are most likely a product of the emergence of Christianity and the growth of European cities. Any woman with Pagan-based knowledge of the healing arts might have been considered a witch by the ever-expanding political powers of the last two millenniums. To avoid punishment, such people lived away from urban centers, often in the woods, adding to the mystique and burgeoning fables of witches as evil, forest-dwelling hags. Today, the witch figures prominently in contemporary fairy tales and folklore, and she is a staple character of Halloween. She no longer heals and ministers; now she casts evil spells and eats children.

Since this is an Archetype, how she appears in your dream is important to your understanding of your own personal development. The areas of life ruled by this Archetype are mysticism, healing, and magic, primarily in the feminine principle, which relates to creativity, receptivity, nurturance, and caretaking. Examine your witch for character, skill, and motivation. Her character will inform you of the levels of good versus evil within your psyche. The power of her skills will inform you of your personal access to the magic in the universe. Understanding what inspires her will get you in touch with your own movement toward integration and away from manipulation.

Any number of hag-like, female characters could be considered the Witch Archetype. In fact, some may be evil, while others may be disenfranchised healers. Given her origins in mysticism and a preponderance of misunderstandings over the centuries, it is important to consider this duality when interpreting the Witch as a symbol. Though she may inspire fear and dread, the witch has powerful magic which, if understood and properly used, can be invaluable to the human experience.

Work

Universal Landscape: Obligations and responsibilities.

Dreaming Lens: Did the dream take place at work? Was it your work place or a fictitious setting? What were you doing there? Who else was present? Was the dream stressful or pleasant?

Personal Focus: We are a society built around jobs and work. Most people relate to their jobs as something that they have to do in order to make ends meet. In this way, your job and your workplace are symbolic representations of all of the responsibilities and obligations that life presents you with.

Very often, dreams about your work are to be taken very literally. You spend a great deal of time there and your dreams may be filled with images from your day; a dream taking place where you work may very well be a compensatory dream helping you cope with stress and wake up the next day to face it all over again. However, such a dream could also be a convenient way for your unconscious to express feelings surrounding other responsibilities and obligations that need attention.

Not all dreams taking place at work are stressful. If this is the case, use your feelings about your job, the environment at work and your coworkers to help you identify what elements of your own personality are being expressed in your dream. Many people have a very different sense of self in the workplace than in other parts of life. Consider your relationship to your work carefully when examining a dream that took place there.

Wound(s)

Universal Landscape: Area of vulnerability; evidence of past hurts.

Dreaming Lens: What type of wound did you sustain? Was it bleeding? Was your life in danger? How old was the wound? Was it in the process of healing? Were you in pain? What caused the wound? Who caused the wound?

Personal Focus: A wound is an indication that something dramatic and dangerous has already occurred. It is not only evidence of the event itself; it is also the residual damage that the wounding event may have left you vulnerable to. While wounds to the body are physical in nature, they can symbolically represent emotional, psychological, and spiritual wounds as well.

The most important thing to consider about a wound in a dream is the state that it has left you in. The greater the risk, the higher the stakes of the life situation the dream is expressing. The presence of infection may be revealing that an old hurt left unattended is festering and causing you pain and discomfort. Anything that results in the loss of blood relates to passion and life force being leaked out or dissipated.

Where on the body you are wounded will also have meaning. Injuries to the feet connect to the direction your life is moving in. If your legs are affected, your ability to move forward may be what is suffering. The belly area relates to instincts and feelings about things that are occurring. The area around the chest points to matters of the heart. The arms are where strength and our sense of capability lie, while the hands are about creativity and skill. Anything that involves the throat may be indicating issues around communication. The face is about the persona and social identity and may also reflect issues of attractiveness and self-esteem. The head is the home of the intellect and if this is wounded, there may be challenges to your ideas and thoughts coming up. Wherever you are wounded, consider the behaviors and actions that might be hindered and add that information to your interpretation. (See also Blood, Cuts/Cutting.)

Zombie

Universal Landscape: Lack of life force.

Dreaming Lens: Was this a nightmare? Were you in danger? Were you a zombie or in danger of becoming one? Were there many or just one? Were you empowered to defend yourself or did you surrender to the zombie's intention?

Personal Focus: The definition of a zombie is one who is no longer alive, but rises to walk again seeking human flesh to eat. The walking dead is a symbolic representation for those moments in life where the very process of living is devoid of any joy or vibrant energy. A zombie in a dream may signal a period of very low energy or a depletion of energy by some situation in your life.

The real danger of a zombie is their ability to transform their victims into zombies as well. In this way, they represent the cumulative effect of depression, fatigue, and a sedentary lifestyle. Additionally, they can also be an image inspired by a person or persons in your life that rob you of joy by virtue of their negative dispositions.

Zombies originated in the media. It is interesting to note that in the films in which they appear, they are seen as menacing and dangerous. This is despite the fact that their slow pace renders them essentially harmless as long as you can move faster than they do. Consider that a life without passion and vibrancy is a thing we fear greatly, both consciously and in our unconscious minds. Look at what in your life may be robbing you of these qualities. Your unconscious mind may be reminding you well in advance that a choice you have made (a job, relationship, living situation, etc.) may be slowly killing off joy.

Zoo

Universal Landscape: The repression of deep, primal urges.

Dreaming Lens: Were you visiting a zoo? What types of animals were in the zoo? Were they real or imaginary? How did you feel about the confinement of the animals? What sort of cages were there? What was the habitat like? Were you the one on display?

Personal Focus: No matter how humane the conditions of a zoo are, there is the inescapable fact that the animals are out of their natural environments and on display. Whether for amusement or educational value, the restraint of an animal is symbolic of the restraint of primal instincts. In a dream, this connects to those urges that our thinking, rational mind keeps beneath the surface of our consciousness.

We project onto caged animals qualities that live inside of us and ponder them from a distance through the bars. The more dangerous the animal, the more primal the urge being repressed. A more docile creature on display might connect to lost innocence. Whatever qualities you ascribe to the zoo animal, it is those qualities that live in yourself which are being compartmentalized by your psyche and exhibited in your dream.

Primates closely resemble human beings. Therefore, a caged monkey or ape could correlate directly with aggressive energy that is being held at bay. You may need to examine a dream zoo from the opposite perspective: there may be spontaneous, aggressive reactions you are having in your life that would be better served by being caged and restrained—visible to others, but safely behind bars.

If your dream connects more to the entertainment element of the zoo experience, you are more likely dreaming of your social interactions with other people. If the sense of the dream is educative in nature, you may have something to learn about your animal instincts. If you are distressed about the confinement of the animals, this may point to levels of compartmentalization in your life that are troubling to you. If safety is the issue of your dream, you might want to look at how fear of losing control may be constraining your freedom.

GLOSSARY OF TERMS

The following terms appear frequently in the Dream Dictionary and understanding them is intrinsic to effective and accurate dream interpretations.

Archetypes: An Archetype is a figure that connects to a specific universal energy. They are larger than life and very particular to the ideas that they embody. The Hero, the Warrior, the King or Queen, the Wise Old Man, the Lover, and the Divine Child are all examples of Archetypes. They each represent basic, primal elements of the human condition. They are signals of powerful expression and should be viewed as important messengers from the unconscious mind. Dreams that feature celebrities or sports figures may be expressing a connection to archetypal energy.

Character Aspects: Any person who appears in a dream is a part of the personality of the dreamer. This is so whether you know the person or not. Human beings tend to compartmentalize their inner experience of themselves, dividing their personality into separate parts. As an example, when faced with a decision, many people will express "part of me wants to do this," and "part of me wants to do that," as if these separate parts had different identities. Within every dream, the characters that appear are representing different aspects of behavior and energy as they live inside your own personality. Many of the terms in the Dream Dictionary point to working with this concept for an accurate interpretation.

Collective conscious: Also known as the "race mind," the collective conscious is made up of a series of ideas that are shared by large groups of people in communal agreement. Many of our moral codes are part of the collective conscious, in that human beings all basically agree that it is wrong to kill or harm others. Changing styles in fashion and art are part of the collective conscious. Newly discovered scientific facts eventually make their way into this realm: The collective conscious once held that the world was flat. Now the collective conscious understands the world to be round.

Collective unconscious: An area of the mind below the unconscious that is thought to be a realm where all human beings are psychically joined to each other. Through this deep and mysterious connection, all people have access to ideas, concepts, ideologies, and instincts that are deeply embedded in the human experience. Discovered through dreams by Carl Jung, he found that people from vastly different cultures were having the exact same types of dreams. He also showed that unrelated early civilizations, separated by vast differences in time and geography, all contained the same basic mythologies that were too similar to dismiss as random. The more scientific concept of genetic or cellular memory can be explained through the presences of the collective unconscious.

Compensatory dreams: To compensate is to restore balance. To some extent, all dreams are compensatory in nature. In fact, the process of dreaming itself is the mind's way of reinstating psychic and emotional balance. In this way, we can wake each day, our brains ready to absorb the next enormous batch of information we receive every waking moment. While this can apply to all dreams in a general sense, there are many dreams that facilitate this process around specific life challenges that affect our equilibrium. Many terms in the Dream Dictionary will invite you to consider them as specifically compensatory and help you answer the question of what in your life may need to be restored to balance.

Conscious mind: The part of our minds of which we are aware. Our thoughts, ideas, fears and cognitive processing are contained in the conscious mind.

Feminine principle: The feminine half of nature; this represents not being female, but all of the traits that are considered to be associated with female energy. They live in us all, male and female alike. These include creativity, sensitivity, emotional expression, the drive to nurture, and flexibility.

Masculine principle: The masculine half of nature; this represents not being male, but all of the traits that are associated with male energy. They live in us all, men and women alike. These include being constructive, power, leadership, aggression, possessiveness, decisiveness, and violence.

Persona: A principle with its origins in Jungian psychology, the persona is the part of the personality that we project out into the world. It connects with how others see and experience who we are, but it is an internal construct that lives within the mind of every individual. The persona includes how people see us, but also how we *want to be perceived* by others. The persona is made up of a combination of our behaviors, styles of communication, choices we make and how we react to the world around us. It is a combination of both the conscious and the unconscious mind. Therefore, it is something of which we are only partly aware. Most people are very identified with their persona, and the process of self-investigation and the search for insight includes recognizing this part of the self and understanding it as separate from who we are as an integrated human being.

Personal unconscious: Synonymous with the unconscious mind, the term Personal Unconscious is the opposite of the collective unconscious. While it means the same thing as the term "unconscious mind," it is sometimes used in the Dream Dictionary to reflect something that is in the mind of the individual as opposed to something that is in the collective unconscious.

Sacrifice: To sacrifice is to willingly let go of something in order to achieve a desired result. What is being released usually has some perceived value. Many ancient cultures sacrificed animals to the gods in order to receive divine blessing. Since an animal had great worth, the act of giving up an object of importance was considered a necessary part of receiving good fortune. This is a notion that has its roots in the cycle of death and rebirth; releasing the old must occur in order to make room for the new. This is an integral part of self-discovery as we uncover, discover, and discard old habits, ideas, and ways of being that no longer serve us. Many dream symbols connect to this process.

The Shadow: The Shadow is the hidden part of the unconscious mind that contains all of the dark, ugly, distasteful, shameful, and rejected elements of a person's sense of self. Any trait in ourselves that we find objectionable can be safely buried in the Shadow, away from our conscious awareness. Socially unacceptable behaviors can be found here, and it is by keeping them at bay that we are capable of functioning in society as law-abiding citizens. However, many much more subtle qualities can be stuck in the shadow as well, especially if they are associated with shame. These things can have a great deal of power over our behaviors and life choices if we don't attend to them. The material that is trapped in the Shadow has more power to run our lives than the things of which we are consciously aware. Dreams are one of the most effective tools available to identify, uncover and free yourself from the grip that most Shadow material can have on you. Dreams that take place at night, that have a dark or sinister sensibility or inspire fearful reactions are often signs that you are dealing with Shadow material.

The Witness: The witness in a dream is the person watching the action take place. Many times, you, the dreamer, are participating in a series of events that make up the story of the dream itself. You may have an independent sense of yourself, but the primary experience of the dream will be connected to your involvement with the occurrences and characters you encounter. Such dreams should be interpreted as reflections of yourself in relation to things that are unfolding in your waking life. In a dream where you are watching what is unfolding without direct involvement, you are in the position of what is known as the Witness. When you dream from the Witness position, the interpretation should focus on psychic and emotional processes that are occurring within the confines of your mind. These dreams are more about your inner experience of growth and wisdom.

Unconscious mind: The much greater part of our mind is the unconscious. It is here that we house our most powerful drives, motivations, hidden agendas (hidden from ourselves), and deepest longings. Dreams are understood to emanate from this area. Additionally, the unconscious is the source of imagination, creativity, libidinal drives, and overpowering impulses. The terms subconscious and unconscious are essentially interchangeable, although I prefer and tend to use unconscious more than subconscious.

Universal: Widely held ideas become universal when they are shared by a considerably large number of people on the planet. This is not to be mistaken with opinions, for that which is universal is not subject to judgment or attitudes. Examples of universal principles are love, aggression, loyalty, wisdom, innocence, to name just a few. Every symbol that appears in a dream has a meaning that can be considered universal; this would most simply be described as that with which the most people on the planet would find agreement if freed from personal opinion and judgment.

INDEX

Abandonment, 82–83

Affair. *See* Infidelity, 225

Age Differences, 83–84

Airplane, 85, 217

Alien, 86–87, 109

Alternate Universe, 87–88

Amputations, 88

Animals, 89–90, 102, 105, 161, 164, 185, 208, 232, 258, 309, 358, 369–370, 374

Anxiety, 285, 297, 304, 328, 330, 337, 352

Arms. *See* Body Parts, 156, 362

Attic, 90–91

Baby, 5, 17–18, 46, 51, 74, 92–93, 118, 280

Bank, 93–94

Bar, 94–95

Barefoot, 96

Basement, 97

Bathing, 357–358

Bathroom, 72, 98–99, 348

Battle. *See* War/Battle

Beach, 41, 99–100

Beams of Light, 100–101, 238

Beast/Human, 101–102

Bed. *See* Bedroom

Bedroom, 55, 103–104

Being Chased, 26, 48, 104–105, 259–260

Birds, 90, 105–106

Black, 128, 143, 147, 319

Blind(ness), 106

Blood, 108–109, 144, 146, 156, 242, 320, 324, 349–350, 368

Blue, 55, 108–109, 127, 144–146, 188, 242

Board Game, 110

Boat, 111–112

Body Parts, 112, 156, 345, 349, 361–362

Bombs, 113

Bones, 121–123, 311, 327

Books, 10, 26, 114–115

Boulders/Rocks, 115–116

Breaking Up, 65, 117, 247

Breasts, 118–119

Breath, 119–120

Breathless, 119–120

Bridge, 120–121

Briefcase. *See* Purse/Briefcase, 285–286

Broken Bones, 121–122

Brother. *See* Siblings, 308, 317

Buddha. *See* Jesus/Buddha, 231

Burning at Stake. *See* Executions, 180–181

Bus, 123–124

Buying. *See* Commerce, 147–148

Candle, 124–125

Candy, 125–126

Car, 6, 49, 51, 55, 64, 101, 124, 126–127, 168, 200–201

Carpets. *See* Floors/Flooring, 192

Cat, 69, 127–128

Celebrities, 128–130, 371

Cell Phone, 130–131, 334

Centaur. *See* Beast/Human

Cheating. *See* Infidelity

Choking, 131–133, 315, 323–324

Christ. *See* Jesus/Buddha, 231

Cigar. *See* Smoke/Smoking, 313

Cigarette. *See* Smoke/Smoking, 313

Circus, 134–135

Climbing, 25, 52–53, 135–137, 256, 320–321, 342

Climbing Stairs, 25, 135–137, 320–321

Cloaked or Hidden Figure, 138

Clocks. *See* Timepieces

Closet, 139–140, 311

Clothes, 70–71, 140–141, 153, 327

Clowns, 134, 141–142

Coffin, 142–143, 209

Colors, 127, 143–147, 166, 188, 270–271, 289–290, 357

Commerce, 147–148

Computer, 60, 148–149, 179

Concealed Identity, 149–150

Cookie, 150–151

Cowboy, 151–152

Criminal, 152, 283, 357

Cross-Dressing, 153–154

Cruise. *See* Boat

Crying, 130, 154–155, 288

Curtains. *See* Window/Window Treatment,

Cut(s), 11, 37, 155–156, 212, 319

Cutting. *See* Cut(s), 155

Dancing, 157, 343

Death, 5, 16, 41, 49, 51, 55, 64, 68, 83, 85, 105, 108, 117, 132, 138, 142–143, 147, 158–161, 174, 180–181, 199–200, 202,

209, 215, 221, 242, 248, 265, 293, 314–315, 319, 323–324, 350, 374

Death, Figure of. *See* Cloaked/ Hidden Figure

Defecation, 159–160

Demons. *See* Possession(Demonic), 279

Deserted Place, 160–161

Devil, 162–164, 279

Dog, 66–67, 69–70, 127, 164–165

Door, 46, 98, 165–166, 231, 246

Downhill. *See* Uphill/Downhill

Dragon, 166–167

Drapes. *See* Window/Window Treatment, 364

Driving, 6, 49, 51, 55, 64, 123, 127, 168, 297, 344

Drowning, 100, 169, 330, 359

Drugs, 170–171, 279

Dungeon, 171–172

Earphones/iPods, 173

Earthquake, 174–175

Egg, 175–176

Electric Chair. *See* Executions, 180–181

Electricity, 176–177

Elevator, 177–179

E-mail, 179–180, 245

Ex-boyfriend. *See* Breaking Up, 117

Ex-girlfriend. *See* Breaking Up, 117

Ex-husband. *See* Breaking Up, 117

Ex Wife. *See* Breaking Up, 117

Exam. *See* also Taking a Test, 76, 85, 284, 330

Executions, 180–181

Explosion. *See* Bombs

Faceless, 182

Face lift/Plastic Surgery, 182

Falling, 26, 48–49, 78, 137, 178, 183–184, 186, 216, 287–288, 332–333

Farm, 185

Fat, 186

Feces. *See* Defecation, 159–160

Feet, 89, 96, 89, 297, 307, 321, 368

Fence, 187–188

Fire, 124–125, 188–190, 192, 209, 223, 304, 313, 318

Fireplace, 189–190

Firing Squad. *See* Executions, 180–181

Fish, 102, 190–191

Floors/Flooring, 192

Flowers, 193–194, 303

Flying, 26, 69, 78, 194, 217, 227, 326, 346

Fog, 195, 237–238

Food, 72, 125, 132, 175, 185–186, 190–191, 196, 233, 294, 306, 309, 333, 339, 354–355

Fountain, 196–197, 361

Freeway. See Road

Frog, 197–198

Funeral, 199

Gaining Weight. See Fat

Game. See Board Game

Garage, 200–201

Garden, 194, 201–202, 303

Gasping. See Breathless

Ghost, 202–204

Gifts, 34, 53, 204–205, 272

Glasses, 205–206

Gloves, 206–207

Gorilla, 207–208

Graves, 209

Green, 109, 144–145, 188, 256, 342

Gun, 209–211

Hair, 211–212, 215

Hands, 89, 112, 122, 156, 206–207, 210, 213–214, 302, 309, 362, 368

Handwriting. See Pencil, 273–274

Hanging. See Executions, 180–181

Hat, 20, 146, 214–215

Headlights. See Beams of Light, 100–101

Heart Attack, 215–216, 301

Hearth. See Kitchen, 150, 233–234

Heights, 216, 300

Helicopter, 101, 217–218

Hidden room, 62, 91, 102–103, 139, 218

High School, 31, 49, 70, 84–85, 219–220

Highway. See Road, 23, 25, 65, 74, 224, 297–298, 347–348

Hooker. See Prostitute, 284

Hospital, 146, 220–221

Hotel, 221–223

House, 71–72, 90–91, 103, 133, 189, 200–201, 218, 222–224, 233, 261, 312, 338, 375

Ice, 58, 64–65, 224–225, 318

Indigo, 144, 146, 188

Infant. See also Baby, 5, 17–18, 46, 51, 74, 92–93, 118, 280

Infidelity, 225–226

Insects, 226–227, 232

Intercourse, 25, 227–228, 237, 307

Internet, 90, 179, 229–230, 261

iPods.See Earphones/iPods

Itch, 45, 230–231

Jail. See Prison/Jail, 283

Jesus/Buddha, 231

Jungle, 232, 344

Killer. *See* Criminal

Kitchen, 150, 233–234

Knife. *See* Stabbing, 319–320

Ladder, 234–235

Languages, 235

Legs. *See* Body Parts, 156, 362

Lesbian Sex, 236–237, 307

Lethal Injection. *See* Executions, 180–181

Light Switch, 240–241

Lighthouse, 101, 237–238

Lightning, 239–240, 336–337

Limbs. *See* Amputations, 188

Lion. *See* Cat, 69, 127–128

Lips, 146, 241–242

Losing Teeth. *See* Teeth Falling Out, 49, 332–333

Losing Weight. *See* Fat, 186

Lost Objects, 139, 242–243

Magician, 37, 244

Mail, 180, 245–247

Mailman, 247

Mansion, 223

Massacre(s), 248–249

Masturbation, 247–248

Medication. *See* Pills, 278

Mermaid. *See* Beast/Human

Mirror, 82, 149, 249–250, 288, 297, 342, 350

Missing Limbs. *See* Amputations

Mittens. *See* Gloves, 206–207

Money, 47, 75, 78, 93–94, 150, 167, 250–252, 264, 284

Monuments, 252

Moon, 253–254, 261, 337

Moonlight. *See* Moon

Motel. *See* Hotel, 221–223

Mother Mary/Quan Yin, 254

Mountains, 255–256

Movies, 1, 257, 343

Murder, 153, 211, 248

Music, 10, 157, 173, 258–259, 261, 263, 275–276

Naked, 48, 143, 220, 259, 358

Nightmares, 4–5, 34, 51–52, 259–261, 290

Numbers, 75–76, 137, 166, 178, 249, 261–264, 319, 321, 335

Nun, 265–266

Obstacles, 47–49, 53, 92, 115–116, 136, 141, 150, 188, 255, 266–267, 287–288, 296, 317, 341

Ocean, 99–100, 102, 111, 190–191, 195, 237–238, 295, 329

Old Man, 17, 37, 74, 164, 267–268, 289, 371

Old Woman, 74, 267, 289

Oral Sex, 268–269, 307

Orange, 144–145, 188

Outlet. *See* Electricity, 176–177

Paint/Painting, 269–270

Paper, 66, 204, 227, 251, 271–272

Parents, 84, 92, 125, 127, 176, 220, 272–273, 300, 309

Pebbles. *See* Boulder/Rocks

Pencil, 273–274

Performing on Stage, 274–275, 284–285

Piano, 275–276

Picture Frame, 277

Pills, 278

Pistol. *See* Gun, 209–211

Plane. *See* Airplane

Plastic Surgery. *See* Face lift/Plastic Surgery

Plug. *See* Electricity, 176–177

Possession (Demonic), 279–280

Pregnancy, 237, 280–281

Priest, 281–282

Prison/Jail, 283

Prostitute, 284

Public Speaking, 94–95, 284–285

Purse/Briefcase, 285–286

Quan Yin. *See* Mother Mary/ Quan Yin, 254

Quicksand, 267, 287–288

Rain, 55, 69, 168, 288, 290, 359

Rainbow, 66, 289–290

Rape, 290–291

Rats, 291–292

Reading. *See* Books

Rebirth/Resurrection, 293

Red, 108–109, 127, 144–145, 166, 188, 212, 241–242, 260

Renting. *See* Commerce, 147–148

Restaurant, 95, 294–295

Restroom. *See* Bathroom, 98–99

Resurrection. *See* Rebirth/Resurrection, 293

River, 239, 295–296, 330, 346

Road, 23, 25, 65, 74, 224, 297–298, 347–348

Robots, 298–299

Rocks. *See* Boulder/Rocks, 115–116

Roller coaster, 299–300

Santa Claus, 300–301

Satan. *See* Devil, 162–164, 279

Scars, 231, 301–302

Scratching. *See* Itch, 45, 230–231

Seeds, 303–304

Seizure, 304

Selling. *See* Commerce, 147–148

Sex, 25, 45, 103, 128, 154, 157, 172, 222, 225, 227–228, 236–237, 247–248, 268–269, 284, 290, 304–307

Sex. *See* also Intercourse, 306

Ship, 341

Shoes, 96, 307

Shotgun. *See* Gun, 209–211

Siblings, 308, 317

Silverware, 309

Singing, 310

Sister. *See* Siblings, 308, 317

Skeleton, 121, 311

Skyscraper, 36, 312

Smoke/Smoking, 313

Snake, 16, 314–315

Snow, 250, 315–316

Soul Mate, 316–317

Special Powers, 317–318

Spider/Spider Web, 318–319

Stabbing, 319–320

Stage. *See* Performing on Stage,
    274–275, 284–285

Stairs, 25, 136–137, 320–321

Stealing, 322–323

Stepladder. *See* Ladder

Stranger. *See* Concealed Identity/
    Stranger, 149

Strangling, 133, 323

Stroke, 73, 324–325

Sun, 145, 253, 290, 325–326, 337

Surgery, 73–74, 182–183, 220,
    302, 326–327

Sweat(ing), 327

Swimming, 99–100, 329–330

Taking a Test, 76, 85, 284, 330

Teachers, 231–232, 331–332

Teeth Falling Out, 49, 332–333

Telephone, 334–335

Television, 11, 27, 151, 257,
    335–336

Temple. *See* Church/Temple

Thunder, 240, 336

Tiger. *See* Cat, 69, 127–128

Timepieces, 337

Tongue, 38, 236, 338–339

Tornado, 340

Traveling, 101, 126, 195, 218,
    238, 295, 297, 324–325, 329,
    341, 344, 346

Tree, 13–14, 300, 304, 342–343

Tribal, 26, 343

Truck, 64, 101, 344–345

Tunnel, 25, 58, 345–346

UFO, 86, 346–347

Uphill/Downhill, 347–348

Urination, 348–349

Vampire, 350–351

Victory/Winning, 351–352

Video Games, 317, 352

Violet, 144, 146–147, 188

Voice. *See* Singing, 310

Volcano, 353–354

Vomiting, 72, 354–355

War/Battle, 113, 355–356

Warehouse, 70–71, 356–357

Washing/Bathing, 357–358

Watches. *See* Timepieces,
    337

Water, 21, 41, 65, 99–100, 111,
    121, 154, 169, 190–192,
    195–198, 224, 238, 287–289,

295–296, 316, 318, 329–330, 345, 358–361

Web. *See* Spider/Spider Web, 318–319

Webs. *See* Obstacles, 267

Wedding, 360–361

Welts, 361–362

Well, 4, 9, 15, 18, 20, 24–25, 29, 32, 34, 55, 58, 61, 63, 75–76, 83, 86, 91, 101, 111, 113, 118, 127, 130, 133–134, 149, 151, 157, 159, 161, 164, 172, 174–175, 178, 183, 186, 188, 197–198, 205, 212, 214–215, 218–220, 222–225, 236, 244, 248, 252, 258, 265, 270, 273, 275, 278, 288, 307, 310, 317, 325, 328, 332, 345, 355–356, 360–361, 367–369, 374

Whispering, 362–363

White, 26, 72, 143, 147, 250, 289, 292

Wig, 112

Wind, 111, 184, 210, 343, 346, 363–364

Winded. *See* Breathless, 120

Window/Window Treatment, 364

Winning, 110, 351–352

Witch, 37, 198, 365–366

Work, 4, 10–11, 15, 17–18, 20, 24–27, 29–35, 37–39, 44, 48, 50–53, 57–60, 62–63, 65–67, 69–70, 77, 84–85, 130, 139, 158, 163, 168, 176–177, 180, 197, 207, 213, 241, 250, 253–254, 261, 263–264, 268, 271, 276, 286, 306, 321, 324, 329, 345, 367

Wounds, 45, 156, 215, 302, 362, 368

Yellow, 74, 144–145, 188

Zombie, 368–369

Zoo, 369–370